Crew Resource Management

Crew Resource Management

From Patient Safety to High Reliability

DAVID MARSHALL

Published and distributed by Safer Healthcare Partners, LLC
Denver, Colorado, USA

Additional copies of this book can be ordered from Safer Healthcare. Safer Healthcare products
are available at special quantity discounts for training and educational purposes.

First Edition, Third Printing

Hardcover
ISBN-13: 978-0-9843851-1-9
ISBN-10: 0-9843851-1-8

Paperback
ISBN-13: 978-0-9843851-2-6
ISBN-10: 0-9843851-2-6

Printed in the United States of America
10 9 8 7 6 5 4 3 2 1

To learn more about the concepts presented in this book including Safer Healthcare's suite of high reliability programs, products and award-winning Crew Resource Management workshops, contact:

Safer Healthcare Corporate Office
and Training Resource Center

Telephone: 1-303-298-8083
Toll-free: (US Only): 1-866-398-8083

For more information visit: www.SaferHealthcare.com

About the Author

David Marshall is President and CEO of Safer Healthcare, a leading education and consulting company based in Denver, Colorado. David is an active speaker and delivers talks and keynote addresses worldwide on Crew Resource Management and the creation of high reliability systems in health care through the development of safety, quality and cost savings programs using Lean principles. He advises boards, executives and organizations in a variety of industries on high reliability concepts, including CRM and Lean programming.

David is a graduate of the College of William and Mary and lives with his wife, Catherine Hance, in Denver, Colorado. His other published works include:

- Using Human Factors to Enhance Patient Safety
- The Human Factors in Healthcare Learning Series
- Crew Resource Management and High Reliability Concepts in Healthcare
- Everyday CRM Skills Handbook

Table of Contents

Contents

Contents

Acknowledgments

I would like to acknowledge the countless individuals that have contributed to this work. In particular, I would like to thank my wife Catherine for her sage advice, steadfast support and encouragement.

In addition, a heart-felt thank you is extended for the tireless efforts of Gary Levi and Pat Johnson in the preparation, research, editing, revising and overall diligent assistance with this book.

Thanks also are due, in no small part, to Scott Shutack for introducing me to this noble journey and pursuit of a formalized CRM solution for healthcare organizations. Other individuals I would like to thank include: Bill Schuler, Travis Maynard, Suzanne Ginsburg, Bill Taggart, Peggy Cain Price, John Weigand, Bob Mansfield, Kevin Shutack, Chuck Fiorella, and my parents, James and Cheryl Chamberlin.

Finally, I would like to thank the hundreds of hospitals and organizations throughout the United States and around the world that have trusted Safer Healthcare and our CRM programs and quality improvement solutions to help make their delivery of patient care safer and more reliable.

Preface

The fact that patient safety is a relatively recent initiative in health care is nothing short of shocking. Emphasizing the reporting, analysis, and prevention of medical errors and adverse health care events should be inherent in the system that we rely on for care. However, the frequency and magnitude of avoidable adverse events was not generally acknowledged or discussed until the late 1990s, when reports in several countries revealed a staggering number of patient injuries and deaths reoccurring each year in our health care systems from generally the same causes.

A decade later, patient safety initiatives and quality improvement programs abound. The problem is these are generally desperate attempts to place Band-aids on systemic problems. These random acts of quality and safety can do more damage than good when applied haphazardly or piecemeal in an organization.

Patient safety and quality initiatives that are being adopted today include the application of lessons learned from business and industry, implementation of advancing technologies, education of providers and the public, and economic incentives for providers and facilities. While well intentioned, these programs must build on a common foundation that is often lacking in health care organizations.

The foundation that is needed, regardless of initiative, is an effective strategy that embraces and hard wires effective teamwork and communication. When analyzing the root causes of patient harm, errors in clinical settings and general dysfunctions in hospitals and care settings, a breakdown in communication is the leading cause of problems and bad outcomes.

One of the best practices in creating teams that perform and communicate reliably in critical situations is Crew Resource Management (CRM). This training methodology used by the commercial aviation industry hard wires the skills and techniques needed to successfully build a culture of quality and safety on a platform of collaboration.

CRM training and skill development, coupled with routine and frequent error and incident reporting, has helped transform commercial aviation into a model of high reliability operating well beyond a level of six sigma quality and safety.

Since 2001, Safer Healthcare has been working with hospitals and care facilities throughout the Americas, Europe, and Asia to successfully transfer and integrate CRM practices into diverse health care settings and cultures.

With a CRM foundation in place, an organization can begin its journey to improve local culture and become a High Reliability Organization. While culture cannot be transformed overnight, concrete steps can be taken in phases to ensure forward progress and ultimate sustainability.

Safer Healthcare is committed to improving patient safety and helping health care organizations begin and sustain this important and critical journey. To those of us privileged to work day-in and day-out with caregivers around the globe, Safer Healthcare is more than a name; it represents our passion and commitment to improve patient safety.

In order to help organizations better understand the requirements and conditions needed to achieve reliability, I have written this book with one simple goal in mind: to give front line caregivers and administrators a text that can serve as a roadmap for this journey. It is my sincere hope that these pages can help caregivers attain an uncompromising level of excellence in the delivery of safe and reliable care. On behalf of the team of experts and support staff at Safer Healthcare, I commit these pages to the delivery of safe and reliable care.

David Marshall
CEO, Safer Healthcare

About this Book

This book is intended as a comprehensive guide to Crew Resource Management and its import and application to health care. It assembles and digests the panoply of publicly available information in order to explain, in one volume, the "what, why, and how" of CRM and its documented contribution to patient safety and high reliability performance.

To that end, this book will:

- Trace CRM's origins.

- Explain CRM's academic and scientific foundation.

- Present the case for using CRM in health care settings.

- Introduce and explain educational and training concepts that are used to hardwire CRM skills.

- Offer specific suggestions, tools, and protocols for instilling, promoting, and sustaining the cultural and behavioral changes necessary for health care organizations to assure continuous high reliability teamwork and standardized communication.

- Make the delivery of patient care safer and more reliable.

Part One

Patient Safety
and Human Factors in the
Delivery of Care

No matter how educated or careful healthcare professionals are, errors will occur. So, the natural question to ask is: "How do we prevent those errors from ever adversely impacting a patient?"

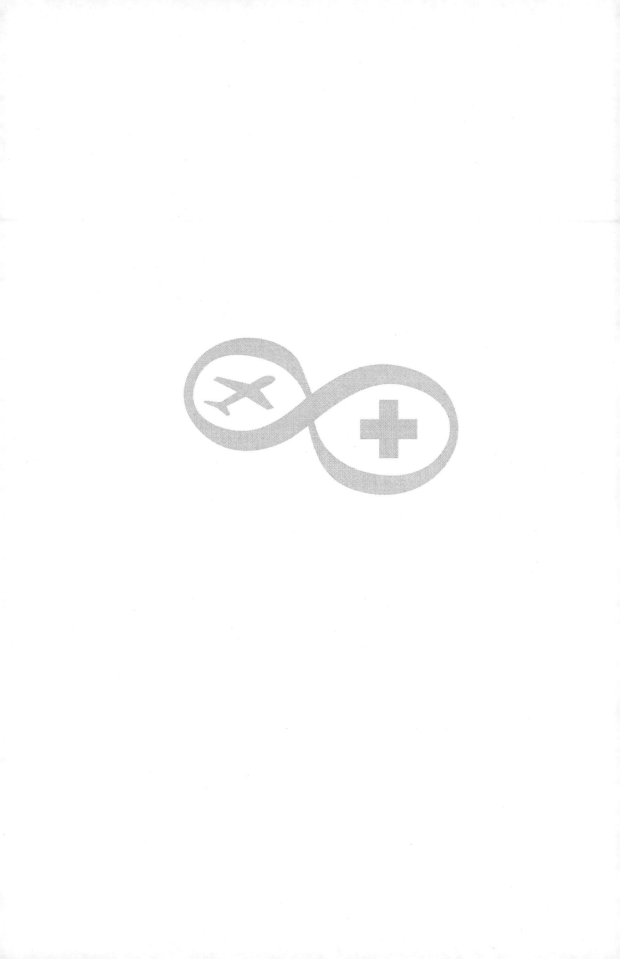

Chapter 1

Introduction to CRM

Key Points in this Chapter

- Because all human beings are fallible and susceptible to error, mistakes will inevitably be made, even by the most proficient and well-intentioned professionals.

- For people with life-or-death responsibility, small mistakes can lead to dire consequences.

- Aviation and medicine have much in common. Both fields are complex and involve high risk. And in both, preventable human error is the main cause of deadly and costly mistakes.

- Preventable medical errors account for more deaths each year than breast cancer, automobile accidents, or drowning.

- Improving patient safety by reducing preventable errors represents the primary pathway for improving health care quality and reducing health care costs.

- Crew Resource Management (CRM), a method developed to reduce human error and improve safety in aviation, has succeeded in doing so, and is now being used in other industries, including health care.

- CRM is now recognized as an evidence-based "best practice" for building sustainable, high reliability performance that reduces medical errors and thereby improves patient safety.

Noble Purpose, Human Limitations

People enter the health care professions for the noblest of reasons: to help others. But health care professionals, like all human beings, are imperfect, fallible, and susceptible to error. This simple, unassailable truth means that in health care—as in every domain of human endeavor—mistakes of commission and omission will be made, even by the most proficient and well-intentioned clinicians.

Most human mistakes are harmless. Car keys are misplaced, written numbers transposed, verbal messages garbled. But when made by people with life-or-death responsibility, small mistakes can lead to dire consequences: friendly fire on the battlefield, jetliners colliding on runways, wrong limbs amputated in operating rooms.

From Tragedy to Enlightenment

It took a landmark tragedy—the largest in aviation history—to indelibly imprint the lesson of human fallibility and rouse a revolution in aviation safety that is now spreading to health care.[1] In 1977, a *preventable error* by a seasoned and respected pilot put two Boeing 747s on the same foggy runway in the Canary Islands, causing a collision that killed 582 people, including the pilot.

That signal disaster, which followed a skein of deadly airline mishaps, led to industry-wide self examination and soon, a startling revelation: human error was the primary cause of *60 to 80 percent* of all aviation accidents.[2] Acting with concerted resolve to close this pronounced safety gap, the aviation

---

1. Aviation's Gift to Health Care: Human Lessons Paid for in Blood. *ABC News.* November 16, 2005. http://abcnews.go.com/Business/FlyingHigh/story?id=1311221 (accessed December 26, 2008).

industry began to study the human factors that cause errors—why and how errors happen—and based on the research, to change systems *and* behaviors.

The change process started in 1979, when a NASA-sponsored workshop led to the development of an error-reducing method called Crew Resource Management (CRM).[3] In 1990, the Federal Aviation Administration (FAA) made CRM training mandatory for all commercial airlines in the United States.[4]

Over time, the CRM movement has succeeded spectacularly at closing the aviation safety gap. Now, according to one FAA official, "Pilots are actually safer on the job than when they are not at work."[5] In fact, [2]CRM training, coupled with consistent and routine error and incident reporting, has helped transform commercial aviation into a model of high reliability, now operating well beyond a level of Six Sigma quality and safety.[6]

---

2. In Aviation, Human Factors are an Entire Field of Study. *Miami Herald.* September 26, 2006. http://www.comairflight5191crash.com/source/news/mcclatchy_092506.htm (accessed December 26, 2008). [Vos 2006] See also Federal Aviation Administration. *Crew Resource Management: An Introductory Handbook.* Final Report, Springfield, Virginia: U.S. Department of Transportation, August 1992, 4.

3. CRM was originally called "Cockpit Resource Management" by the FAA. Crew-based training is referred to by various names within commercial and military aviation, including Aeronautical Decision Making (ADM), Aircrew Coordination Training (ACT), FliteDeck Management, Cockpit Resource Management, Cockpit Management Resources, and Situational Awareness.

4. For a detailed history of how CRM evolved, see Helmreich, R.L.; Merritt, A.C., and Wilhelm, J.A. "The Evolution of Crew Resource Management Training in Commercial Aviation." *International Journal of Aviation Psychology,* 1999: 9(1), 19-32.

5. Nicholas Sabatini, Associate Administrator for Aviation Safety, Federal Aviation Administration, September 26, 2006, quoted by Aram Gesar in "Travel Safety Update." *Airguide Online,* Monday, October 2, 2006. http://www.allbusiness.com/government/government-bodies-offices-government/7982241-1.html (accessed July 30, 2009).

6. "Six Sigma," a concept many businesses use to evaluate performance, signifies the fewest errors and therefore the highest quality/performance level.

Because the CRM method at its core aims to eliminate or mitigate preventable human error, CRM principles have been found adaptable to other high-intensity, high-risk spheres such as the military, nuclear power plants, and health care.

Natural Links between Aviation and Health Care

Aviation and health care have much in common. Both fields are extremely complex, requiring that highly trained personnel function ably under considerable stress. In both, human beings are entrusted with the safety of others, and the available literature is replete with evidence that human factors cause the vast majority of harmful mistakes. Instructive parallels between aviation and health care will therefore be highlighted throughout this book.

The Health Care Quality Gap

In 1999, the Institute of Medicine reported that 44,000 to 98,000 Americans die each year from preventable medical errors, at an estimated annual cost of $29 billion.

As in aviation before the advent of CRM, the health care system is grappling with its own significant gap. Despite the best intentions and efforts of all concerned and the staggering sums of money spent on preventable patient safety claims, an acknowledged "quality gap"—a quality *chasm*—persists.[7]

---

7. See, for example:

   (a) *Closing the Quality Gap: The Role and Importance of "True Benchmarking."* The MCM Group, February 2005, 1. www.themcmgroup.com/PDFs/ Closing_the_Qualty_Gap.pdf (accessed January 14, 2009).

   (b) Agency for Healthcare Research and Quality (AHRQ). *Closing the Quality Gap: A Critical Analysis of Quality Improvement Strategies, Volume 1.* Rockville, MD: U.S. Department of Health and Human Services; 2004. Available at: http:// www.ahrq.gov/downloads/pub/evidence/pdf/qualgap1/qualgap1.pdf (accessed January 14, 2009).

   (c) Institute of Medicine. *Crossing the Quality Chasm: A New Health System for the 21st Century.* Washington, DC: National Academy Press; 2001.

For health care, the quality problem is compounded by spiraling costs. Health care decision-makers must somehow find a way to simultaneously improve quality and reduce costs in today's volatile economy.

Closing the Gap: Evidence-Based Practices

As a practical matter, the debate has ended about how to best attack health care's quality/cost conundrum. According to the overwhelming consensus of authority from the Institute of Healthcare Improvement (IHI) to the (Institute of Medicine) IOM, the ultimate solution lies in evidence-based practices— sustainable best practices that are backed by credible research.

Moreover, it is now recognized that evidence-based practices apply not only in the clinic, but also to the business of delivering health care. More pointedly, an expanding reservoir of evidence shows that continuously improving quality across an entire health care enterprise inherently saves money. Politics aside, this concept is a pillar of current health care reform initiatives on both sides of the political aisle.[8]

Improved Patient Safety

Research and historical data strongly support the conclusion that improved patient safety represents a primary pathway for bridging the quality chasm and reducing costs in the delivery of health care.

This is perhaps most clearly signaled in the IOM landmark 1999 report "To Err is Human: Building a Safer Health

---

8. Office of Management and Budget. "President Obama's Fiscal 2010 Budget: Transforming and Modernizing America's Health Care System, FY 2010 Fact Sheet." http://www.whitehouse.gov/omb/fy2010_key_healthcare (accessed July 25, 2009)

System." In that report, IOM stated that 44,000 to 98,000 Americans die each year from preventable medical errors, at an estimated annual cost of $29 billion. IOM therefore urged that patient safety become top priority in the U.S. healthcare system.[9] To put the IOM findings and their continued relevance into sharper perspective, as late as 2005, preventable medical errors accounted for more deaths than breast cancer, automobile accidents, or drowning.[10]

Although the primary goal of implementing CRM within an industry is to improve safety by preventing accidents and providing a safer work environment, it is widely accepted that a fully implemented CRM training program can positively affect the performance of individual crews, resulting in more efficient and less costly operations.[11]

9. Institute of Medicine. *To Err is Human: Building a Safer Healthcare System.* Washington, DC: National Academy of Sciences; 2001, 1.

10. D. L. Hoyert, H.C. Kung, B.L. Smith. *"Deaths: preliminary data for 2003."* National Vital Statistics Reports, Vol. 53, No. 15. Hyattsville, Maryland: National Center for Health Statistics, 2005. Referenced in Susan Mann, MD, Ronald Marcus, MD, Benjamin Sachs, MB, BS. "Lessons from the cockpit: How team training can reduce errors on L&D. "*Contemporary OB/GYN.* January 1, 2006. http://contemporaryobgyn.modernmedicine.com/obgyn/content/printContentPopup.jsp?id=283481 (Accessed December 24, 2008).

11. Federal Railroad Administration. *Rail Crew Resource Management (CRM):The Business Case for CRM Training in the Railroad Industry.* Final Government Report, Washington, DC: U.S. Department of Transportation, September 2007 [Federal Railroad Administration September 2007], 3.

Health Care Adapts Slowly

Notably, the IOM report was published 20 years after the post-Canary Island NASA conference. Despite the compelling links between aviation and medicine, the avoidable errors/patient safety imperative has emerged relatively recently in private organized health care. And for many reasons (discussed in greater detail later in this book), private organized health care has been adapting somewhat gradually.

Healthcare Follows Aviation's Lead

Following aviation's lead, a crucial—arguably the *most* crucial—objective for today's complex, interdisciplinary health care organization (HCO) is to improve health care quality by reducing preventable errors, which in turn makes patients safer.

This objective, of course, is the right thing to do. After all, the first rule of medicine is "Do no harm." As it happens, the right thing is also the profitable thing: the moral mandate aligns with the business payoff noted above. Improving quality via reducing errors inherently saves money by:

- Improving efficiency
  Better resource utilization and allocation

- Reducing risk
  Reductions in malpractice suits and insurance premiums

- Helping retain employees
  Increasing morale and employee satisfaction

Patient safety initiatives have focused primarily on reporting, analyzing, and preventing medical errors and adverse events. But to avoid adverse events sustainably in the clinical setting—at the "sharp end,"[12] where interactions between professionals and patients actually occur[13]—specific, easily adopted and sustainable tools and protocols are needed to prevent errors or to intercept, eliminate, or mitigate them.

Given the parallels between aviation and medicine, respected leaders[14] have consistently asserted that the CRM model, which has generated proven error-reducing tools and protocols for aviation, would translate well to health care. And over the past several years, CRM has been formally introduced into hospitals throughout the United States, Asia, Canada, Europe, and Australia.

These initial efforts have more than confirmed that the CRM solution translates to health care. CRM is now recognized as an evidence-based "best practice" for building and sustaining high reliability performance that reduces medical errors, thereby improving patient safety and reducing costs. CRM practices, in fact, have been formally incorporated into various accreditation standards.[15]

The conclusion that CRM constitutes evidence-based best practice has been consistently reinforced by a growing chorus of credible sources. For example, in January 2009 *The New England Journal of Medicine* reported that following a simple surgical checklist—a basic CRM tool—could cut the death rate

12. For the remainder of this book, the term "sharp end" will be used without quotation marks.

13. David C. Classen, MD, MS, and Peter M. Kilbridge, MD. *The Roles and Responsibility of Physicians to Improve Patient Safety within Health Care Delivery Systems.* Academic Medicine, October 2002, Vol. 77, 964. (Classen and Kilbridge 2002)

14. See, for example, Helmreich, R., et al. *Applying aviation safety initiatives to medicine.* Focus on Patient Safety. A newsletter from the National Patient Safety Foundation. Vol.46: Issue 1 2001.

15. See, for example:

    (a) Joint Commission on Accreditation of Health Care Organizations. "Preventing ventilator-related deaths and injuries." *Sentinel Event Alert*, Issue 25, February 26, 2002.

    (b) Joint Commission on Accreditation of Health Care Organizations. "Preventing infant death and injury during delivery." *Sentinel Event Alert*, Issue 30, July 21, 2004.

    (c) Joint Commission on Accreditation of Healthcare Organizations. 2007 National Patient Safety Goals, 3-5.http://www.jointcommission.org/NR/rdonlyres/ F04D6D9C-7EB8-46D2-B2E5-98E4A33F193E/0/08_LAB_NPSGs_Master.pdf (accessed July 22, 2009); 2008 National Patient Safety Goals (Laboratory), 3-6.

from surgery almost in half, reduce complications by more than a third, and save U.S. hospitals about $15 billion per year.[16] On average, this would translate to approximately $3 million in savings per hospital.

How and Why CRM Works

Research shows that workplace errors in general, and medical errors in particular, flow from a finite list of human factors. Among those factors, The Joint Commission on Accreditation of Healthcare Organizations (JCAHO or The Joint Commission) has found that the most common cause of medical error is poor communication among health care workers. At the heart of poor communication is an unfortunate but natural combination of persistent cultural and systemic impediments.

By far, the most common cause of medical error (from prescription and medication mistakes to wrong site surgeries) is poor communication among health care workers.

---

16. Simple checklist cuts surgical deaths in half. Associated Press. January 14, 2009. www.msnbc.msn.com/id/28662096/ (accessed January 23, 2009), referring to Alex B. Haynes, M.D., M.P.H., Thomas G. Weiser, M.D., M.P.H., William R. Berry, M.D., M.P.H., Stuart R. Lipsitz, Sc.D., Abdel-Hadi S. Breizat, M.D., Ph.D., E. Patchen Dellinger, M.D., Teodoro Herbosa, M.D., Sudhir Joseph, M.S., Pascience L. Kibatala, M.D., Marie Carmela M. Lapitan, M.D., Alan F. Merry, M.B., Ch.B., F.A.N.Z.C.A., F.R.C.A., Krishna Moorthy, M.D., F.R.C.S., Richard K. Reznick, M.D., M.Ed., Bryce Taylor, M.D., Atul A. Gawande, M.D., M.P.H., for the Safe Surgery Saves Lives Study Group. *A Surgical Safety Checklist to Reduce Morbidity and Mortality in a Global Population*, N Engl J Med 2009;360:491-9.

Cultural and Systemic Impediments to Effective Communication

- Traditionally, pilots (before the advent of CRM) and doctors were not often challenged, or even approached, by those of lesser rank.

- The proliferating complexity of modern health care and the attendant specialization have actually *increased* the risk of things going wrong. This position is plausible because, on one hand, complexity drives interdependence among the many participants caring for each hospital patient. But on the other hand, clinicians are typically compartmentalized into separate disciplines. The result is a "silo approach" to health care.[17] Although technical training can assure proficiency and decision-making acumen for isolated tasks, it does not address the potential for errors arising from absent or deficient cross-silo communications and fragmented decision making.

- Even when clinicians try to communicate outside their silos or areas of expertise and subjectively believe they communicate well, objective evidence shows that their peers and subordinates often report the opposite.

Research also shows that through CRM-based training, clinicians can acquire the skills and behaviors necessary to redress the human factors that impede communication and lead to medical errors. Moreover, these skills are relatively easy to adapt, learn, deploy, and sustain.

CRM and Culture Shift

The journey from awareness to results can be arduous. CRM grew out of the seminal insight that to improve aviation safety, a fundamental, *cultural* shift would be necessary.

---

17. Susan Mann, MD, Ronald Marcus, MD, Benjamin Sachs, MB, BS. Lessons from the Cockpit: How team training can reduce errors on L&D. Contemporary OB/GYN (Jan 1, 2006). Available at: http://contemporaryobgyn.modernmedicine.com/obgyn/content/printContentPopup.jsp?id=283481 (Accessed December 24, 2008).

Commercial aviation organizations would first have to genuinely commit to improve quality and safety, and only then seek to instill that commitment enterprise-wide.

Health care organizations face the same daunting threshold challenge.[18] The CRM solution for health care is grounded in the unvarnished, paradigm-shifting recognition that in a hospital setting, a physician acting alone and in "silo" isolation cannot effectively manage all aspects of a patient's care. He or she needs help, support, and input from an array of personnel with specialized expertise.

Technical expertise is not enough. Efficient, effective, and safe care requires that all efforts be coordinated and complementary and that good communication threads through it all. Simply put, to improve quality and patient safety, health care professionals must work as interdisciplinary teams.

As Chapter 11 will discuss in greater detail, research has proved what seems empirically apparent: good teamwork not only increases effectiveness; it also reduces errors. In the clinic, when each person has a clearly defined role, understands the plan of care, has input into the process, and is valued for his or her unique contribution—all essentials of CRM-trained teamwork skills—those individuals perform better, make fewer mistakes, and are more satisfied with their jobs.

CRM training breaks down cultural and systemic barriers to performance by instilling teamwork and communication across the complex, high-risk, and high-stress disciplines involved in delivering care to patients. When infused HCO-wide, CRM promotes an organic shift to a "safety culture" (discussed in greater detail elsewhere in this book) and ultimately, the HCO's transformation into a High Reliability Organization.

---

18. Given the vast size, complexity, and dynamic changeability that characterize the current health care system, its slow embrace of patient safety imperatives may be more understandable.

In the clinical setting—at the sharp end, where interactions between teams of professionals and patients actually occur—specific, easily adopted and sustainable tools and methods are needed to prevent or to intercept and eliminate errors. CRM has become recognized as a best practice for building high reliability performance that reduces medical errors and thereby improves patient safety.

CRM has become recognized both inside and outside of the healthcare community as a best practice for building high reliability performance that reduces medical errors and improves quality and patient safety.

High Reliability Organizations (HROs)

High Reliability Organizations (HROs) are organizations or systems that operate in hazardous conditions but have fewer than their fair share of adverse events. Commonly discussed examples include air traffic control systems, nuclear power plants, and naval aircraft carriers.

It is worth noting that, in the patient safety literature, HROs are considered to operate with nearly failure-free performance records, not simply better than average ones. This shift in meaning is somewhat understandable given that the "failure rates" in these other industries are so much lower than rates of errors and adverse events in health care…

The point remains, however, that some organizations achieve consistently safe and effective performance records despite unpredictable operating environments or intrinsically hazardous endeavors…

Common HRO characteristics include:

- **Preoccupation with failure** and the acknowledgment of the high-risk, error-prone nature of an organization's activities and the determination to achieve consistently safe operations.

- **Commitment to resilience** and the development of capacities to detect unexpected threats and contain them before they cause harm, or bounce back when they do.

- **Sensitivity to frontline operations** and an attentiveness to the issues facing workers at the frontline.

- **Management units at the frontline are given some autonomy** in identifying and responding to threats, rather than adopting a rigid top-down approach.

- **A culture of safety**, in which individuals feel comfortable drawing attention to potential hazards or actual failures without fear of censure from management.

Extracts of definition of HROs from AHRQ Patient Safety Network Glossary. http://www.psnet.ahrq.gov/glossary.aspx#H, accessed July 20, 2009.

Chapter 1
Core Conclusions and Summary

- Improving the overall quality of health care is a national imperative.

- At the sharp end of health care quality are highly trained yet fallible human beings entrusted with life-or-death decisions. In medicine, as in aviation and other high-risk industries, a person's very humanity contributes to errors—the cause of most adverse events.

- Reducing human error in health care reduces adverse advents and thereby improves patient safety. At the core of reducing human error is effective teamwork and communication, but cultural and systemic impediments to patient safety persist.

- CRM, an error-reducing method adopted from the aviation industry, is based on proven principles for overcoming these human-factor impediments and improving safety. CRM offers specific tools and protocols that are relatively easy to adopt and sustain, teaching clinicians to interact as part of a well-defined team. This fundamental culture shift leads to improved staff attitudes and performance, thereby increasing favorable outcomes, reducing error, and consequently, reducing medical malpractice claims and premiums.

- CRM methodology offers to health care what it delivered for aviation: scalable, repeatable front-line skills and techniques that have proved effective for improving safety and performance. When CRM is hard-wired to an organizational commitment to patient safety, attaining the necessary culture shift organically through tangible improvements becomes distinctly achievable.

- The culture of any organization cannot be transformed overnight. But concrete CRM methods deployed in strategically managed phases can help an HCO evolve ultimately into a High Reliability Organization.

Chapter 2

The Origin, History and Evolution of CRM

Key Points in this Chapter

- CRM grew out of the aviation industry's recognition that human beings are fallible and will inevitably make mistakes.

- Human beings are individuals, with a rich diversity of personalities, cultural backgrounds, talents and skills. CRM was developed to help keep the traits that make each person unique from causing harm to others.

- CRM is by design a flexible, systemic method for increasing safety and optimizing human performance by (1) recognizing the human factors that cause errors, (2) recognizing that in complex, high-risk settings, teams rather than individuals are the most effective operating units, and (3) instilling practices that use all available resources to reduce the adverse impacts of those human factors.

- CRM is not (1) a quick fix to improve patient safety, (2) cook-book medicine, (3) a way for management to dictate clinician behavior, or (4) a scheme to undermine a team leader's authority. In fact, authority should be *enhanced* through the use of CRM.

- CRM has evolved through five previous generations, each improving the methodology.

The Seeds of CRM

CRM grew out of the aviation industry's surrender to two fundamental and incontrovertible realities:

- Human beings are fallible and will inevitably make mistakes.

- Human beings are individuals, with a rich diversity of personalities, cultural backgrounds, talents and skills. Whether by nature or nurture, some are better at communicating, some better at performing under stress.

In aviation and in medicine, these quintessentially human traits collide against a professional environment in which adverse events are starkly and objectively measured: people get hurt or killed. Safety improvement initiatives based on reducing human error demand a standardized, scalable, and sustainable method for preventing *un-standard* human factors from causing adverse events. Simply put, CRM methods help keep the traits that make each person wonderfully unique from causing harm to others.

A system not designed to expect and safely absorb human error will constantly suffer from those human mistakes.[19]

CRM has been studied from various scholarly and scientific angles, and several training approaches have been developed. Given this variation, it is useful to consider what CRM is and what it is not.

---

19. Aviation's Gift to Health Care: Human Lessons Paid for in Blood. ABC News. November 16, 2005. http://abcnews.go.com/Business/FlyingHigh/story?id=1311221 (accessed December 26, 2008).

CRM Defined

Crew Resource Management (CRM) is a flexible, systemic method for optimizing human performance in general, and increasing safety in particular, by (1) recognizing the inherent human factors that cause errors and the reluctance to report them, (2) recognizing that in complex, high risk endeavors, teams rather than individuals are the most effective fundamental operating units, and (3) cultivating and instilling customized, sustainable and team-based tools and practices that effectively use all available resources to reduce the adverse impacts of those human factors.

What CRM Is

CRM has been variously described and defined by academics, consultants and various organizations. For the purpose of understanding its import and application in the aviation context, it can be defined as the following:

- A method created to optimize human and crew performance by reducing the effect of human error through the use of all resources, including people, hardware (technology) and information (process)[20] to solve problems.

- A systems approach to safety that emphasizes the inherent nature of error, promotes a non-punitive culture,[21] and centers on clear, comprehensive standard operating procedures (SOPs).[22]

---

20. See, for example:

    Federal Aviation Administration. "FAA Advisory Circular AC 120-51E." U.S. Department of Transportation, January 22, 2004. [Federal Aviation Administration January 22, 2004]

    Robert Gould. "Human Factors and National Goals." *Flight Safety Foundation/Human Factors & Aviation Medicine*, January/February 1990, Vol. 37 No. 1: 1-4, 3. [Gould January/February 1990]

- A comprehensive, operationally focused, and "self-convincing and hands-on"[23] system of proactively applying human factors to improve crew performance.

- A system that includes the following critical elements:

- Focuses on how crew member attitudes and behaviors affect safety.

- Adopts the crew rather than the technically competent individual as the standard training unit.

- Employs active training; the participants learn by participating rather than being lectured to.

- Imparts leadership and teamwork skills.

- Promotes crew member input teams while preserving authority and chain of command.

- Gives individuals and crews the opportunity to review and analyze their own performance and make appropriate improvements.[24]

What CRM Is Not

Given the relatively recent emergence of CRM in health care and the system's apparent resistance to its adoption, highlighting what CRM is *not* may be as instructive as stating what *is*.

---

21. Stephen M. Powell; Ruth Kimberly Hill, RN. My copilot is a nurse—using crew resource management in the OR. AORN Journal. January 2006, Vol 83, No 1; 178-204, at 201.

22. Gould January/February 1990, 3.

23. Federal Aviation Administration January 22, 2004; Gould January/February 1990, 3.

24. Helmreich, R.L., Merritt, A.C., & Wilhelm, J.A. (1999). The evolution of Crew Resource Management training in commercial aviation. International Journal of Aviation Psychology, 1999: Vol. 9, No. 1: 19-32, 2. [Helmreich, Merrit, and Wilhelm 1999]

As this book will demonstrate, CRM is not:

- A quick fix to improve patient safety. An organizational mindset and cultural shift are required.

- A stand-alone system that operates in isolation from other training activities.

- A passive series of classroom lectures.

- Cook-book medicine.

- A psychological or personality assessment tool.

- A way for company management to dictate and control behavior.

- A method of managing by committee or undermining the team leader's authority. In fact, authority should be *enhanced* through the use of CRM. This is so because (1) all team members direct information to the team leader, and (2) although all team members have the chance to be heard, the final decision on any course of action still rests with the team leader.

Tragic Airline Mishaps Impel Culture Change

A series of aviation disasters in the 1970s triggered the tectonic shift that led to CRM. These included the 1977 Canary Islands disaster referred to in the Introduction, in which two Boeing 747s collided on a runway, killing 582 people. In 1972, a Lockheed L-1011 (Eastern Air Lines Flight 401) crashed in a Florida swamp, killing 99 passengers, as the crew worked to repair a burned-out light bulb. United Airlines Flight 173, making its final approach to Portland International Airport after a routine flight on December 28, 1978, ran out fuel and crashed into a residential area, killing eight passengers and two crew members, and seriously injuring 23 others.

In each case, tragedy traced back to human failing:

- In his haste to take off, the captain of the Boeing 747—a highly seasoned professional—mistakenly assumed a critical pre-flight step had been performed and barreled down a foggy runway without first obtaining takeoff clearance.

- EAL 401 crashed, in essence, because someone forgot to fly the plane. The National Transportation Safety Board (NTSB), after investigating, found (NTSB, 1973) that the autopilot was inadvertently switched from "Altitude Hold" to "Control Wheel Steering" mode when the captain accidentally leaned against a yolk, causing the plane to enter a gradual descent. No one in the crew noticed or heard the system's altitude alert warning because the crew was distracted by the landing gear light and the flight engineer was not in his seat when the alert sounded and thus could not hear it.

- UA 173 experienced a similar landing gear light problem. The experienced captain noticed that the plane's nose gear light failed to turn green to indicate it was properly deployed. With the control tower's permission, the pilot circled the plane and ran through his checklists to troubleshoot the problem, but the nose gear light stayed red. While circling, the first officer and flight engineer told the pilot that the plane was running low on fuel. The pilot apparently ignored the warnings. Post-crash analysis revealed that the green light bulb for the nose gear had simply burned out; the landing gear had been deployed the entire time. The NTSB found that the crash was caused by the captain's failure to accept input from junior crew members and a lack of assertiveness by the flight engineer.[25]

---

25. Stephen A. Albanese, MD. From the cockpit to the OR. The American Academy of Orthopaedic Surgeons/The American Association of Orthopaedic Surgeons, September 2007. http://www.aaos.org/news/bulletin/sep07/managing6.asp (accessed 12.22.2008). [Stephen A. Albanese 2007]

In all of these cases, the aircraft were mechanically sound,[26] the pilots and their crews technically competent. The systems and procedures in place simply did not catch these fatal mistakes in time. In short, the system was flawed.

NASA took the lead to explore with greater urgency how to fix the system, convening a June 1979 workshop to evaluate the causes of aviation accidents.[27] As the above episodes imply, the workshop led to an alarming discovery: human error caused most aviation accidents[28]—in fact, *60 to 80 percent* of them[29]. This problem was compounded by failures in leadership, interpersonal communication, and decision making in the cockpit.[23,30]

The 1979 workshop did not operate in a vacuum. NASA had, in fact, pioneered research into human factors and performance in aviation and aerospace in the early 1970s, at its Ames Research Center in California. NASA's "human factors in aviation safety" program began in 1973 when a series of interviews were conducted with airline crew members. One typical comment was: "My company trains pilots well but not captains." In a noted NASA-sponsored study,[31] H.P. Ruffel-

---

26. In 1983, Boeing reported that nearly three-quarters of all fatal commercial jet accidents involved planes that were technically capable of a safe landing. This reinforced the earlier research reflecting that many accidents began with a relatively minor mechanical malfunction but because of human factors, unraveled into disaster.

27. "Resource Management on the Flight Deck" gathered constituents from aviation research, training, and operations to share information about aircrew coordination training.

28. Vos 2006.

29. Ruffell-Smith, H.P. (1979). A Simulator Study of the Interaction of Pilot Workload with Errors, Vigilance, and Decisions. NASA TM-78482, Moffett Field, CA.

30. In 1975, well before the NASA workshop, the Federal Aviation Administration (FAA) became involved with the forerunner to CRM. The FAA agreed to a request from Northwest Airlines to allow a new type of training, which later became known as Line Oriented Flight Training (LOFT). LOFT uses simulators and structured scripts or scenarios to train flight crews. Although LOFT is mentioned at various times and is a recognized method for promoting continuous quality, a detailed exposition of LOFT is beyond the scope of this book.

Smith (1979) used simulators to examine crew behaviors and performance in both routine and emergency situations. Ruffel-Smith's study demonstrated that the better crew resources were utilized and the more effectively crew members communicated, the better the crew performed.[32]

Other NASA-sponsored research projects suggested that grafting CRM concepts onto existing training programs in flight operations (such as Line Oriented Flight Training or LOFT) would help resolve human factor-related problems. This research recognized that improved technology and operating process would represent only a partial route to better performance and safety; the full solution depended on the crew.[33] That way, all resources would be utilized to drive improvement.

> *NASA-sponsored research recognized that improved technology and operating process would partly solve human factor-related problems, but that the full solution depended on the crew.*

Following NASA's lead, the FAA, in the early 1980s, incorporated a CRM-type platform into its regulatory program. The stated objective was to work with the aviation industry to develop a draft Notice of Proposed Rule-Making that would address crew coordination concepts and CRM. On January 13,

---

31. Helmreich, Merrit, and Wilhelm 1999.

32. This conclusion has been validated many times over. For example, the NTSB report on the fatal crash of a Lockheed Electra in Reno, Nevada, on January 21, 1985, reflected that attitudes and cockpit resource management are directly related to individual and crew performance.

33. NASA/Industry Workshop on Line-Oriented Flight Training, NASA Ames Research Center, Moffett Field, California. January 13-15,1981

1981, at another NASA/Industry Workshop,[34] the FAA's Charles Huettner said:

> We are embarking on an adventure into the flight training techniques of the future. In recent years a growing consensus has occurred in industry and government that training should emphasize crew coordination and the management of crew resources.

The Six Generations of CRM

Since its introduction in the early 1980s, there have been six generations of CRM.[35] Each successive generation was enhanced to build upon the successes and lessons learned. Following are overviews of each generation.

First Generation
Cockpit Resource Management

With crew-based training validated in concept, United Airlines (UA) initiated the first formal CRM[36] training course in 1981. This initiative followed the alluded to rash of serious accidents, none of which were attributable to a specific problem (including a mechanical failure) that would have prevented a safe flight.

UA developed its program[37] with the input of experts on improving business management. Other airlines took the same management-focused approach in their early CRM programs.

---

34. The information on this section draws heavily on Helmreich, R.L., et al.

35. Rhona Flin, Paul O'Connor, Margaret Crichton. Safety at the Sharp End: A Guide to Non-Technical Skill. Ashgate Publishing, Ltd., 2008, at 247.

36. At first "CRM" stood for "Cockpit Resource Management," but when it was recognized that the necessary teamwork extended beyond the cockpit to the entire crew, the name changed to "Crew Resource Management."

37. The United Airlines Command/Leadership/and Resource Management program (C/L/R).

Some of them, following the results of NASA's research, included full-mission LOFT training in addition to classroom work. UA made its C/L/R program available to other carriers, but they were slow to respond. However, UA continued to fine-tune its program, making it an integral part of UA's own flight officer training. Consistent with the FAA recommendations, the main tenets of the program were to institute:

- A comprehensive system for improving crew performance.

- An operational focus on safety improvement.

- A study of how team member attitudes and behaviors affect safety.

- A training method using the team, not the individual, as the training unit.

- Active training where the participants experience and participate.

In retrospect, the business management focus of these first-generation programs proved unduly narrow. Virtually all of those programs—somewhat reflexively on the heels of the NTSB's damning report on UAL 173—emphasized correcting deficiencies in individual behavior such as a lack of assertiveness by juniors and authoritarian behavior by captains. The programs featured psychological testing and explored abstract concepts such as "leadership." They advocated general strategies of interpersonal behavior but did not clearly define appropriate cockpit behavior.

Overall, despite these shortcomings, the early CRM programs were generally well received. That said, some pilots resisted, denouncing them as "charm school" or attempts to manipulate their personalities.[38, 39]

Second Generation
Crew Resource Management

During the middle and second half of the 1980s, many commercial airlines, domestic and foreign, developed and implemented their own CRM programs. By the time NASA held its May 1986 industry workshop, a new generation of CRM courses had emerged.[40] These newer programs expanded the scope of the first-generation efforts, embracing more modular, "real world" operations.

Second-generation programs emphasized cockpit group dynamics—team dynamics—and led to a name change, from "Cockpit" to "Crew" Resource Management. The expanded training included new topics such as team building, briefing strategies, situational awareness, and stress management and featured distinct modules on decision making and breaking error chains that can cause catastrophe. These refinements were intended partly to address pilots' resistance to first-generation programs, but also to translate abstract concepts into everyday operational tools.

However, in order to teach CRM concepts, many of the second-generation courses still relied on exercises and games (such as "Lost on the Moon" and "Win as Much as You Can") unrelated to aviation. Therefore, although the new courses were better received by trainees than those of the first generation, the criticism persisted that the training was heavily laced with "psycho-babble"; for example, the notion of "synergy" in group dynamics was often condemned by participants as useless jargon.

---

38. Helmreich, et al, 7, 9.

39. For a more detailed discussion on attitudes and other barriers to CRM, see Chapter 8 of this book.

40. Delta Airlines' CRM program typified the new generation.

Third Generation
Further Expanding the Scope

In the early 1990s, the CRM training began to aim at increased relevance. CRM was integrated with technical training, focusing on specific skills and behaviors that would help pilots function more effectively in actual flight deck operations. Several airlines introduced modules connecting CRM and flight deck automation.

Significantly, third-generation CRM programs also expanded to address:

- Issues related specifically to the aviation system in which crews function. This included the elements of organizational culture that affect safety.

- The recognition and assessment of human factor issues.

As the name change suggests, training in Crew Resource Management was extended to other groups that shared the responsibility for aviation safety, including flight attendants, dispatchers, and maintenance personnel. Many airlines, in fact, initiated joint cockpit-cabin CRM training. A number of carriers developed CRM training specifically for captains, related to the leadership demands that accompany command. Advanced CRM training was given to check airmen and others responsible for training and evaluating crew members.

Third-generation CRM programs filled the identified need to expand the emphasis on, and the definition of, the flight crew. But they may also have had an unintended consequence: diluting the original CRM mandate to reduce human error.

Fourth Generation
Integrating CRM and Establishing Formal Procedures

In 1990, the FAA issued an advisory circular on CRM; comprehensive CRM training became not only a reality, but a regulatory *requirement*. The FAA also introduced another major change with its Advanced Qualification Program (AQP).

AQP allowed carriers to develop customized CRM training for their own organizations. In exchange for this greater flexibility, carriers would be required to:

- Provide both CRM and LOFT for all flight crews.

- Integrate CRM concepts into technical training.

- Create detailed analyses of training requirements for each aircraft.

- Develop programs for addressing human factors in each aspect of training.

Most major U.S. airlines and several regional carriers chose AQP. A consensus found that the AQP approach improved flight crew training and qualifying.

To assimilate CRM into actual operations, airlines began to formalize CRM concepts by adding specifically prescribed behaviors to their checklists. This was done to ensure that decisions and actions would be informed by "bottom line" considerations and that the basics of CRM would be observed, particularly in non-standard situations.

By making CRM an integral part of all flight training, the fourth generation of CRM made progress in solving the persistent problems with human error. But even more progress was needed.

Fifth Generation
Error Management

The fifth generation of CRM aimed at resolving reported deficiencies in the previous iterations. For example, previous training regimens had prescribed specific behaviors but did not explain the reasons for doing so.

Dr. Robert Helmreich (a preeminent CRM pioneer) and his colleagues set out to fix the education shortfall by defining a single, *universal* rationale that could be supported by pilots worldwide. They circled back to the basics:

> Returning to the original concept of CRM as a way to avoid error, we concluded that the overarching justification for CRM should be error management....Effective error management is the hallmark of effective crew performance and the well-managed errors are indicators of effective performance.[41]

The Helmreich team advocated sharply defined justification accompanied by proactive organizational support. The fifth generation of CRM would:

- Introduce and emphasize the concept of *error management*: managing and living with human error.[42]

- Flow from the recognition that "human error is ubiquitous and inevitable—and a valuable source of information."[30]

---

41. See also Does CRM Need A New Name? Air Safety Week, February 28, 2005. http://findarticles.com/p/articles/mi_m0UBT/is_8_19/ai_n11844074, accessed February 4, 2008.

42. Helmreich, et al, at page 8.

Therefore, CRM would concentrate on error countermeasures that would apply to each situation, with three strata of defense (the "error troika"):

An Illustration of the "Error Troika"

Source: Helmreich, et al, 8.

1. Avoiding error altogether. (For example, advance briefing on landing approach procedures and potential pitfalls, combined with intra-crew communication and verification.)

2. Identifying and trapping incipient errors before they are committed. (For example, cross-checking navigation information before executing on it.)

3. Mitigating the consequences of errors that do occur. (For example, remembering to fly the plane after a warning alarm sounds.)

Fifth-generation CRM would include formal instruction about the limitations of human performance, including the nature of cognitive errors and slips and the performance-degrading effects of stressors such as fatigue, work overload, and emergencies.[43, 44]

Fifth-generation CRM posited that in order for the error management approach to achieve full traction, organizations should (1) affirmatively concede that errors will inevitably occur and (2) adopt a non-punitive approach to all errors (except for willful violations of rules or procedures).

As suggested above, fifth-generation CRM also stressed data gathering and reporting. Doing so would advance deeper understanding, but also help gauge program success. The FAA took the cue and, in 1997, enacted Aviation Safety Action Programs (ASAP), intended to encourage aviation organizations to take proactive safety measures and freely report incidents.[45] American Airlines (AA) was an early adopter, working in cooperation with both the FAA and the pilots' union. Through AA's confidential, non-punitive reporting program, pilots reported safety concerns and errors. The AA program was a resounding success: during its first two-years, nearly six thousand reports were received. The data generated by its ASAP helped AA refine and improve its CRM training program.

---

43. Federal Aviation Administration. Aviation Safety Action Programs (ASAP). Advisory Circular (AC) No: 120-66. January 8, 1997.

44. This recommendation was made to counter research reflecting that pilots generally, and from all regions of the world, held unrealistic and incorrect attitudes about the adverse impact of stressors on their performance. Helmreich also noted, significantly for the thrust of this book, that an *"attitude of personal invulnerability is a negative component of the professional culture of pilots and physicians* [emphasis added].*"* A more detailed discussion on harmful attitudes and other barriers to safety is contained in Chapter 8 of this book.

45. See, for example, Delta Reinstates Pilot Aviation Safety Action Program. Press Release, Delta Air Lines, Inc. January 28, 2009.

Although each ASAP requires delicate negotiation among the carrier, the FAA, and the pilots' union (which seeks to protect the confidentiality and non-punitive nature of incident reports), ASAP continues today to be a vital element of airline safety.[46]

Sixth Generation
Threat Management

CRM has evolved to a sixth generation, which builds on the fifth generation's "error management" theme. The sixth generation recognizes that the fifth generation's focus on pilot error—the sharp end—was appropriate; it further addresses the reality that flight crews must not only cope with human error inside the cockpit but also with threats to safety arising from the work environment as a whole.

Thus, in the sixth generation, the CRM lens has been widened from "error management" to "threat management."[47] These days, "traditional" CRM skills and methods are applied not only to eliminate, trap, or mitigate errors, but to identify systemic threats to safety.

46. Helmreich, R.L. "Red Alert." *Flight Safety Australia.* September-October 2006: 24-31.

47. Earl L. Wiener, Barbara G. Kanki, Robert L. Helmreich. Cockpit Resource Management. San Diego, CA: Academic Press, 1993, 489.

Chapter 3

CRM Embraced by
Other Industries

Key Points in this Chapter

- CRM has expanded its focus to address the root causes of preventable errors, both organizational and individual.

- There is no universal CRM training program. But there are universal CRM *principles* based on scientific and empirical evidence about avoidable human error.

- CRM methodology has proved readily adaptable to other high-risk industries — most recently, to health care.

- CRM came to medicine in evolved form, as a validated, evidence-based, best practice.

- The term "error" is somewhat a misnomer. In the CRM/patient safety context, "errors" actually mean correctable shortfalls and represent the recognized root causes of harm.

- CRM skills and tools address these shortfalls and have proved effective in health care, as they have in aviation.

- In clinical performance, failure or defect rates between 2% to 5% have been the tolerated norm, but are much too high.

Evolution Reveals Universal Principles

CRM has been an integral part of the airline industry since the late 1970s and has evolved steadily through six generations. CRM's early iterations, derived from corporate management principles, focused on individual styles and skills. By 1988, fifth-generation CRM had expanded into error management. Finally, in 2001, sixth-generation CRM further widened to involve threat *and* error management.

CRM is less about universal programs and more about universal principles, principles based on scientific evidence about human factors—the common threads that bind us all. Simply put, CRM is "evidence based" in the strictest sense of the term.

Given the measured expansion and maturity of CRM, it may seem somewhat surprising that there is no standard, universal CRM training program. As previously noted, the FAA allows air carriers to customize their own CRM programs. Therefore, training programs vary from carrier to carrier. Furthermore, these programs continue to evolve as aviation technology changes and more is learned about group dynamics.

Despite this variation, the foundation of CRM is on firm ground. As developed and explained over the years by Helmreich and other CRM pioneers, CRM is less about universal *programs* and more about universal *principles*, principles based on scientific research and validated evidence about human factors—the common threads that bind us all. Simply put, CRM is "evidence based" in the strictest sense of the term.

Through the steady evolution of CRM, we better understand the common causes of human error and how to help each other recognize, avoid, and manage them.

CRM programs share several universal themes. Educational programs often include content about the limitations of human performance and the stressors that precipitate errors, including fatigue, emergencies, work overload, teamwork, situational awareness, effective communication, conflict resolution and decision making.

Universal Principles, Universally Translatable

Over time, CRM methodology has proved readily adaptable to other industries and pursuits. These adaptations have happened for two main reasons. First, CRM is grounded in well-settled principles of human psychology. Second, CRM's inherent flexibility enables any organization to tailor programs to meet its own performance improvement needs.

Dr. Helmreich and his colleagues have consistently promoted CRM's adaptability. In their 1993 book, *Cockpit Resource Management*,[48] they wrote:

> The success that CRM has enjoyed in the last decade in the cockpit could clearly be exported to other high-risk domains, such as nuclear power production, military operations, high-technology medicine, law enforcement, construction, and shipping, just to name a few.[49]

Following this authoritative lead, other industries adopted CRM throughout the 1980s and 1990s, including the military, the maritime trades, and the railroads.[50]

Given the similarities between aviation and medicine, the adaptability and validity of CRM is quite natural. In both cases,

---

48. See also Helmreich, R.L. "Red Alert," 26.

49. Federal Railroad Administration September 2007.

50. Hoyert, Kung and Smith 2005.

professionals work in teams with leaders in traditionally strong roles[51] — the pilot or the doctor — who are prone to believe that their performance is not affected by outside stressors. Teams can spend hours performing mundane tasks and then be called upon to act swiftly under extreme stress.

There are also the tragic similarities noted above. Inarguably, thousands have died, at staggering economic cost, from preventable medical errors—again, more than from breast cancer, automobile accidents, or drowning.[52] In fact, the yearly loss of life caused by preventable medical errors in the United States is roughly equivalent to the number of deaths that would be caused by a jumbo jet full of passengers crashing every day.[53]

In health care, as in aviation, "errors" actually mean correctable shortfalls in leadership, team work, task allocation, communication, situational awareness, and decision making, which represent the root causes of harm.

The parallels between aviation and health care also apply to the *types* of errors that occur and the tools available to manage them. In both fields, "errors" actually mean correctable shortfalls in leadership, team work, task allocation, communication, situational awareness, and decision making, which represent the root causes of harm and denote the failure to marshal the available resources. The available CRM skills and tools address each of these shortfalls.[54]

---

51. These entrenched traditions are discussed in greater detail in chapter 8 of this book.

52. Wachter RM. The end of the beginning: patient safety after "To Err is Human". Health Affairs (Millwood). (suppl web exclusives). July-December 2004:W4-534-545, as cited in David A. Marshall, Diane A. Manus, MPA, RHIA. A Team Training Program: Using Human Factors to Enhance Patient Safety. AORN Journal, December 2007, 86: 6, 994-101, 995.

53. Stephen A. Albanese 2007.

54. Specific health care-related CRM skills and tools are discussed later in his book, particularly in Part IV of this book.

The link between CRM and health care was succinctly summarized by Dr. Stephen A. Albanese in his 2007 article, "From the Cockpit to the OR":

> CRM training, therefore, emphasizes the role of human factors in high-stress, high-risk environments. The training encompasses a wide range of knowledge, skills, and attitudes including communications, situational awareness, problem solving, decision making, and teamwork. Various CRM models—all based on the same basic concepts and principles identified in the [1979] NASA workshop—have since been successfully adapted to different industries and organizations. Over the past 20 years, these principles have gradually been incorporated into various components of the healthcare system.[55]

The salient message about CRM and medicine is this: CRM came to medicine in evolved form. After several generations of evolution, refinement, and proof of concept, it had been firmly established as an evidence-based best practice that was inherently dynamic and flexible. It was presented to health care as a proven solution, ready to be adapted to each HCO's specific challenges.

The salient message about CRM and medicine is this: CRM came to medicine in evolved form. It presented to health care as a proven evidence-based best practice, ready to be adapted to each HCO's specific challenges.

---

55. National Transportation Safety Board. United Airlines Flight 232 McDonnell Douglas DC-1040, Sioux Gateway Airport, Sioux City, Iowa July 19, 1989. Aircraft Accident Report, Washington, D.C. 1990, 76.

Overwhelming Consensus: CRM Works

CRM clearly makes intellectual sense, but does it actually work, in both aviation and health care? The simple answer: yes.

To be fair, some skeptical commentators in each field have pointed to a dearth of hard outcomes data. On the other hand, the research for this book has not produced a single credible source that asserts that CRM does *not* work, and proliferating reports—both empirical and statistical—leave little reasonable doubt about its effectiveness. For example:

- In July 1989, on United Airlines Flight 232 to Los Angeles from Chicago, one of the engines failed in flight. All three hydraulic lines necessary for controlling flaps, rudders, and other flight controls were severed. The plane crash landed in Sioux City, Iowa. Although 111 were killed, 184 survived. The crew attributed this minimized loss of life to their CRM training.

- In NTSB reports following two commercial airline accidents, it was noted that one of the crews had attended CRM training. The NTSB found that CRM training played a positive role in preventing a much more serious accident.[56]

- After implementing CRM, the U.S. Coast Guard reported a 74% reduction in injuries and fatalities.[57]

---

56. Lieutenant Commander Valerian Welicka, USCG (DC), presentation at International Association of Fire Chiefs (IAFC) headquarters, June 14, 2001.

57. Helmreich, Merrit, and Wilhelm 1999. Along the same lines, see:

   a) Pizzi, Goldfarb and Nash 2001.

   b) Health Service Performance Improvement Branch, New South Wales, Australia. "A Multi-disciplinary Human Factors Training Course." 2007 NSW Health Awards Entry. http://www.archi.net.au/documents/e-library/health_administration/health_awards/health-workforce/2007_0078.doc (accessed July 18, 2009).

- Dr. Helmreich and John Wilhelm, after collecting results for NASA from several CRM programs, reported a change in individuals' attitudes. Among all program participants, 70% to 80% found CRM training very useful or extremely useful, and a similar proportion believed CRM would improve flight safety.[58]

- From the advent of a formalized CRM program in 1980 through 2009, air disasters have dropped from approximately 20 per year to one to two per year.[59]

- As previously mentioned, *The New England Journal of Medicine* reported in January 2009 that following a simple surgical checklist—a basic CRM tool—could cut the death rate from surgery almost in half, reduce complications by more than a third, and save U.S. hospitals about $15 billion per year.[60]

Restating this theme in the reverse, the FAA, in the *Federal Register*, recently reported the consequences of not having effective CRM training:

> We evaluated part 135 accidents from March 20, 1997, through March 7, 2008. During this time period, there were 24 accidents (18 involving

---

58. Mr. Chris Hart, FAA (DC), presentation at IAFC headquarters, September 18, 2000.

59. Simple checklist cuts surgical deaths in half. Associated Press. January 14, 2009. www.msnbc.msn.com/id/28662096/ (accessed January 23, 2009), referring to Alex B. Haynes, M.D., M.P.H., Thomas G. Weiser, M.D., M.P.H., William R. Berry, M.D., M.P.H., Stuart R. Lipsitz, Sc.D., Abdel-Hadi S. Breizat, M.D., Ph.D., E. Patchen Dellinger, M.D., Teodoro Herbosa, M.D., Sudhir Joseph, M.S., Pascience L. Kibatala, M.D., Marie Carmela M. Lapitan, M.D., Alan F. Merry, M.B., Ch.B., F.A.N.Z.C.A., F.R.C.A., Krishna Moorthy, M.D., F.R.C.S., Richard K. Reznick, M.D., M.Ed., Bryce Taylor, M.D., Atul A. Gawande, M.D., M.P.H., for the Safe Surgery Saves Lives Study Group. A Surgical Safety Checklist to Reduce Morbidity and Mortality in a Global Population, N Engl J Med 2009;360:491-9.

60. "Risk of an Accident Caused by the Absence of CRM Training." Proposed Rules. Federal Aviation Administration. Federal Register, May 1, 2009, Vol. 74, No. 83: 20267.

airplanes and 6 involving helicopters) with causal factors directly related to a lack of effective CRM. These accidents were responsible for 83 fatalities (66 involving airplanes and 17 involving helicopters) and 12 serious injuries (all involving airplanes).[61] ...[In sum,] CRM's contribution to improvement in overall safety is generally accepted throughout the industries in which it is practiced.[62]

More results specific to health care are presented in Chapter 6 of this book.

CRM and Six Sigma

Six Sigma is a business method pioneered by General Electric that involves developing and using specific protocols and tools to achieve improvements in quality and performance in process-based businesses and professions.[63]

In essence, Sigma is a statistical construct intended to reflect the degree of variation or deviation (standard deviation) in any process from its stated specifications. "Six Sigma" equates to six deviations from the standard—99.9997% defect free—and translates into 3.4 defects per million opportunities. Using this statistical yardstick, organizations can create

---

61. Federal Railroad Administration September 2007, 2.

62. Herman Maskelly, Global Productivity Solutions. "Application of Lean/Six Sigma Methods to Mortgage Related Legal Services." Presentation to Mortgage Bankers Association Conference. Tampa, FL, March 27, 2007. http://www.mortgagebankers.org/files/Conferences/2007/ 2007TechConference/4ApplicationofLeanSixSigma-HermannMiskelly.pdf (accessed July 20, 2009).

63. The name "sigma" derives from the Greek letter and is often used to refer to the standard deviation of a normal distribution. By definition, 95% of a normally distributed population falls within two standard deviations of the average (Two Sigma). This leaves 5% of opportunities as "abnormal" or "unacceptable."

objective, fact-based measurement protocols that enable them to monitor, analyze, and continuously improve their processes.

99% Error-Free Performance is Insufficient

Six Sigma is based on the pursuit of near perfection. Its premise: 99.9% performance is insufficient, because at 99.9%:

- Post offices in New York State would lose 81,828 pieces of mail per day.

- Chicago O'Hare Airport would have 1,284 unsafe arrivals/departures per year.

- Doctors in New York hospitals, state-wide, would drop 288 babies per year.[64]

At 99.7% (Three Sigma), within the current estimated performance range for health care:[65]

- Virtually no modern computer would function.

- 10,800,000 health care claims would be mishandled each year.

- 18,900 U.S. Savings Bonds would be lost every month.

- 54,000 checks would be lost each night by a single large bank.

- 4,050 invoices would be sent out incorrectly each month by a modest-sized telecommunications company.

---

64. Thomas Pyzdek. The Six Sigma Handbook (Chapter 3). Tucson, AZ: Quality Publishing, 1999.

65. The traditional performance rage for health care has been between Three and Four Sigma, and AHRQ, as noted above, acknowledges this. Along these same lines, also see Crago 2000.

- 540,000 erroneous call details would be recorded each day from a regional telecommunications company.

- 270,000,000 erroneous credit card transactions would be recorded each year in the United States.[66]

Relating the Six Sigma yardstick to health care, the AHRQ Glossary's definition of Six Sigma[67] states as follows:

> ...having 5% of a product fall outside the desired specifications would represent an unacceptably high defect rate. What company could stay in business if 5% of its product did not perform well? ...would we tolerate a pharmaceutical company that produced pills containing incorrect dosages 5% of the time? Certainly not. But when it comes to clinical performance—the number of patients who receive a medication, the number of patients who develop complications from a procedure—we routinely accept failure or defect rates in the 2% to 5% range, orders of magnitude below Six Sigma performance.[68]

Not every process in health care requires such near-perfect performance. In fact, one of the lessons of Reason's Swiss cheese model[69] is the extent to which low overall error rates are possible even when individual components have many "holes." However, many high-stakes processes are far less forgiving, since a single "defect" can lead to catastrophe (e,g., wrong-site surgery, accidental administration of concentrated potassium).

---

66. United States Department of Health and Human Services, Agency for Healthcare Research and Quality. AHRQ Patient Safety Network Glossary http://www.psnet.ahrq.gov/glossary.aspx#refsixsigma1 [AHRQ Glossary]

67. AHRQ Glossary, citing M.R. Chassin. "Is health care ready for Six Sigma quality?" The Milbank Quarterly. 1998 Vol. 76, 565-591, 510.

68. AHRQ Glossary.

The Five Features of Six Sigma

General Electric also developed a Six Sigma approach commonly deployed in health care. This approach consists of five elements represented by the acronym DMAIC:

- **Define** – specify the purpose and scope of each task, including background information, needs, and requirements.

- **Measure** – record and compare results.

- **Analyze** – identify defects and their root causes.

- **Improve** – develop, test, and implement data-based solutions that address the root causes.

- **Control** – sustain the gains by standardizing new methods and processes.

Although, as the AHRQ Glossary notes, this process resembles the "Plan-Do-Study-Act" (PDSA) approach to continuous quality improvement, the resemblance can be misleading. PDSA aims at incremental improvements; Six Sigma, however, typically strives for quantum leaps in performance—which, by their nature, often necessitate major organizational changes and substantial investments of time and resources at all levels.

---

69. According to the AHRQ Glossary, Reason's "Swiss cheese model" illustrate[s] how analyses of major accidents and catastrophic systems failures tend to reveal multiple, smaller failures leading up to the actual hazard....[E]ach slice of cheese represents a safety barrier or precaution relevant to a particular hazard. For example, if the hazard were wrong-site surgery, slices of the cheese might include conventions for identifying sidedness on radiology tests, a protocol for signing the correct site when the surgeon and patient first meet, and a second protocol for reviewing the medical record and checking the previously marked site in the operating room. Many more layers exist. The point is that no single barrier is foolproof. They each have "holes"; hence, the Swiss cheese. For some serious events (eg, operating on the wrong site or wrong person), even though the holes will align infrequently, even rare cases of harm (errors making it "through the cheese") will be unacceptable. (http://www.psnet.ahrq.gov/glossary.aspx#S, accessed July 20, 2009)

Thus, according to the AHRQ Glossary:

> A clinic trying to improve the percentage of
> elderly patients who receive influenza vaccines
> might reasonably adopt a PDSA-type approach
> and expect to see successive, modest
> improvements without radically altering
> normal workflow at the clinic. By contrast, an
> ICU that strives to reduce the rate at which
> patients develop catheter-associated
> bacteremia virtually to zero will need major
> changes that may disrupt normal workflow. In
> fact, the point of choosing Six Sigma is often
> that normal workflow is recognized as playing
> a critical role in the unacceptably high defect
> rate.

As the figure on the following page shows, as a result of
using CRM, the U.S. domestic airline fatality rate is well
beyond the Six Sigma level. It also shows that physician
prescription writing is at Four Sigma, slightly better than the
accuracy rate for restaurant bills and about the same as airline
baggage handling.

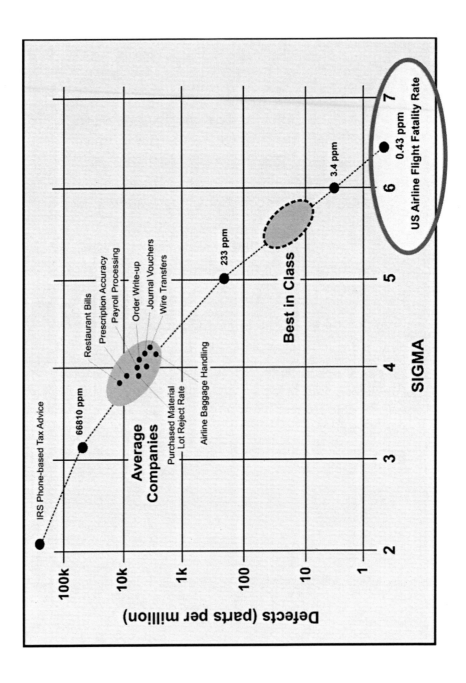

Part Two

Making the Case
for Change in Health Care

*Healthcare organizations have a moral imperative
to deliver safe and reliable care to the communities
and patients that they serve.*

Chapter 4

The Etiology of Error

Key Points in this Chapter[70]

- Managing human factors to improve performance in health care, and with it patient safety, begins with recognizing human limitations and the inevitability of error.

- The challenge in delivering health care is to keep the inevitable mistakes from harming patients and practitioners.

- Research has shown that the causes of human error are the same for all occupations.

- Threats to patient safety can originate from individual *and* organizational factors.

- The shaping perspective of CRM is aligned with the idea that recognizing and managing threats to patient safety is, quintessentially, a systemic pursuit. Individual "errors" are seen as consequences of systemic factors rather than blameworthy personal defects.

---

70. This section draws heavily from the following sources:

    a)   Charles Vincent, Sally Taylor-Adams, Nicola Stanhope. *Framework for analysing risk and safety in clinical medicine*. BMJ April 11, 1998 Vol. 316:1154-1157.

    b)   J. Bryan Sexton, Eric J Thomas, Robert L Helmreich. *Error, stress, and teamwork in medicine and aviation: cross sectional surveys*. BMJ March 18, 2000 Vol. 320:745-749.

    c)   Robert L Helmreich. *On error management: lessons from aviation*. BMJ March 18, 2000 Vol. 320:781-785

Where Errors Come From

As Part One of this book has articulated, managing human factors to improve performance in health care, and with it patient safety, begins with recognizing human limitations.[71] Specifically, errors will inevitably occur in every human endeavor, regardless of technical acumen and the best intentions, and even in the best organizations. The challenge in delivering health care, then, is to prevent the limitations on human performance from harming patients and practitioners.[72]

Knowing that human performance will never be perfect, the challenge in delivering health care is to keep the inevitable mistakes from becoming consequential and harming patients and practitioners.

In order to reduce the impact of human limitations—human error—it therefore becomes crucial to understand the nature and extent of error and the conditions that breed error.[73] Extensive research into those causes, in fact, set the stage for the development and success of CRM in aviation. The same researched conclusions apply in exporting CRM to health care.[74]

---

71. James Reason. *Human error: models and management.* BMJ March 18, 2000 Vol. 320:768-770, 768.

72. Michael Leonard, MD. "Lessons from the Sharp End: Critical Components of Successful Patient Safety Work." *Focus in Patient Safety (a Newsletter from the National Patient Safety Foundation).* 2003 Vol. 6:2, 1.

73. Robert L Helmreich. *On error management: lessons from aviation.* BMJ March 18, 2000 Vol. 320:781-785, 781.

Research into human error has confirmed, not surprisingly, that error flows from the physiological and psychological limitations of humans. What may be somewhat surprising and instructive is that the root causes of human error (that is, the factors that degrade performance and result in adverse events) are essentially identical for all occupations.[75][76]

Dr. Helmreich, James Reason, and other prominent authorities have traced adverse outcomes attributable to human error, linking them to individual patient, individual provider, team, and environmental origins. The origins of harmful error were found to include cultural factors—organizational (systemic), professional, and national (ethnic). Most recently in the CRM context, as already noted, all of the factors that can lead to error have been analyzed under the general label "threats," since each can be the root cause of, and even increase the likelihood of, errors and consequent adverse events.

Researchers analyzing these root cause factors have given them different and sometimes overlapping labels. Generally, however, there are two main categories of threat to patient safety: (1) individual and (2) organizational. Within either category, a particular type of threat can be either active or latent.

Formal labels aside, CRM methodology is built on the recognition that both individual behaviors *and* organizational traits often coincide to increase patient risk. The figure on the following page illustrates certain behaviors—implicating both individual and organizational elements—that increase risk in clinical settings to patients.

---

74. Well-researched examples and support for this fundamental principle— emphasized throughout this book—are abundant, and elevate it beyond credible debate. See, for example, Reason, March 18, 2000.

75. James Reason. *Human Error.* Cambridge, UK: Cambridge University Press, 1990, 2.

76. This is another reason why the CRM connection to both aviation and health care is on well-fixed footing.

The Shaping Perspective of CRM

While recognizing that preventable medical error can be traced to individual and organizational factors, the shaping perspective for CRM is aligned with the dominant theme in Reason's work: recognizing and managing threats to patient safety is, quintessentially, a *systemic* pursuit. In this overarching light, individual "errors" are seen as consequences of systemic factors rather than blameworthy personal defects. CRM therefore is aimed at addressing and mitigating the actual root causes of adverse events.[77]

For each HCO, recognizing and managing threats to patient safety is a *systemic* pursuit.

Behaviors that Increase Risk to Patients

Communication Failure to inform team of patient issues Failure to discuss alternative procedures Failure to introduce personnel Failure to debrief
Leadership Failure to establish leadership within team Lack of clear reporting channels and team cohesion
Interpersonal Relations / Conflict Overt hostility Frustration Passive behavior
Preparation, Planning and Vigilance Lack of team briefing Lack of contingency planning Failure to monitor situation (lack of situational awareness)

Adapted from Helmreich March 18 2000. 783.

---

77. Helmreich March 18, 2000, 783.

Chapter 5

Sources of Threat
Specific Types and Examples

Key Points in this Chapter

- Threats to patient safety can be active or latent.

- Active threats are acts or omissions of individuals at the sharp end that can have immediate adverse consequences.

- Latent threats are systemic (including cultural) conditions that can breed unnecessary harm to patients.

- Individual errors can result from both cognitive limitations (such as stress or fatigue) and behavioral limitations (such as lack of assertiveness or low morale).

Notwithstanding the overall systemic perspective of CRM, specific types and examples of failure are vitally instructive. They represent the basic drivers for and inform specific CRM methods, tools, and skills.

Active Threats

Active failures, the most visible threats to safety, are the sharp-end acts or omissions of individuals that can have immediate adverse consequences: for example, those of pilots and air traffic controllers on the aviation side and anesthetists, surgeons, and nurses on the medical side.[78]

Active failures include, for example:

- Action or procedural slips or failures, such as entering the wrong information into a computer, picking up the wrong syringe, or performing surgery on the wrong site.

- Cognitive failures, such as memory lapses or mistakes through lack of technical knowledge or skill or from misinterpreting a situation.[79]

- Violations, that is, deviations from safe operating practices, procedures, or standards, such as a deliberate failure to comply or running through a checklist from memory.

- Communication failures, such as missing information, transposed numbers, or a garbled exchange.

---

78. Some researchers consider individual patient-related variables, such as difficult airways or undiagnosed conditions, as "active" or "immediate" threats.

79. Additional specific examples of cognitive threats are presented later in this chapter.

The last point warrants special emphasis, particularly with respect to CRM. The Joint Commission, after analyzing medical errors in 2005, observed that nearly 70% of reported sentinel events were caused by communications breakdowns, with at least half of them occurring during handoffs.[80] Effective communication, as later text will reflect, is a main focus of CRM training and a key to improved clinical performance.

Latent Threats

According to Reason, latent threats are the systemic (including cultural) conditions that can breed unnecessary harm to patients.

Latent conditions include:

- Rapid change within an organization.

- Incompatible goals (for example, conflict between financial and clinical needs).

- Inadequate equipment or facilities—even poor lighting.

- Inadequate or ineffective supervision.[81]

- A stressful work environment.

- Heavy workloads, including those resulting from staff scheduling policies.

- Inadequate or ineffective teamwork.

---

80. Joint Commission on Accreditation of Healthcare Organizations (Joint Commission or JCAHO). Improving handoff communications; meeting national patient safety goal 2E. Jt Perspectives Patient Saf. 2006;6(8):9-15.

81. See, for example, Steven J. Henkind, MD, PhD; J. Christopher Sinnett, MA, MBA. *Patient Care, Square-Rigger Sailing, and Safety.* Journal of the American Medical Association (JAMA), 2008;300(14):1691-1693.

- Inadequate or ineffective communication/norms of communication; this overlaps with "active" communication failures as noted above.

Limitations of Human Performance

At the sharp end, academic labels matter less than reality. CRM methods are grounded in the understanding that patient safety is jeopardized by the all-too-real limitations of human beings, both cognitive and behavioral.

Cognitive Limitations

Limited Memory Capacity, Multitasking, Interruptions and Distractions

The contemporary clinic environment is extremely fragmented. However, the human brain can hold only five to nine bits of information in short-term memory.[82] A busy clinician—with the pager going off, talking on the phone, and trying to talk with two people at once while conveying patient information—can easily exceed that capacity. The substantial increase in auto accidents caused by drivers talking on cell phones illustrates this limitation.[83]

If a clinician is interrupted during a critically important task, it often takes a formal cue to turn attention back to the original activity.

---

82. Benjamin J. Sadock, Harold I. Kaplan, Virginia A. Sadock. *Kaplan & Sadock's Synopsis of Psychiatry (10th ed)*. Philadelphia, PA: Lippincott Williams & Wilkins; 2007, 147.

83. Michael Leonard 2003, 1.

Stress

One of the better established (yet often overlooked) findings in stress research is that as stress or arousal increases, an individual's thought processes and breadth of attention narrow.[84] To put it another way, when humans are under significant stress, their performance degrades. According to some studies, under stress, the error rate in performing even routine tasks can be as high as 30%.[85]

Stress also increases the risk of developing tunnel vision—not being able to see the forest for the trees: in CRM parlance, loss of situational awareness. This is what happened to the crew of UA 173, which became so absorbed in troubleshooting a faulty light bulb that the plane ran out of fuel and crashed.

Sources of stress include sudden surges of intense activity, as well as unremitting organizational pressure to perform.

Fatigue

Long hours of work and fatigue are typical of the medical professional. Ironically, this ingrained tradition is at odds with proven medical science: fatigue impairs the ability to process complex information and care for patients. In fact, after 24 hours without sleep, cognitive performance is equivalent to a blood alcohol level of .10%.[86]

---

84. J. Bryan Sexton, Eric J Thomas, Robert L Helmreich. *Error, stress, and teamwork in medicine and aviation: cross sectional surveys.* BMJ March 18, 2000 Vol. 320:745-749, 746.

85. See, for example, Charles P. Shelton. *Human Interface/Human Error.* Research Study, Pittsburgh, PA: Carnegie Mellon University, Spring 1999. http://www.ece.cmu.edu/~koopman/des_s99/human/ (accessed July 20, 2009).

86. M. Rosekind, Gander, P. H., et al. "Managing fatigue in operational settings 2: An integrated approach." *Hospital Topics*, Summer 1997, Vol. 75:31-35.

Behavioral Limitations

Behavioral limitations relate to each person as an individual, whether by nature or nurture (including work environments). These link to, or may overlap with, some of the factors already cited, and include:

- Complacency.

- Low morale.

- Individual lack of assertiveness. This may include cultural perceptions of class or status.

- Fear, including fear of reporting errors.

Chapter 6

Best Practices
Managing Human Factors
in Health Care

Key Points in this Chapter

- Patient safety—and how to manage the human factors that can threaten it—have been intensely debated. However, it is universally agreed that patient safety is a problem and something *must* be done to improve it.

- The evidence is overwhelming that CRM is a "best practice" that works in other fields.

- The current debate, therefore, about CRM and health care is about means, methods, and demonstrable results—specifically, whether CRM truly works in the health care field.

- Although each item of data is subject to dispute, a growing number of specific examples, including those cited by the American Medical Association, supports the conclusion that CRM methodology works in health care.

The efficacy of CRM has been established, in part, because CRM has been evaluated throughout its evolution. CRM training was developed interactively—introducing and testing the effectiveness of different strategies—which allowed for the best possible results.[87]

Patient safety and managing the human factors that can threaten it have inspired intense study and debate. Credible researchers and thought leaders have produced hundreds, if not thousands, of books, studies, and articles on these subjects.

But the debate must be properly framed, because there is virtual unanimity on the fundamental premise: patient safety is a problem and something *must* be done to improve it. The research for this book has unearthed no one who suggests that improving patient safety is a bad idea.

The appropriate field for the debate, therefore, is about means, methods, and demonstrable results. Specifically, the ongoing debate is about:

- Whether CRM truly works.

- Even if CRM works in aviation and other high-risk endeavors, whether it is truly translatable to health care.

- Even if CRM is translatable to health care, whether the techniques and tools thus far deployed have truly worked.

---

87. David P. Baker, Sigrid Gustafson, J. Mathew Beaubien, Eduardo Salas, Paul Barach. "Medical Team Training Programs in Health Care." 253-266. Agency for Healthcare Research and Quality (AHRQ): Advances in Patient Safety: Vol. 4 - Medical Team Training Programs, April 27, 2005. (Baker 2005)

CRM Success in Other Fields

In 1981, United Airlines started the first CRM training program in aviation. Since then — more than 25 years later— United has not had a single hull loss accident related to crew factors.

In other high reliability domains, including aviation, air traffic control, space travel, the military, nuclear power plants, railroads, and firefighting, the benefits of CRM as a best practice have been well-documented.[88] Here are a few specific examples:

- In one of the earliest studies (1990), Helmreich and colleagues analyzed more than 2,000 line flights and LOFT sessions, and reported that as a result of the CRM training, the overall percentage of crews rated by Check Airmen and LOFT instructors as "above average" increased, while the percent rated "below average" decreased.[89]

- As previously noted, United Airlines started aviation's first CRM training program in 1981. Since then, more than 25 years later, United has not had a single hull loss accident related to crew factors. The commercial aviation industry now operates beyond Six Sigma-

---

88. This overall conclusion is amply supported in the literature. See, for example:

   a) M. Leonard, S. Graham, D. Bonacum. "The human factor: the critical importance of effective teamwork and communication in providing safe care." *Quality and Safety in Health Care*, 2004, Vol. 13(Suppl 1):i85–i90, 85: "Other high reliability domains, such as commercial aviation, have shown that the adoption of standardised tools and behaviours is a very effective strategy in enhancing teamwork and reducing risk."

   b) James Reason. Human error: models and management. BMJ March 18, 2000;320:768-770: "… success stories involved nuclear aircraft carriers, air traffic control systems, and nuclear power plants." (Reason 2000)

89. This Helmreich study and other early aggregated evidence of the effectiveness of CRM are summarized in Making Health Care Safer: A Critical Analysis of Patient Safety Practices. AHRQ July 20, 2001 (AHRQ 2001). http://www.ahrq.gov/clinic/ptsafety/pdf/ptsafety.pdf.

level (near-perfect performance), with only one in five million flights ending in a fatal accident.

- Recognizing that CRM programs succeeded in reducing the number of airline accidents, the NTSB in 1999 recommended that a "Train CRM" program be developed for the U.S. railroad industry (NTSB, 1999). The final report, issued in 2007, noted the positive effects of CRM training.[90]

- In October 2008, *The Journal of the American Medical Association* (JAMA) observed that six years after CRM training was implemented in the United States Coast Guard (USCG), handoffs were "proven to be nearly failsafe," and "fleet-wide, vessel mishaps had decreased by more than 65%."[91] Overall, USCG has reported that since adopting CRM, its injury rate has decreased 74%.

In March 2008, AHRQ noted that viewed in isolation, each piece of evidence concerning the effectiveness of CRM training in aviation might be disputed. Overall, however:

> ...The pattern of results suggests that CRM training does improve the margin of aviation safety. In short, the scientific evidence appears to support a reasonable inference that gains achieved during training in critical teamwork-related competencies can transfer directly to actual flights and flight safety, provided the application of learned skills by the trained individuals is consistent.[92]

---

90. U.S. Department of Transportation, Federal Railroad Administration. Final Report: Rail Crew Resource Management (CRM): Pilot Rail CRM Training, Development, and Implementation. Washington, DC 20590. February 2007.

91. Steven J. Henkind, MD, PhD; J. Christopher Sinnett, MA, MBA. Patient Care, Square-Rigger Sailing, and Safety. JAMA, October 8, 2008; 300(14):1691-1693. (Steven J. Henkind and J. Christopher Sinnett October 8, 2008)

92. Medical Teamwork and Patient Safety: The Evidence-based Relation. AHRQ March 27, 2008 (AHRQ 2008). http://www.ahrq.gov/qual/medteam/medteamwork.pdf, 22.

Despite a perceived absence of definitive cause and effect data, the sheer weight, volume, and consistency of the available evidence seems more than sufficient to overcome any meaningful dispute that CRM training is a firmly established best practice that truly works in high-risk industries.

CRM Applies to Health Care

Some skeptics have gone so far as to concede that CRM works in other high-risk realms, but question whether CRM principles apply to health care. This skepticism, however, also seems contrary to a considerable and expanding body of evidence. In addition to the thorough and copious research of Helmreich and Reason, as previously described, consider the following:

- The Joint Commission, having documented the striking parallels[93] between aviation and health care, in 2005 recommended CRM training to improve health care.[94] The Joint Commission has continually monitored the path of CRM and has consistently reinforced its support.

- In 1999, President Clinton established the Quality Interagency Coordination (QuIC) Task Force to develop a Federal plan for reducing the number and severity of medical errors. One of the QuIC's primary recommendations was the adaptation of CRM to medicine.[95]

---

93. Dr. Reason refers to these parallels as "defining cultural characteristics" (BMJ 2000; 320:770). These characteristics are discussed in greater detail in Chapter 8 of this book.

94. Health Care at the Crossroads: Strategies for Improving the Medical Liability System and Preventing Patient Injury 2005, 4.

95. AHRQ 2008,1.

- A 2006 Australian government-commissioned review of best practices in safety and reliability noted as follows:

  > Observations of deficiencies in training of medical personnel and a greater awareness of the need for effective teamwork and communication has led to growing consensus in health care of the benefits of CRM-style training.[96]

- In 2007, The National Quality Forum stated that CRM applies to and can yield notable improvements out of "the work we do every day."[97]

- AHRQ, in 2008, noted the "common sense conceptual link between CRM training and enhanced patient safety" and concluded:

  > the component theories of CRM are applicable to any medical domain in which effective teamwork has been shown to reduce errors and enhance patient safety.... [T]eams yield valuable process-oriented benefits, including cohesion, retention, peer respect, and positive morale. Given the pervasiveness of these findings, the inference that successful teamwork might substantially reduce severe life-threatening medical errors is not unreasonable. Therefore, we consider [CRM]...to be entirely relevant to medical team training.[98]

---

96. National Rail Resource Management Project: Review of Best Practice, Implementation Issues and Task Analysis. Public Transport Safety Victoria and Independent Transport Safety and Reliability Regulator, NSW. Albert Park, Victoria, Australia. March 31, 2006, 40.

97. *Safe Practices for Better Healthcare—2006 Update: A Consensus Report.* National Quality Forum 2007, 55.

98. AHRQ 2008 24-25.

- In 2008, the American Medical Association (AMA) recognized the "meaningful parallels," particularly regarding shift changes and handoffs, between the USCG's CRM practices and medicine, and noted that the lessons learned and strategies used "may be applicable to health care."[99]

In sum, it seems apparent that CRM training is transferable to health care.

The Measurement Problem

The conclusion that CRM training is truly compatible with health care leaves the final crucial question raised at the beginning of this chapter: have the techniques and tools thus far deployed truly worked? This question is straightforward, reasonable, and expected. But the answer is less than straightforward, for many reasons.

First, CRM is relatively new to health care, and in contrast to aviation it has not had six generations of evolution. Although the early research suggests that CRM training has been well received and that errors have been reduced,[100] relatively few studies exist to "prove" that CRM works in health care.[101]

Some skeptics, discounting The Joint Commission's consistent advocacy of CRM and the supporting voices of AHRQ and the AMA, point up the differences (rather than the striking similarities) between aviation and health care. Some

---

99. Steven J. Henkind and J. Christopher Sinnett October 8, 2008, 1692-1693.

100. David M. Musson, MD, PhD and Robert L. Helmreich, PhD. "Team Training and Resource Management in Health Care: Current Issues and Future Directions." *Harvard Health Policy Review.* Spring 2004 Vol. 5, No. 1: 25-35, 30. (Musson 2004)

101. See, for example, AHRQ 2001, 506; AHRQ 2008, 22, 28, 35, 38, 42; Baker 2005, 2656; Musson 2004, 29.

believe that IOM's original report, *To Err Is Human,* exaggerated the magnitude of the patient safety problem.[102] Therefore, many hospital decision makers are cautious, awaiting definitive, *scientific* proof of outcomes before committing time and resources to CRM training.

According to AHRQ, another reason for the dearth of hard data is the relatively low base rate at which serious medical errors occur or are reported.[103] Dr. Reason calls this the "paradox of reliability"; in his view, reliability is a "non-event" because "successful outcomes rarely call attention to themselves."[104]

This impediment of proof has been carefully considered by AHRQ, Reason, and Helmreich, and ultimately, all have argued it away. Helmreich and his colleague David Musson assert that because CRM centers on human behavior, scientific proof may be elusive and to demand or expect it illusory. They explain it this way:

> Many of the most important threats in flight safety are rare and strict scientific validation of the effectiveness of an intervention to prevent them is exceedingly difficult. *Things are often done because it seems to all involved to be the safest way to get the job done* [italics added]....The scientific model for funding research, with its emphasis on reproducibility and scientific rigor may suit the development of pharmacologic and therapeutic interventions but may not be completely

---

102. Robert J. Blendon, Sc.D., Catherine M. DesRoches, Dr.P.H., Mollyann Brodie, Ph.D., John M. Benson, M.A., Allison B. Rosen, M.D., M.P.H., Eric Schneider, M.D., M.Sc., Drew E. Altman, Ph.D., Kinga Zapert, Ph.D., Melissa J. Herrmann, M.A., and Annie E. Steffenson, M.P.H. "Views of Practicing Physicians and the Public on Medical Errors." *New England Journal of Medicine*, December 12, 2002 Vol. 347, No. 24: 1933-1940, 1933. (NEJM 2002)

103. AHRQ 2008, 42.

104. Reason 2000, 769.

appropriate for matters that are more sociological and anthropological than healthcare agencies are used to supporting.

…Health care may be well advised to examine how other industries have supported such research, and how successful interventions were employed, rather than attempt to adopt specific training elements or seek validation of every component of complex and institutionally specific training programs. *A random, double blind, placebo-controlled study of the utility of team training programs may be both virtually impossible and potentially meaningless in its results* [italics added]. It is important to recognize that while this study design may be the gold standard for validation in medicine, it may not be appropriate for complex socio-technical interventions. This does not mean that the intervention itself is inappropriate.[105]

This opinion is echoed by Richard N. Wissler, M.D., PhD:[106]

The continued pursuit of patient outcome data distracts from other team training accomplishments….CRM improves the workplace environment; this should be an inducement to all of us….Any industry should see these effects of team training as a positive outcome, and worth considerable investment [and] we should not lose the benefits of CRM by insisting on a link to patient outcome data.

---

105. Musson 2004, 34.

106. Richard N. Wissler, M.D., Ph.D. Resolved: Crew Resource Management in Medicine is a Fad (Part II). Presentation to Society for Obstetric Anesthesia and Perinatology (SOAP) 2007: May 18, 2007 http://www.soap.org/Wissler-SOAP-2007-safety-debate.pdf (accessed February 22, 2009).

General Sentiment

Helmreich's and Wissler's urgings, persuasive by themselves, do not stand alone. Despite the inherent difficulties in producing hard data and the attendant caution of many decision makers, the evidential case for CRM in health care—general and specific—is proliferating from all quarters, goes beyond what AHRQ has called CRM's "face validity,"[107] and in the aggregate is both widespread and convincing:

- In her article "Lessons from the Cockpit," Dr. Susan Mann and colleagues wrote:

  > ...while this approach [CRM] may meet some resistance, we're convinced by the data—and our own clinical experience— that it will provide a safety net that helps reduce preventable errors and medical malpractice suits.[108]

- The *British Medical Journal* (BMJ), JAMA, and *The Journal of Critical Care* have all published research describing the positive impacts of CRM.[109]

- In a 2006, the American Academy of Orthopaedic Surgeons stated that "Crew resource management (CRM) is essential to achieving reliable excellence in surgery."[110]

---

107. AHRQ 2001, 507.

108. Susan Mann, Ronald Marcus and Benjamin Sachs, 2006,1.

109. What Pilots Can Teach Hospitals About Patient Safety. New York Times. October 31, 2006. http://www.nytimes.com/2006/10/31/health/ 31safe.html?_r=1&n=Top%2fReference%2fTimes%20Topics%2f (accessed December 23, 2008).

110. American Academy of Orthopaedic Surgeons / American Association Orthopaedic Surgeons (AAOS). Newsletter. Spring 2006. ww3.aaos.org/ member/safety/psmo/newsletter/patletter_spring06.cfm (accessed February 26, 2009).

- In his 2008 book, *The Future of Medicine: Megatrends in Health Care That Will Improve Your Quality of Life*, Stephen C. Schimpff wrote that CRM is an effective system for reducing preventable errors that will "reinforce the desired changes in both the process and the individual's behavior....[CRM is] still rarely used in most hospitals, but its day will come."[111]

- In March 2008, AHRQ concluded that Anesthesia Crisis Resource Management (ACRM), MedTeams, and Medical Team Management (MTM) programs have, when viewed together, provided documented improvements in patient safety.[112]

- Another 2008 study of CRM training for surgeons showed "a significant correlation between the use of CRM practices and their perceived utility in improving team coordination and reducing error."[113]

- In his 2008 book *Health Organizations*, James A. Johnson wrote that the success of CRM is evident and that the available evidence suggests that CRM "has been helpful in deterring potentially false self-perceptions of good performance during fatigue...[and] that CRM style training for tactical teams in healthcare are highly relevant, including operating rooms, labor and delivery rooms, and cardiac arrest response teams."[114]

---

111. Stephen C. Schimpff. *The Future of Medicine: Megatrends in Health Care That Will Improve Your Quality of Life*. Nashville TN: Thomas Nelson Inc., 2007, 217, 237.

112. AHRQ 2008, 38.

113. Stephanie Guerlain, Florence E. Turrentine, David T. Bauer, J. Forrest Calland, Reid Adams. "Crew resource management training for surgeons: feasibility and impact." Cognition, Technology and Work. September 2008 Vol. 10, No.4: 255–264.

114. James A. Johnson, *Health Organizations*, Jones & Bartlett Publishers, 2008, 118-119.

Specific Findings

Various studies and reports on CRM-based training, communication, and teamwork in specific settings—some scholarly, some anecdotal and subjective—have credited CRM and related tools with the following positive results:

- A 58% reduction in emergency room errors;[115] another study reported a reduction in the error rate from nearly 31% to 4.4%.[116]

- A 50% reduction in surgical counts errors.[117]

- A greater than 50% reduction in observed L&D adverse outcomes over four years,[118] and at Beth Israel Deaconess Medical Center (BIDMC), between 2001 and 2004, a 47% drop in the adverse outcomes index among gestations under 37 weeks and a 14% drop for gestations over 37 weeks; total improvement for the entire patient population was 16%.[119]

---

115. M. J. Shapiro, J. C. Morey, S. D. Small, V. Langford, C. J. Kaylor, L. Jagminas, S. Suner, M. L. Salisbury, R. Simon, G. D. Jay. "Simulation based teamwork training for emergency department staff: Does it improve clinical team performance when added to an existing didactic teamwork curriculum?" *Quality & Safety in Health Care* 2004 Vol. 13:417-421. (Shapiro 2004)

116. John C. Morey, Robert Simon, Gregory D. Jay, Robert L. Wears, Mary Salisbury, Kimberly A. Dukes, Scott D. Berns. "Error Reduction and performance improvement in emergency department through formal teamwork training: evaluation results of the MedTeams project." *Health Service Research* December 2002: 37: 1553.

117. R.M. Rovers, Diane Swain, and Bill Nixon. "Using aviation safety measures to enhance patient outcomes. " *AORN Journal* 2003, 77-158.

118. American College of Obstetricians and Gynecologists (ACOG). (2004, May3). Press release: Beyond blame: Ob-gyns investigating model reforms on patient safety. http://www.acog.org/from_home/publications/ press_releases/nr05-03-04.cfm (no longer available).

119. Susan Mann, MD, Ronald Marcus, MD, Benjamin Sachs, MB, BS. "Lessons from the cockpit: How team training can reduce errors on L&D." *Contemporary OB/GYN.* January 2006 Vol. 51 No. 1: 34-41. (Mann 2006)

- Expanding on its success in L&D, BIDMC began a program to eliminate catheter-related bloodstream infections (CRBIs). The rates for CRBI, at 9.1 infections per 1,000 line days in 2004, dropped to 2.8 in 2005, 1.1 in 2006, and 0.4 in 2007—saving an estimated 12 lives.[120]

- Improved perinatal outcomes.[121]

- For diabetes care in an inner-city primary care clinic, improved process redesign and standardized care approaches, and significant improvements in microalbumin testing and associated patient outcome measures.[122] The study reporting these results concluded as follows:

  > The CRM approach provided tools for management that, in the short term, enabled reorganization and prevention of service omissions and, in the long term, can produce change in the organizational culture for continuous improvement.

- A significant improvement in interprofessional teamwork in a multidisciplinary obstetrical setting.[123]

120. "Teaching Hospitals Battle Hospital-acquired Infections." Association of American Medical Colleges (AAMC). *AAMC Reporter,* November 2007. http://74.125.47.132/search?q=cache:smuN1cdMc3QJ:www.aamc.org/newsroom/reporter/nov07/quality.htm (accessed March 2, 2009). (AAMC 2007)

121. Meredith Rochon, Thomas Hutchinson, Francine Miranda, James Reed, Erika Linden and L. Wayne Hess. "Crew resource management (CRM) improves perinatal outcomes." *American Journal of Obstetrics and Gynecology.* Volume 197, Issue 6, Supplement, December 2007: S25.

122. Cathy R Taylor, Joseph T Hepworth, Peter I Buerhaus, Robert Dittus, Theodore Speroff. "Effect of crew resource management on diabetes care and patient outcomes in an inner-city primary care clinic." *Quality & Safety in Health Care* 2007;16:244-247.

123. Guy Haller, Philippe Garnerin, Michel-Ange Morales, Ricardo Pfister, Michel Berner, Olivier Irion, François Clergue and Christian Kern. "Effect of crew resource management training in a multidisciplinary obstetrical setting." *International Journal for Quality in Health Care* 2008 20(4):254-263.

- After airline pilots taught team training at Children's Hospital of Boston, medical error rates "dropped to zero." At another New England Hospital, CRM team training resulted in lower death rates for cardiac surgery.[124]

- Fewer malpractice suits and postsurgical infections, reduced length of stay, and increased employee satisfaction.[125]

Without question, formal CRM programs that are integrated within clinical settings through a robust training program produce results. Having answered the question of what benefits CRM will provide to organizations, the following chapter will address the individual caregiver.

124. Gerald B. Healy, M.D. "Ending medical errors with airline industry's help." *The Boston Globe*, January 8, 2008. http://www.boston.com/news/health/articles/2008/01/08/ending_medical_errors_with_airline_industrys_help/ (accessed February 23, 2009).

125. "What Pilots Can Teach Hospitals About Patient Safety." *New York Times*. October 31, 2006. http://www.nytimes.com/2006/10/31/health/31safe.html?_r=1&n=Top%2fReference%2fTimes%20Topics%2f (accessed December 23, 2008).

Chapter 7

CRM: What's In It For Me?

Key Points in this Chapter

- Despite the compelling case for CRM's applicability to and value for health care, some clinicians and hospital leaders, before making patient safety a higher priority and embracing CRM, seek an answer to "What's in it for me?" (WIIFM).

- For these holdouts, the CRM solution offers ample moral, personal, *and* business incentives.

- Although improving patient safety is plainly the right thing to do, patient safety is not a top priority in many HCOs, often taking a back seat to financial and production concerns.

- On the personal side, research has shown that increasing patient safety is a "win-win" proposition for health care workers, associated with reduced risk/fear of malpractice claims and increased morale/job satisfaction.

- On the business side, medical teams trained in CRM can perform more work at a lower cost while improving patient safety.

The case for CRM's overall applicability to, and effectiveness in, health care has been made and is compelling.

But to some, the evidence cited may not prove sufficiently persuasive to inspire an enthusiastic embrace of CRM as a solution that can work for them in the "real world." One commentator has candidly distilled this obstacle as follows:

> Rule number one is always "What's in it for me?" (WIIFM). The people doing the work need to see an upside.[126]

Along these same lines, The Joint Commission's Dr. Dennis O'Leary has observed that hospital leaders appear to need more justification to make patient safety a higher priority for their organizations.[127]

For those holdouts, the CRM solution offers ample moral, personal, *and* business incentives.

Moral Incentives

Improving patient safety is simply the right thing to do. Yet in many HCOs, patient safety is not a top priority.

Above all, health care organizations have a moral imperative to deliver safe care.[128] Although this seems axiomatic, the debate over patient safety continues.

The research reviewed for this book has revealed a quality/ safety paradox. The consensus view is that health care

---

126. Michael Leonard 2003, 2.

127. Medscape. "Improving Patient Safety: Conference Report." Medscape Money & Medicine 4(1), 2003. http://www.medscape.com/viewarticle/ 456622_4 (accessed February 25, 2009). (Medscape 2003)

128. William B. Weeks, MD, MBA, CHE James P. Bagian, MD, PE. "Making the Business Case for Patient Safety." *Joint Commission Journal on Quality and Safety.* January 2003 Vol. 29, No. 1:51-54,53

professionals generally have entered the field to help people, and health care institutions exist for the same overarching purpose. Yet according to both patients and practicing physicians, patient safety is not a top priority in many HCOs, often taking a back seat to financial and production concerns.[129]

This juxtaposition has placed these HCOs in a curious position, in effect arguing that because the pressure is so intense, and because everyone is too busy and health care too complicated, the necessary investment in improving the safety of patients cannot be allowed to get in the way of curing them. Implicit in this "argument" is the idea that it is somehow tolerable to expose patients to harm from something other than their original disease—or to make their original condition worse.

Under any analysis, this position is untenable: improving the safety of patients is plainly the right thing to do.[130]

Personal Incentives

For those working in a clinical environment, CRM training and techniques help make their day-to-day work safer, simpler and easier.[131] It enables the creation of highly effective—highly

---

129. See: NEJM 2002, 1935:

> Neither physicians nor the public named medical errors as one of the largest problems in health care today. The problems cited most frequently by physicians were the costs of malpractice insurance and lawsuits (cited by 29 percent of the respondents), the cost of health care (27 percent), and problems with insurance companies and health plans (22 percent). In the survey of the public, the issues cited most frequently were the cost of health care (cited by 38 percent of the respondents) and the cost of prescription drugs (31 percent). Only 5 percent of physicians and 6 percent of the public identified medical errors as one of the most serious problems.

130. On February 9, 2009, Ann Blouin, RN, PhD, and member of The Joint Commission, noted that failure to improve patient safety might jeopardize an HCO's accreditation as well as CMS funding. She also said, however, that HCOs are not motivated to improve merely to retain their CMS funds and accreditation: "they want to do better because it's the right thing to do." (Ann Blouin 2009)

reliable—teams.[132] As reflected in the specific findings listed above, research has shown that increasing patient safety is a "win-win" proposition for health care workers and is associated with:

- Reduced risk/fear of malpractice claims,[133] and reduced malpractice premiums for physicians who participate in CRM training.[134]

- Increased morale/job satisfaction.[135]

- Everyone participates, everyone benefits.

A Sidebar on Nurses

Nurses have probably been the strongest sharp-end advocates of CRM. They have reported, for example:

- More respect from doctors after CRM was initiated.

- Greater job satisfaction and reduced turnover because of the perception that their input is valued by doctors.[136]

Reduced turnover is enormously beneficial to hospitals. Hospitals with high nursing turnover rates had 36% higher costs per discharge than hospitals with turnover rates of 12% or less. Hospitals with a lower turnover rate also reported lower risk-

---

131. Michael Leonard 2003, 2.

132. *The Harvard Business Review* has stated that "people want to belong to something that they think is effective." (Ross December 2006, 8).

133. See, for example, "Managing Expectations for Surgery New Tools Help Hospitals Explain Procedures, Risks; Protection From Malpractice." *Wall Street Journal.* December 14, 2005, D5. (WSJ 2005)

134. Baker 2005, 255; Mann 2006; WSJ 2005.

135. See, for example, "What Pilots Can Teach Hospitals About Patient Safety." *New York Times.* October 31, 2006.

136. Stephen M. Powell 2005.

adjusted mortality scores as well as lower severity-adjusted length of stay, compared with hospitals having 22% or higher nursing turnover rates.[137]

Myriad sources have cited these additional personal benefits from CRM team training:

- Enhanced problem-solving skills.

- Increased knowledge of interpersonal dynamics.

- Broader knowledge of business processes.

- New skills for future leadership roles.

- Increased quality of work life.

- Feelings of satisfaction and commitment.

- A sense of being part of something greater than what one could accomplish alone.

The Business Case

Medical teams trained in health care CRM can perform more work at a lower cost of quality without compromising patient safety.[138]

Still, as Dr. O'Leary has said, hospital leaders need more justification. They need a strong *business* case to initiate patient safety programs and, by extension, to adopt CRM. This section will show that a combination of regulatory, accreditation, and cost factors delivers a powerful business case for improving patient safety and for adopting CRM.[139, 140]

---

137. L. Gelinas, C. Bohlen. "The Business Case for Retention." *Journal of Clinical Systems Management*, 2002, Vol. 4, No. 78, 14–16, 22.

138. Garrison, R. H., & Noreen, E. W. (2003). Managerial accounting. New York:McGraw-Hill, 63,69.

The Regulatory Environment

First, by way of perspective, the system-wide imperative to close the acknowledged health care quality gap has triggered a paradigm shift—from "managed care" to "care management" or "disease management." The original managed care approach in which dollars drove or were perceived to drive health care decisions has been roundly discredited. The new care management paradigm is patient-centric, aimed at improving the quality of care and service so that patients will get the right treatment at the right time and in the right setting—and get better faster. With this fundamental change in thinking has come the consensus that delivering higher quality health care translates into lower costs.[141]

Second, even if this conclusion were groundless, it has nevertheless been a driving principle of government regulators for the last few years. A prime example is the Medicare Prescription Drug, Improvement and Modernization Act of 2003 (DIMA), which was signed into law on December 8, 2003.[142] Following its enactment, the Centers for Medicare and Medicaid Services (CMS)—now the largest consumer of health care services in the world—launched a National Healthcare Quality Initiative, which recognized that quality services and

---

139. Medscape. "Improving Patient Safety: Conference Report." Medscape Money & Medicine 4(1), 2003. http://www.medscape.com/viewarticle/ 456622_4 (accessed February 25, 2009). (Medscape 2003)

140. Some remain unmoved. While arguing for the business case, Dr. O'Leary nevertheless conceded that it may fall outside the rubric that demands a measurable return on investment. According to Dr. O'Leary, the fundamental problem is that the organizations investing the money and resources to improve safety are "not the same people who realize the returns. If [hospitals] were to continue investing aggressively in patient safety, that could be a prescription for going out of business," he said (Medscape 2003). That said, the proliferating cache of information (as sampled in this chapter) amply supports the business case.

141. Closing the Quality Gap: The Role and Importance of "True Benchmarking". The MCM Group. February 2005. www.themcmgroup.com/PDFs/ Closing_the_Qualty_Gap.pdf (accessed February 27, 2009).

quality outcomes of patient care are paramount, and that economical consumption of resources will naturally follow.[143] Among the vast changes enacted under DIMA, hospitals receive additional reimbursements by demonstrating quality improvement. One of the earliest beneficiaries of this initiative was Kettering Medical Center, which in 2003 received $1.2 million for achieving high quality levels in 2002.[144]

Third—and of enormous significance[145]—the unmistakable trajectory of the quality movement and its regulatory support has culminated in the Medicare "Do Not Pay" regulations, which became effective on October 1, 2008.[146] In the wake of these regulations, patient safety at hospitals has taken on "new financial urgency;" previously, HCOs resistant to voluntary quality improvement were actually getting paid for additional services necessitated by avoidable errors involving Medicare patients. This refuge is now gone. Simply put, Medicare will no longer pay for certain specified conditions (including some referred to as "never events")[147,148] that could reasonably have

---

142. As an interesting aside, and perhaps a precursor to the "Do Not Pay" rules, at the 2003 conference of the Council on Health Care Economics and Policy (CHCEP), a consensus noted that under the traditional managed care model, health care resources are too often overused, underused, or misused—all indicia of poor quality. Elliott S. Fisher, MD, MPh, one of the presenters, estimated that as much as 30% of Medicare spending was wasted on potentially harmful services. (The Kaiser Family Foundation 2003, 18)

143. John Hartley, MHA [charter member, NAHQ]. Interview by Joann Genovich-Richards, PhD MBA MSN RN. *Upcoming challenges for the healthcare quality professional.* National Association for Healthcare Quality. *JHQ Online.* Sept/Oct 2004:W5: 20-21. http://www.nahq.org/journal/online/sep_oct/Hartley_Interview.pdf (accessed February 27, 2009).

144. Kettering Medical Center marketing department. Federal government to pay Kettering Hospital $1.2 million for high quality levels in 2002: CMS offers hospitals incentives to improve [press release]. July 15, 2003.

145. As early as 2001, the AHRQ report "Making Health Care Safer: A Critical Analysis of Patient Safety Practices" stated: "Given the traditional American dependence on education, competition, and other non-coercive mechanisms of change, the shift toward a regulatory approach is evidence of the depth of concern this issue [patient safety] has engendered." (AHRQ 2001, 611)

146. Centers for Medicare & Medicaid Service [CMS]: Proposed Rules. *Federal Register*, Wednesday, April 30, 2008, Vol. 73, No. 84, 23528, 23547-23562. (CMS Proposed Rules, 2008)

been prevented through the application of evidence-based guidelines, and HCOs may not bill beneficiaries for those costs.[149]

> ... [We adopt the] broad principle of Medicare not paying for preventable health care associated conditions.... [P]aying hospitals for serious preventable events is contrary to the promise that hospital payments should support higher quality and efficiency.[150] Linking a payment incentive to hospitals' prevention of avoidable or preventable HACs [Hospital Acquired Conditions] is a strong approach for encouraging high quality care. Combating these HACs can reduce morbidity and mortality as well as reducing unnecessary costs.[151]

As the largest insurer in the United States, Medicare's decision to refuse payment for HCAs has had predictably concussive impact, for both public and private payers:[152]

---

147. See, for example, CMS Press Release: Medicare and Medicaid Move Aggressively to Encourage Greater Patient Safety in Hospitals and Reduce Never Events. Thursday, July 31, 2008. http://www.cms.hhs.gov/apps/media/press/release (accessed February 27, 2009).

148. As of this writing, there are 10 such conditions: (1) Stage III, IV pressure ulcers; (2) fall or trauma resulting in serious injury; (3) vascular catheter-associated infection; (4) catheter-associated urinary tract infection; (5) foreign object retained after surgery; (6) certain surgical site infections; (7) air embolism; (8) blood incompatibility; (9) certain manifestations of poor blood sugar control; and (10) certain deep vein thromboses or pulmonary embolisms. (CMS Proposed Rules, *Federal Register*, 2008: 23642-3)

   Of these, foreign object retained after surgery, air embolisms, and blood incompatibility are considered "never events."

149. See: "Medicare Will Not Pay for Preventable Conditions Acquired at Hospitals." The Henry J. Kaiser Family Foundation. *Kaisernetwork.org. Kaiser Daily Health Policy Report*, August 20, 2008. http://www.kaisernetwork.org/daily_reports/rep_index.cfm?DR_ID=46979 (accessed February 28, 2009). (Kaiser Family Foundation 2008)

150. Id., 23561.

151. Id., 23643.

152. NYT 2008.

- When the "Do Not Pay" rule became effective, CMS sent a letter to state Medicaid directors advising them how to adopt the same criteria. And during 2008, four state Medicaid programs (including New York), announced they would not pay for as many as 28 specified HCAs.

- Some of the country's largest commercial insurers have followed suit, including WellPoint, Aetna, Cigna and Blue Cross Blue Shield plans in seven states.

- Several state hospital associations (including Minnesota) have brokered voluntary agreements that providers will not bill for medical errors.

- In April 2008, Maine became the first state to pass a law banning billing and payment for medical errors.

Adverse events in hospitalized patients have been associated with increased costs of care, both direct and indirect. Therefore, additional investment to enhance patient safety is warranted from a business perspective as well as a response to this unmistakable regulatory trend. In response to the worry expressed by Dr. O'Leary, in the long run giving top priority to patient safety may become critical to an organization's very survival: regardless of what the regulators do, health care purchasers will increasingly demand safe care.[153] And contrary to the belief that patient safety initiatives are prohibitively expensive, many—like CRM in particular—are not. *Harvard Business Review*, for example, stated in 2005 that big gains can be achieved through small changes.[154]

---

153. William B. Weeks January 2003, 53.

92

Accreditation

AHRQ and The Joint Commission both acknowledge the value of teamwork in the professional medical environment. Team training is now becoming a standard for accreditation and for ongoing in-service staff education and training. For example:

- On February 26, 2002, The Joint Commission, to reduce ventilator-related deaths and injuries, recommended that JCAHO-accredited organizations initiate interdisciplinary team training for staff caring for ventilator patients. On July 30, 2004, The Joint Commission issued a similar recommendation relating to infant death and injury during delivery.[155]

- Improved communication among caregivers was a Joint Commission National Patient Safety Goal in both 2007 and 2008 (laboratory). Specifically, JCAHO required organizations to establish processes to eliminate communication errors, such as:

    - Having individuals verify verbal and telephone orders and critical test results by reading back the complete order or test result.

    - Standardizing a list of abbreviations, acronyms and symbols that are *not* to be used throughout the organization.

---

154. Steven J. Spear. "Fixing Healthcare from the Inside." *Curing U.S. Healthcare, 2d Edition. Harvard Business Review On Point Collection.* September 2005, Article 1: 2-19, 3. (HBR 2005)

155. Joint Commission on Accreditation of Health Care Organizations. "Preventing ventilator-related deaths and injuries." *Sentinel Event Alert*, Issue 25, February 26, 2002. Joint Commission on Accreditation of Health Care Organizations. "Preventing infant death and injury during delivery." *Sentinel Event Alert*, Issue 30, July 21, 2004.

- Implementing a standardized approach to "hand off" communications, including an opportunity to ask and respond to questions.[156]

- The Accreditation Council for Graduate Medical Education (ACGME) recently required surgical residents-in-training to demonstrate their mastery of several teamwork-related competencies.[157]

Costs: Direct and Indirect

Health care decisions makers are understandably interested in finding out whether patient safety improvements will enhance the bottom line—they seek a direct costs, hard data analysis. Indirect costs are generally of secondary interest, perhaps because they are traditionally difficult to measure. Both cost classes will be addressed, in reverse order.

Indirect Costs

They are difficult to measure, but no less real. In the patient safety context, there are two streams of indirect cost.

Patient-Related Cost

Patients injured as a result of medical errors experience direct costs, through higher copayments for the services rendered, and indirect costs, such as lost income, increased disability rates, and increased burden on caregivers.[158]

---

156. Joint Commission on Accreditation of Healthcare Organizations. 2007 National Patient Safety Goals, 3-5.(accessed July 22, 2009); 2008 National Patient Safety Goals (Laboratory), 3-6.

157. AHRQ 2008, 26; Susan Mann, Ronald Marcus and Benjamin Sachs Jan 1, 2006,2.

158. Baker 2005, 255.

Organization-Related Cost

An exclusive focus on direct costs obscures the organizational costs associated with adverse events. Those indirect costs include litigation: although error-related litigation rates are relatively low, when litigation occurs, substantial additional HCO resources are consumed in investigating errors, mounting a defense, responding to discovery requests, and paying settlements and awards. Also, preventable errors generate substantial personnel, regulatory, and marketing costs that may impair profitability and compromise organizational performance.[159, 160] (See figure below.) According to Weeks and Bagian, "Marketing costs of adverse events—in lost public confidence and tarnished reputation—due to vulnerable systems are likely to be incalculable and threaten organizational survival."

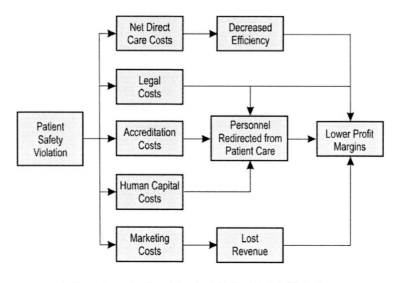

Indirect Organizational Costs of Patient Safety Violations
Source: Adapted from William B. Weeks, 52.

---

159. William B. Weeks, 52.

160. As practical matter, the improved processes introduced by CRM protocols also help HCOs manage staffing and scheduling more cost-effectively.

Direct Costs

For many, the moral, legal, and indirect cost rationales for adopting team-based training in general and CRM in particular have been, in themselves, sufficient to decisively demonstrate its value-add to HROs. That said—and Dr. O'Leary's diplomacy aside—the accumulating economic evidence is dramatic and no less telling.

As previously mentioned, *The New England Journal of Medicine* reported in January 2009 that using a simple surgical checklist—a basic CRM tool—could cut the death rate from surgery almost in half, reduce complications by more than a third, and save U.S. hospitals about $15 billion per year.[161]

Similarly dramatic results have been reported in ICUs. In 2001, Dr. Peter J. Pronovost, a professor at Johns Hopkins University School of Medicine (and a prominent voice in patient safety), began a mandatory five-step checklist program at Johns Hopkins Hospital. Over a 27-month period, the 10-day line infection rate of patients in the ICU dropped from 11% to 0%. During that time, only two line infections occurred. The hospital estimated that use of the checklist prevented 43 infections and eight deaths, saving $2 million.

This same protocol was then applied to 103 ICUs in Michigan (representing 85% of all ICU Michigan hospital beds) for an 18-month period (March 2004-September 2005). The results were remarkable. After only three months of the

---

161. Simple checklist cuts surgical deaths in half. Associated Press. January 14, 2009. www.msnbc.msn.com/id/28662096/ (accessed January 23, 2009), referring to Alex B. Haynes, M.D., M.P.H., Thomas G. Weiser, M.D., M.P.H., William R. Berry, M.D., M.P.H., Stuart R. Lipsitz, Sc.D., Abdel-Hadi S. Breizat, M.D., Ph.D., E. Patchen Dellinger, M.D., Teodoro Herbosa, M.D., Sudhir Joseph, M.S., Pascience L. Kibatala, M.D., Marie Carmela M. Lapitan, M.D., Alan F. Merry, M.B., Ch.B., F.A.N.Z.C.A., F.R.C.A., Krishna Moorthy, M.D., F.R.C.S., Richard K. Reznick, M.D., M.Ed., Bryce Taylor, M.D., Atul A. Gawande, M.D., M.P.H., for the Safe Surgery Saves Lives Study Group. A Surgical Safety Checklist to Reduce Morbidity and Mortality in a Global Population, N Engl J Med 2009; 360:491-9.

program, the median rate of catheter-related bloodstream infection per 1,000 catheter days dropped to zero from an average 2.7 infections—a 66% reduction. This improvement was sustained throughout the 18 months of monitoring. This program, the details of which were reported in *The New England Journal of Medicine*,[162] saved an estimated 1,500 lives, saved between $175 million and $200 million—and cost only $500,000 to administer.[163] This represented a financial return on investment with direct correlation to quality and safety.[164]

Other HCOs have reported notable CRM-related results. Beth Israel Deaconess Medical Center (BIDMC or Beth Israel), an early adopter of the patient safety culture and advocate of CRM,[165] began team training in 2002. From the outset, and as briefly mentioned above, BIDMC has reported consistent improvement in reducing preventable errors and managing errors and related economic benefits:

- On the L&D side, malpractice claims, suits, and observations (monies placed in reserve for potential claims) dropped by more than 50% in the period from

---

162. Peter Pronovost, M.D., Ph.D., Dale Needham, M.D., Ph.D., Sean Berenholtz, M.D., David Sinopoli, M.P.H., M.B.A., Haitao Chu, M.D., Ph.D., Sara Cosgrove, M.D., Bryan Sexton, Ph.D., Robert Hyzy, M.D., Robert Welsh, M.D., Gary Roth, M.D., Joseph Bander, M.D., John Kepros, M.D., and Christine Goeschel, R.N., M.P.A. "An Intervention to Decrease Catheter-Related Bloodstream Infections in the ICU." *The New England Journal of Medicine* December 28, 2006 Vol. 355: No. 26: 2725-2732.

163. As reported, for example, in:

   European Hospital. "Simple checklists could save healthcare billions." *EHOnline*, April 1, 2008. (accessed April 1, 2008). (EH 2008)

   MedicineNet.com. "Program Seeks to Reduce ICU Infections" [report of telephone conference with Peter J. Pronovost, M.D., Ph.D., professor, Johns Hopkins University School of Medicine, Baltimore]. HealthDay News, Ocotber 1, 2008. (accessed March 1, 2009).

164. Inexplicably, these impressive results were largely ignored by both the North American and the international medical and consumer press (EH 2008).

165. "Conferences with Patients and Doctors: A 38-Year-Old Woman With Fetal Loss and Hysterectomy (Benjamin P. Sachs, MB, BS, Discussant)" *Journal of the American Medical Association (JAMA)*, August 17, 2005 Vol. 294, No. 7 833-840, 837.

2002 to 2005. The money set aside for cases also dropped 50%, a savings of several million dollars.[166]

- Beth Israel's CRBI team training initiative (mentioned previously) cost $37,500 to implement and has translated into a cost savings of $1.3 million,[167]—a remarkable 3400% return on investment.

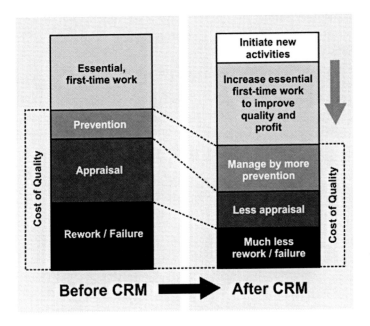

Cost of Quality
Source: Adapted from Garrison 2003, Stephen M. Powell, 2005

As the above analysis reflects, one of the primary and demonstrable economic by-products of CRM training is dramatically reduced malpractice claims and reduced premiums. Liability cost savings have been reported in the emergency department and in anesthesiology, as well as L&D. A closed claim review of ED errors—an area of pronounced focus for improvement[168]—revealed that after CRM training,

---

166. Mann 2006.

167. AAMC 2007.

the projected liability cost savings averaged $3.45 per patient visit.[169] According to another study published in 2007 in the *Journal of the American College of Surgeons*, which reported on the benefits of surgical time outs (a standard CRM practice):[170]

- Team training "substantially lessens target events with a frequency that is actually cost beneficial to the hospital."

- Anesthesiology is a "shining example" of how improved quality and safety translates to lower malpractice insurance premiums.

However, that study also observed that the personal economic gain from team training has not yet been widely recognized among surgeons.[171]

The fact that CRM has been associated with greater job satisfaction among nurses—and therefore lower turnover—also has positive economic consequences. According to one often-cited (and previously mentioned) study, hospitals with high nursing turnover rates had 36% higher costs per discharge than

---

168. In a 2007 interview for *Newsweek*, Dr. Frederick Blum, past president of the American College of Emergency Physicians said that absent grand solutions from government (which as suggested above, may already be on the way), hospitals will have to focus on internal steps like CRM:

    You just keep chipping away at the stone and hope that at some point, someone will say, "We've got to fix this," he said. "Hopefully it won't take a catastrophic failure for others to realize the state of emergency the emergency health-care system is in." (How to Stop the Bleeding 2007)

169. Shapiro 2004, as cited in Stephen M. Powell, Capt., BA, ASO, Robert N. Haskins, Capt., BSS Wayne Sanders, BS. "Improving Patient Safety and Quality of Care Using Aviation CRM." *Patient Safety & Quality Healthcare* July / August 2005. http://www.psqh.com/julaug05/delivering.html (accessed February 22, 2009).

170. Terry Altpeter, RN, PhD, Kitty Luckhardt, LPN, John N Lewis, MD, PhD, Alden H Harken, MD, FACS,Hiram C Polk Jr, MD, FACS. "Expanded Surgical Time Out: A Key to Real-Time Data Collection and Quality Improvement." *Journal of the American College of Surgeons* 2007 Vol. 204:527–532, 530, 531.

171. Id., 531.

hospitals with turnover rates of 12% or less. Hospitals with a lower rate of turnover also had lower risk-adjusted mortality scores as well as lower severity-adjusted lengths of stay compared with hospitals having 22% or higher nursing turnover rates.[172]

In 2005, the *Harvard Business Review* viewed the error management crisis through a different lens—as a value-generating opportunity.[173] The table below represents projected savings to hospitals in the United States with reductions in medical errors by 50% and 90%.

Medical Errors in U.S. Hospitals

National estimate of current annual level	50% Reduction	90% Reduction
974,000 patients injured	487,000 patients injured	97,400 patients injured
98,000 patient deaths	49,000 patient deaths	9,800 patient deaths
$17 billion to $29 billion in costs	$8.5 billion to $14.5 billion in costs	$1.7 billion to $2.9 billion in costs

Source: Adapted from IOM, HBR, 2005,6.

---

172. L. Gelinas and Bohlen, C. "The Business Case for Retention." *Journal of Clinical Systems Management* 2002 Vol. 4, No. 78, 14-16, 22.

173. HBR 2005, 6.

WIIFM Conclusions

CRM is relatively new to medicine and some HCO decision makers have lingering reservations, citing a paucity of scientific studies that definitively "prove" CRM works. Metaphorically, the skeptics seem to demand the highest possible resolution for an already unambiguous photograph. The ever-rising current of evidence rather convincingly shows that CRM works—specifically, CRM improves teamwork and performance and reduces errors—and is translatable to health care.

Moreover, CRM methodology has evolved from a wide-angle, top-down perspective that aligns with sound business principles. Those principles take into account the relationship between individual tasks and overall business goals: the manner in which HCO physicians, nurses, pharmacists, technicians and other personnel work and perform every day impacts, if not dictates, the organization's profitability and financial health.

The benefits of improved, CRM-driven teamwork are well-documented. By developing and installing CRM to support its pressing error management imperatives, an HCO can realize numerous benefits that nourish the bottom line, including:

- Deeper overall commitment to corporate mission, more flexible response to change, increased ownership and stewardship.

- Increased job satisfaction, and therefore reduced turnover and absenteeism.

- Improved quality and productivity.

- Reduced costs.

- Increased patient satisfaction.

Furthermore, in relative terms, the money spent to install a CRM program is less a cost than a value-adding investment in individual and organizational competence that yields significant returns. To again echo the Harvard Business School, building this competence "is both achievable and creates a huge value opportunity with relatively little attached cost...[We know of] nothing else that can give you so much bang for the buck in terms of significantly increasing the value of an organization."[174]

Baker has distilled the myriad virtues of CRM programs succinctly:

> ... [T]hey work, they're sustainable (despite staff turnover and new faces each day on the team), they save money, they save lives, and they improve morale. [They] also contribute to continuous self-education, continuous quality control... [, and] some malpractice insurers have lowered their rates for CRM-trained professionals.[175]

174. Richard Luecke. "Make Better Decisions." *Harvard Management Update.* April 2006. Vol. 11, No.4, 4-7, 5.

175. Baker 2005, 255.

Part Three

Overcoming Barriers
and Adopting CRM

Improving patient safety flows from a single—but arguably the most important—safe practice: the creation of a health care culture of safety.[176]

---

176. National Quality Forum. "Safe Practices for Better Healthcare – 2006 Update." Consensus Report. Washington DC 2007, 38. (NQF 2007)

Chapter 8

Assaulting Tradition

Key Points in this Chapter

- Despite the evidence that CRM works, saving lives and money, many HCOs have not yet responded.

- To reduce the threat of human error factors and improve patient safety, HCOs must create a sustainable culture of safety via an enterprise-wide commitment.

- The five hallmarks of a positive safety culture in an HCO are: (1) a fundamental acknowledgment that life-threatening human error is inevitable; (2) a willingness to direct resources toward improving safety; (3) a commitment to collaboration across ranks; (4) a blame-free environment; and (5) a commitment to constantly learn and improve.

- Putting financial performance above safety is not consistent with a safety culture.

- The term "culture" in the patient safety context involves many interlaced top-end and sharp-end (organizational and individual) cultural streams, any one of which can adversely impact the goals of CRM.

- The culture of medicine has traditionally held that if highly trained practitioners try hard and pay attention, their performance will be error-free.

- Behaviors and attitudes in operating rooms, emergency rooms, and intensive care units are similar to those that existed in cockpits before CRM.

- Professional culture is crucial to the success of any patient safety/ CRM program. Without buy-in and participation of physicians, the program is doomed to fail.

Demonstrably, CRM works; it is readily translatable to health care; and when properly deployed, it saves lives and money. Although those barriers to adoption have been dispatched, research nevertheless shows that even though patient safety is a public health priority,[177] many HCOs have not yet responded to the patient safety movement in general and team-based/CRM best practices in particular.

Culture-Based Resistance to Change

This resistance, according to the overwhelming preponderance of authority, is attributable to culture: confronting current cultures and establishing new ones.

To reduce the threat of error from human factors and improve patient safety, HCOs must first create and sustain a culture of safety.[178] That conclusion—reached by a chorus of credible sources inside and outside medicine—challenges, if not rejects, the existing systemic culture:

> An emphasis on financial performance, capital preservation, and liability avoidance prioritized over safe care would not be acceptable behavior and would not be consistent with a culture of patient safety.[179]

This idea is not new. In fact, The Joint Commission has long identified problems with HCO culture and communication as the most prevalent root causes of error-related death and

---

177. See, for example, Vinette Langford, RN, MSN and Victoria H. Rollins, MHA, RN, CPHRM. "Building a Culture of Safety: Creating a Reliable and Sustainable Patient Safety Infrastructure through Teamwork Training." *Patient Safety and Quality Healthcare*. September/October 2007, 1. http://www.psqh.com/sepoct07/culture.html (accessed 12.15.08). (Vinette Langford 2007)

178. National Quality Forum. "Safe Practices for Better Healthcare – 2006 Update." Consensus Report. Washington DC 2007, 38. (NQF 2007)

179. NQF 2007, 44 (Footnote 13).

injury[180] and in 2001 imposed patient safety goals that urged hospital leadership to create a "non-punitive culture of safety." The IOM's *To Err Is Human* recommended that "health care organizations and the professionals affiliated with them should make continually improved patient safety a declared and specific aim by establishing patient safety programs."[181]

Safety Culture as a Concept

The term "safety culture" first appeared after the Chernobyl disaster in 1986. That signal event, as well as others of that decade such as the pesticide plant explosion in Bhopal, was found attributable to human factors that festered in what the UK Parliament elegantly called an "impoverished safety culture."[182, 183] Similarly, investigators of the *Columbia* space shuttle tragedy concluded that NASA's internal culture (including apparent complacency) was a major contributor. NASA's organizational culture had as much to do with this accident as foam did.[184]

---

180. "Fostering Teamwork Between Sterile Processing and the OR." *Infection Control Today Magazine*, October 1, 2003. http://www.infectioncontroltoday.com/articles/406/406_3a1topics.html# (accessed March 5, 2009).

181. John R. Meurer, Linda N. Meurer, Jean Grube, Karen J. Brasel, Chris McLaughlin, Stephen Hargarten, Peter M. Layde. "Combining Performance Feedback and Evidence-based Educational Resources." In *Advances in Patient Safety: From Research to Implementation*, 2005: Vol. 4, 237-252, 248. Rockville, MD: Agency for Healthcare Research and Quality (AHRQ 2005)

182. *Managing Human Error.* London, UK: Parliamentary Office of Science and Technology [UK], 2001, 5. (Managing Human Error, 2001)

183. These events, and the perceived organizational complicity in them, aroused sufficient public outcry in the UK that its Law Commissions recommended creating a new a criminal offense called "corporate killing," which would apply when an organization's "conduct in causing death fell far below what could reasonably be expected." (Managing Human Error 2001,7)

184. Columbia Accident Investigation Board (CAIB). *Final Report on the Columbia Space Shuttle Accident, Volume 1.* Washington DC: U.S. Government Printing Office, 2003 (CAIB 2003), 12.

NASA's Organizational Culture

It is both ironic and tragic that NASA's organization culture was a root cause of the *Columbia* Space Shuttle catastrophe, since NASA was the moving force behind CRM at its inception, and doubly so considering the *Challenger* disaster. These separate incidents graphically demonstrate, as one close observer of NASA's organizational culture said, that "cultural norms tend to be fairly resilient ... The norms bounce back into shape after being stretched or bent. Beliefs held in common throughout the organization resist alteration." The Columbia Accident Investigation Board (CAIB) viewed "this cultural resistance as a fundamental impediment to NASA's effective organizational performance." (CAIB 2003, 101,102)

The CAIB report, as it relates to organizational culture, is particularly instructive in the health care/CRM context. For example, the reports says:

The dramatic Apollo 11 lunar landing in July 1969 fixed NASA's achievements in the national consciousness, and in history. However, the numerous accolades in the wake of the moon landing also helped reinforce the NASA staff's faith in their organizational culture. Apollo successes created the powerful image of the space agency as a "perfect place," as "the best organization that human beings could create to accomplish selected goals." During Apollo, NASA was in many respects a highly successful organization capable of achieving seemingly impossible feats.

The continuing image of NASA as a "perfect place" in the years after Apollo left NASA employees unable to recognize that NASA never had been, and still was not, perfect, nor was it as symbolically important in the continuing Cold War struggle as it had been for its first decade of existence. NASA personnel maintained a vision of their agency that was rooted in the glories of an earlier time, even as the world, and thus the context within which the space agency operated, changed around them. (CAIB 2003, 102)

The consensus demand for creating a safety culture in health care centers on a simple but frequently overlooked guiding precept: systems produce performance, not individuals. The current pay-for-performance movement, for all its surface merit, is—at least according to one outspoken commentator—playing at the fringes of the patient safety problem because

> tinkering with pay…appears to be easier than fixing organizational cultures and leadership capabilities…[and] does not seem to require the systemic intervention along multiple dimensions implied in the idea of building high performance work arrangements.[185]

As a practical matter, this means that in order for CRM methodology to achieve maximum effect, an organization-wide commitment to safety must come first. This commitment entails cultural changes that spread wide and run deep, incising long-held beliefs about practicing health care and the business of delivering it.[186] A "new mental model" is required, with new technologies and training.[187]

But in the health care domain, the term "culture" has several layers of complexity and meaning, with both top-end and sharp-end implications.[188] In order to prepare a fertile field for CRM,

---

185. Jeffrey Pfeffer PhD. Testimony to United States House of Representatives Committee on Oversight and Government Reform/Subcommittee on Federal Workforce, Postal Service, and the District of Columbia Hearing on the Status of Federal Personnel Reform. Washington, DC, March 8, 2007. http://www.evidence-basedmanagement.com/research_practice/commentary/pfeffer_congressional_testimony_08mar2007.html (accessed March 6, 2009).

186. It is recognized, however, that this imperative is superimposed on the already intense pressure facing health care decision makers. The Joint Commission, for example, notes that "increasing costs, increasing demand for services, and unfavorable reimbursement policies mean that patient 'throughput' – the time in which patients move into, through, and out of the health care setting—must be accelerated to maintain revenues. This acceleration of the care process heightens the risk of medical error, and compromises effective patient-practitioner communications." (Health Care at the Crossroads: Strategies for Improvng the Medical Liability System and Preventing Patient Injury 2005, 9)

187. Vinette Langford 2007,1.

several interlaced cultural streams must be taken into account, because (as Helmreich has pointed out) any one of them "can deflect the goals of CRM."[189]

Instilling a Safety Culture

There is no dispute that establishing and fostering a safety culture is fundamental to effective error management and optimal patient safety. Although volumes have been written about what constitutes a "safety culture," the term eludes standard definition.[190] That said, certain common and readily discernible characteristics have emerged, sometimes by describing and contrasting the attributes of medicine's traditional culture.

The culture of medicine holds to the following traditional belief: its practitioners are so highly trained that if they try hard and pay attention, their performance will be error-free.[191] Competence has been equated with near-perfect performance.

---

188. Steven J. Spear. "Fixing Healthcare from the Inside." *Curing U.S. Healthcare, 2d Edition. Harvard Business Review On Point Collection.* September 2005, Article 1: 2-19, 3. (Spear 2005)

189. Much of the culture-related information in the following paragraphs was distilled from the following interrelated sources by Helmreich and colleagues:

Robert L. Helmreich and John A.Wilhelm. "CRM and Culture: National, Professional, Organizational, Safety." The Norwegian University of Science and Technology (NTNU).

Helmreich, R. L. (1998). "Culture, Threat, and Error: Assessing System Safety." Paper presented at the Safety in Aviation: The Management Commitment: Proceedings of a Conference. Royal Aeronautical Society, London. (Helmreich, Culture, Threat, and Error: Assessing System Safety 1998)

Robert L. Helmreich, PhD FRAES and Jan M. Davies, MSc MD FRCPC. "Culture, threat, and error: lessons from aviation." *Canadian Journal of Anesthesia*, June 19 2004, Vol. 51:R1-R4.

190. For example, See, Laura T. Pizzi, PharmD, Neil I. Goldfarb, and David B. Nash, MD, MBA. "Promoting a Culture of Safety," Chapter 40 in *Making Healthcare Safer: A Critical Analysis of Patient Safety Practices.* Agency for Healthcare Research and Quality (AHRQ), 447-457. Rockville, MD: U.S. Department of Health and Human Services, 2001[Pizzi et al 2001]: "...an exact definition of a safety culture does not exist," 448.

Mistakes have been considered a personal failing.[192] The National Quality Forum (NQF) has called this the "culture of name, blame, and shame."[193] Understandably, this collective mindset, which is based on unrealistic expectations, inhibits the open admission and discussion of errors and the process of learning from and managing them.[194] This represents, according to NQF, a "major barrier to performance improvement."[195, 196] and diverts attention from the systems consciousness necessary to improve patient safety. In her 2004 study, Amy Edmonson noted:

> Given that human error will never disappear from organizational life, an important management issue thus becomes the design and nurturance of work environments in which it is possible to learn from mistakes and collectively to avoid making the same ones in the future.[197, 198]

---

191. This idea links directly to the professional culture of physicians, discussed in greater detail below. The inference may be made that in some ways the culture of HCOs has been influenced by—or approximates a macrocosm of—that professional culture. In support of the proposition that each has shaped the other, see, for example, Vinette Langford (2007, 1): "The healthcare industry is held increasingly to a standard of flawless performance in an environment where it can be very difficult to manage human error." This link makes perfect sense, given that many hospital leaders are clinicians who have been promoted into those positions (Singer and Tucker, 25).

192. Amy C. Edmonson. "Learning From Mistakes Is Easier Said Than Done: Group and Organizational Influences on the Detection and Correction of Human Error." *The Journal of Applied Behavioral Science*, March 2004, Vol. 40 No. 1: 66-90, 70. (Edmonson March 2004)

193. NQF 2007, 59.

194. Amy C. Edmonson. "Learning From Mistakes Is Easier Said Than Done: Group and Organizational Influences on the Detection and Correction of Human Error." *The Journal of Applied Behavioral Science*, March 2004, Vol. 40 No. 1: 66-90, 70. (Edmonson March 2004)

195. NQF 2007, 59.

196. As suggested above, the cultural barriers have been perpetuated by the preoccupation with the bottom line typical of the managed care era, coupled with (as NQF points out) an underlying fear of malpractice liability (NQF 2007, 59).

For some organizations, their safety culture has become "impoverished" and eroded beneath them, with deadly consequences. As happened at NASA leading up to the *Challenger* tragedy, repeated behaviors that stray from best safety practices eventually become normal and ingrained as complacent culture. Corners are cut, safety checks bypassed, and red flags ignored.[199] In the health care context, Mark Chassin and Elise Becher have referred to this phenomenon as the "culture of low expectations": when a system routinely produces errors (for example, making entries on the wrong chart, miscommunications between team members), providers in the system become habituated to malfunction. What should be recognized as a warning of impending danger is ignored as normal operating procedure.[200]

This sketch of what a safety culture is not points to an outline of what it is. The research about high reliability organizations leads to the conclusion that conceptually, for an organization to attain and sustain a safety culture, it must demonstrate, through its norms and processes and the behaviors of its people, a constant commitment to safety as a top priority—a commitment that is manifest in a shared value and belief permeating all levels of an organization, from frontline personnel to executive management.

---

197. Edmonson March 2004, 87.

198. On this theme, Edmonson also wrote:

   These findings provide evidence that the detection of error is influenced by organizational characteristics, suggesting that the popular notion of learning from mistakes faces a management dilemma. Detection of error may vary in such a way as to make those teams that most need improvement least likely to surface errors—the data that fuel improvement efforts. This has important implications for quality improvement efforts that rely upon work teams' participation in detecting and correcting error... (Edmonson March 2004, 86-87).

199. Vaughan Diane. *The Challenger launch decision: risky technology, culture and deviance at NASA*. Chicago, IL: University of Chicago Press, 1996.

200. Mark R. Chassin (MD, MPP, MPH) and Elise C. Becher (MD, MA). "The wrong patient." *Annals of Internal Medicine,* June 2, 2002 Vol. 136, No. 11: 826-833, 830.

A culture of safety serves as an institutional conscience....It is how individuals view the world around them and respond when faced with a visible challenge—and when no one is looking.[201]

A safety culture concentrates on systems and processes rather than individuals and fosters open and honest communication, but nevertheless gives its people a safe harbor for their candor.

---

201. Georgia W. Peirce. "Building the Foundation for a Culture of Safety." *Focus on Patient Safety: a newsletter from the National Patient Safety Foundation,* 2005; Vol. 8, No. 1: 1-3, 1 (Peirce 2005). http://npsf.org/paf/npsfp/fo/pdf/ Focus2005Vol8No2.pdf (accessed December 27, 2008).

Safety Culture: Five Essential Hallmarks

The assembled research into organizational culture reflects five common and essential hallmarks of a positive safety culture in an HCO (and by extension, an HRO):[202]

1. Reality Check

    A fundamental acknowledgment that its activities are inherently high risk and that life-threatening human error is inevitable.

2. Investment

    Willingness to direct resources toward improving safety by managing the threat of error. This means:

    *   Deploying proven threat and error-management resources and protocols—such as CRM—that recognize the intrinsic value of, and promote, teamwork.

    *   Proactively providing training and skill building (with regular reinforcement) not only to medical teams but also to instructors and evaluators.

---

202. These hallmarks are abundantly reflected and reinforced with virtual unanimity throughout the research for this book, including as contained in or summarized in the following sources:

Reason 2000.

Pizzi et al 2001, 448.

Singer and Tucker 2005, 25.

Powell and Hill, 2006.

Stephen M. Powell; Ruth Kimberly Hill, RN. "Home Study Program: My copilot is a nurse—Using crew resource management in the OR." *AORN Journal*. January 2006, Vol 83, No 1; 178-204.

Vinette Langford 2007,1.

NQF 2007, 37-38.

3.   <u>Collaboration</u>

A commitment to seek solutions to vulnerabilities through collaboration across ranks;[203] this is often referred as "flattening the hierarchy" and is discussed in greater detail later in this chapter.

4.   <u>Blameless Safe Harbor</u>

A blame-free environment in which individuals are encouraged and enabled—through multiple, easy-to-use channels or perhaps check-off forms—to report errors or close calls without fear of reprimand or punishment. Expanding on this idea:

- Engineering a just culture is an essential early step in creating a safe culture.[204]

- Trust is a critical element of a safety culture, since it is the lubricant that enables free communication and encourages highly attuned vigilance for "red flags."

- Trust is achieved by demonstrating a non-punitive attitude toward error (not to be confused with intentional or reckless violations of policy)[205] and showing in practice that safety concerns are addressed.[206]

---

203. See, for example, Pamela H. Mitchell, Lynne S. Robins, Douglas Schaad. "Creating a Curriculum for Training Health Profession Faculty Leaders," in Volume 4, *Advances in Patient Safety,* Agency for Healthcare Research and Quality (AHRQ), 299-312. Rockville, MD: U.S. Department of Health and Human Services, 2005, 304-5.

204. Reason 2000, 768.

205. Helmreich raises an important qualifier: "An error-tolerant culture accepts errors but does not tolerate violation of formal rules, especially those validated as error avoidance or mitigation strategies." (Helmreich Winter 2001, 2).

The British Parliament sounded a similar chord: "It has also been found that workers in poor safety cultures have a 'macho' attitude to breaking safety rules, and tend to ascribe the responsibility of safety to others." (Managing Human Error, 2001)

206. Helmreich, Culture, Threat, and Error: Assessing System Safety 1998, 10.

- You have to create a culture in which people feel free to commit candor....The goal is not to blame but to understand. Accepting failure is pretty easy; to understand it is the hard part.[207]

5.   <u>Thirst for Knowledge</u>

The system would seek and maximize any opportunity to learn and improve, and support and encourage every effort aimed at ensuring safety.[208] This equates to an unwavering commitment to systematically identify and mitigate safety threats and learn from mistakes by:

- Gathering and analyzing data about errors and close calls.

- Based on that evidence, creating new ways (or adjusting current ways) to prevent or manage future occurrences.[209]

The positive non-punitive attributes listed above contribute to a self-sustaining cycle of learning,[210] which "cascade[s] down to ever more junior workers...building exceptionally adaptive and self-renewing organizations."[211]

A safety culture, therefore, concentrates on systems and processes rather than individuals and fosters open and honest communication, but nevertheless gives its people safe harbor for their candor.

---

207. "Leaders: Don't Go It Alone. A conversation with Warren Bennis". *Harvard Business Review*, December 2006, Vol. 11, No. 12, 9-10, 9, 10.

208. Peirce 2005, 3.

209. This resembles, in essence, the "Plan-Do-Study-Act" concept.

210. Edmonson March 2004, 80.

211. Spear 2005, 7.

Organizational Culture

Organizational culture is closely related to, but distinguishable from, safety culture. It refers to the policies, procedures, processes, and behaviors that characterize how an institution actually functions—"the way we do things here." Perhaps this distinction is best viewed as how a safety culture (or the lack of it) manifests itself: if the safety culture is the computer's operating system, then organizational culture is the software application.

Even in an established safety culture, organizational factors "can lead the best-qualified and motivated to err."[212] These factors, latent and diverse, may include:

- Environmental traits such as chains of command, the openness of communication between management and employees, the commitment of resources to training, and the level of teamwork among groups.

- Operational realities such as inadequate equipment, flawed procedures, and fatigue-inducing schedules.

As already suggested, organizational culture is a powerful force that can be positive or negative and can persist indefinitely through reorganizations and the change of key personnel.[213] A negative organizational culture can result in a CRM initiative being dismissed as yet another fashionable "me too" exercise rather than a reflection of the organization's core values and standards.

Hence, routines and SOPs can be either friend or foe to improving patient safety. CRM methods have been proved to promote improvement by becoming routine, second nature. On

---

212. Helmreich, Winter 2001,1.

213. CAIB 2003, 97.

the other hand, persistent "just because" routines that are artifacts of organizational inertia—and indicia of "cultures of low expectations" such as the pre-*Challenger* NASA—impede the necessary organizational sea change that is the predicate for sustainable high reliability performance.[214]

Sharp-End Cultural Streams

National/Ethnic Culture[215]

National/ethnic culture is the real-world amalgam of norms, values, and resulting behaviors extant in an increasingly diverse health care workforce, which can influence HCO behavior and performance.[216]

This stream is generally given low emphasis but merits close attention, because as Helmreich has pointed out:

> No national culture is optimal for safety. Because cultural values are so deeply ingrained, it is unlikely that exhortation, edict, or generic training programmes can modify

---

214. Amy C. Edmonson; Richard M. Bohmer; Gary P. Pisano. "Disrupted Routines: Team Learning and New Technology Implementation in Hospitals." *Administrative Science Quarterly,* Vol. 46, No. 4 (December 2001), 685-716 [Edmonson, Bohmer, and Pisano 2001], 685.

215. In his work, Helmreich refers only to "national culture." It seems, however, that awareness of ethnic influences—which cut across national boundaries—ought to be part of the overall patient safety equation.

This idea also implicates what has become known as "cultural competence." A detailed treatment of that subject is beyond the scope of this book. But, in concept, cultural competence requires, among other things, that HCOs (1) have defined values and principles, and (2) instill policies, structures, behaviors, and attitudes that enable them to work effectively across cultures. (See, for example, Georgetown University Center for Child and Human Development n.d.)

Although the health care industry has pioneered this field as it relates to patients, it seems no less germane to interactions among health care employees in general, and because delivery of safe healthcare and CRM requires effective teamwork, clinical team members in particular.

them. The challenge is to develop organisational initiatives that are congruent with cultures while enhancing safety... Error management can serve as a universally valued goal that can be embraced by individuals from every culture.[217]

National/ethnic culture also plainly ties back into organizational and safety culture. Ingrained individual reverence for rules, routines, and SOPs may either promote or undermine patient safety. These values, if aligned with a positive culture, would be beneficial, but if aligned with a flawed system, potentially disastrous.

Professional Culture

Professional culture, according to Helmreich, reflects the composite attitudes and values associated with a particular occupation.[218]

The mass of available research suggests that professional culture is particularly crucial to the success of any patient

---

216. Helmreich has pointed out several dimensions of national culture that are relevant to both aviation and medicine. For example, people from individualistic cultures tend to focus on the self, autonomy, and personal gain; those from collectivist cultures show primary concern for the group, harmonious relationships, and deference to leaders. Some cultures impart a belief that rules should not be broken and that written procedures are needed for all situations. Many Asian cultures are generally rule-oriented while the United States, the United Kingdom, and other nations of the British Commonwealth reflect much lower concern for rules and written procedures. In the clinic, as in the cockpit, national culture influences how juniors relate to seniors, including their willingness to speak up with critical information. Cultures that value harmony and teamwork may also support autocratic leadership and inhibit input from juniors. A belief in strict adherence to rules may portend difficulty in dealing with unforeseen emergencies. In contrast, leaders from cultures that do not highly value adherence to Standard Operating Procedures (SOPs) may be able to deal creatively with problems not covered by SOPs. (Helmreich, Culture, Threat, and Error: Assessing System Safety 1998, 2-3) This last point also links to the sterotypical beliefs and attitudes of physicans discussed in the following "Professional Culture" section of this chapter.

217. Helmreich, Culture, Threat, and Error: Assessing System Safety 1998, 3.

218. Helmreich, NTNU.

safety/CRM program. More pointedly, it is the fulcrum upon which the program will flourish or fail. The experts' plain message is this: even when all of the other cultural planets are aligned, without buy-in and participation of physicians—at the very tip of the sharp end—the program is doomed.

Again, instructive parallels have been drawn between aviation and medicine, pilots and physicians. Overall, pilots and physicians share an ardent commitment to excellence, a strong work ethic, and pride in the job.[219] In both cases, highly trained but fallible humans are expected by their organizations, the public, and themselves to perform well in complex, high stress environments and in close quarters (such as the cockpit or the OR/ED) with team members that may be total strangers—all with the lives of others staked on their routine decisions. Because of their superior expertise and the ultimate sharp-end responsibility that depends on it, pilots and physicians have traditionally led, and set the tone for, their work teams.[220,221]

In aviation, before the advent of CRM, proficiency was considered the prime factor in assessing a pilot's ability to perform safely under extreme pressure. This became known as "the right stuff," and whoever had it was held in the highest esteem and was accorded reverence and elevated status. Books and movies have romanticized the exploits, leadership, and raw courage of pilots, test pilots, and astronauts.[222] They acquired an aura of machismo,[223] rugged individualism, and flawless invulnerability.

---

219. Helmreich,Winter 2001.

220. David A. Marshall, Danae A. Manus, MPA, RHIA. "A Team Training Program: Using Human Factors to   Enhance Patient Safety." *AORN [Association of periOperative Registered Nurses] Journal*, December 2007, Vol. 86, No. 6: 994-1011 (Marshall 2007), 995.

221. Stephen A. Albanese 2007.

222. For example, "The Right Stuff," a 1983 film adapted from Tom Wolfe's 1979 book of the same name, is about the test pilots involved in high-speed aeronautical research at Edwards Air Force Base as well as those selected to be astronauts for Project Mercury, the United States' first foray into human spaceflight.

Somehow, when these individuals found themselves in a work group setting, their special and revered status transmuted into leadership of, and managerial authority over, their flight crews. Moreover, commercial pilots were often recruited from the military and brought with them a culture that valued respect for authority and reluctance to question orders, even in situations where the orders contradicted standard operating procedures.[224, 225] By extension, junior crew members were expected to do the same and dared not challenge the pilot.

Physicians acquired a similar—and similarly well-deserved—aura.[226] Medical training emphasizes individual skills and performance; physicians tend to practice as individuals.[227] Over time, this paradigm has served well. In the OR, for example:

> This context and its traditions are neither arbitrary nor irresponsibly harsh but, instead, reflect a well-established process that functions effectively. Surgeons have years of specialized training, are medically and legally responsible for patients' care, and conventional surgical technology allows them the highest quality, most direct access to data on a patient's well-being in the OR. [This] kind of top-down, one-way communication that was problematic in learning MICS

---

223. Stephen M. Powell, Capt., BA, ASO, Robert N. Haskins, Capt., BSS Wayne Sanders, BS. "Improving Patient Safety and Quality of Care Using Aviation CRM." *Patient Safety & Quality Healthcare*. July/August 2005. http://www.psqh.com/julaug05/delivering.html (accessed February 22, 2009) [Powell et al 2005], 3.

224. David P. Baker, Sigrid Gustafson, J. Mathew Beaubien, Eduardo Salas, Paul Barach. "Team Training in High-risk Contexts." Chapter 3 in *Medical Teamwork and Patient Safety: The Evidence-based Relation*. Literature Review. AHRQ Publication No. 05-0053, April 2005. Agency for Healthcare Research and Quality, Rockville, MD. http://www.ahrq.gov/qual/medteam (accessed March 11, 2009), 23. [Baker et al 2005]

225. The individual-based image has managed to co-exist with, and is perhaps somewhat at odds with, military-based values of respecting authority and following orders.

[minimally invasive cardiac surgery] can be essential to saving lives in critical moments during conventional cardiac surgery.[228]

The long-practiced "top-down, one way communication" model aligns with the macho stereotype. It also aligns with the "traditional hierarchical medical structure that assumes no physician can make a critical error."[229] As previously mentioned, a physician's technical acumen and hard work historically have become equated—within HCOs and for individual physicians—with an unrealistic expectation of near-perfect performance. Mistakes are considered a personal failing; they denote incompetence.[230]

Thus is exposed the negative underside of these positive individual attributes, and a serious impediment to improved safety. As Reason has said:

> The person approach has serious shortcomings and is ill suited to the medical domain. Indeed, continued adherence to this approach is likely

---

226. Here is a excerpted summary of an episode from the television show, *Grey's Anatomy*:

Addison arrives at Seattle Grace with her brother Archer, who's collapsed due to a parasite in his brain. ...Derek announces that surgery is not an option as Archer has eight cysts in his brain, any one of which could burst during surgery and kill him. Derek consults with the best doctors and they all agree the case is hopeless. "I need to believe that you can do this, that you can save my brother. I need you to be a God, just today," Addison begs him....

Derek decides it's doable ["I can fix this," he says] and talks a reluctant Archer into having the surgery....

A pregnant patient with an aneurysm, whose surgery was delayed due to the Archer emergency, begs Derek to do her surgery tonight, rather than make her wait until the next morning. There's a complication during the craniotomy but Derek, with Lexie's help, solves the problem.

...Derek walks in [to the bar], to loud cheers. "You were a god today. You slew dragons and you walked on water," Addison tells him.

(*Grey's Anatomy*. "Before and After," Season 5, Episode 515, February 12, 2009, http://abc.go.com/primetime/greysanatomy/index?pn=recap#t=131878&d=172093, accessed March 11, 2009)

227. Powell et al 2005, 3.

228. Edmonson, Bohmer, and Pisano 2001, 710.

> to thwart the development of safer healthcare institutions....[B] y focusing on the individual origins of error it isolates unsafe acts from their system context.... [I]t is often the best people who make the worst mistakes—error is not the monopoly of an unfortunate few.[231]

For both pilots and physicians, the unrealistic but embedded image of invincibility is conversely associated with an unrealistic (but according to Helmreich "universal") denial of vulnerability to what Helmreich calls "the multiple stressors of the occupation," including overwork, fatigue, and personal problems. The assembled research reflects that most physicians and nurses believe that they perform effectively even when fatigued; in fact, according to one study, 70% of consultant surgeons and 47% of consultant anesthesiologists denied that fatigue degraded their performance. Most physicians believe that their decision making is as good in emergencies as in normal situations and that their performance is not affected by personal problems.[232]

As previously mentioned, however, these beliefs are more folklore than fact and contrary to the scientific evidence. One physician has concisely concluded that "in both the cockpit and the OR, a lead professional sets the tone of the team's work. And in both places, fatigue and routine are the enemies of precision."[233]

Moreover, as Helmreich points out, the "macho" attitude of invulnerability can lead to risk taking, failure to rely on fellow

---

229. "Aviation's Gift to Health Care: Human Lessons Paid for in Blood." *ABC News*. November 16, 2005.

230. Edmonson March 2004, 70; NQF 2007, 37-38.

231. Reason 2000,768.

232. Helmreich, NTNU; Powell et al 2005, 3; J. Bryan Sexton, Eric J. Thomas, and Robert L. Helmreich. "Error, stress, and teamwork in medicine and aviation: cross sectional surveys." *BMJ*, March 18, 2000, Vol. 320:745-749 [Sexton et al 2000], 745.

233. Stephen A. Albanese 2007.

team members, and error.[234] As a by-product, a steep hierarchy defined by rank and status is often manifested in autocratic team leadership that confers decision-making power on the doctor.[235] In the OR, for example, surgeons are considered "kings" likely to resist flattening steep team hierarchies; one study observed that only 55% of consultant surgeons rejected steep hierarchies.[236]

For patients undergoing surgery, the biggest risk may be the power structure in the operating room.[237]

Traditionally, the utmost and deserved respect for, and elite status of, physicians has mutated into fear of them by nurses and other staff. One dated but illuminating study on how pharmacists interact with physicians observed:

> Pharmacist-physician communication is especially problematic because many of the acts pharmacists routinely perform (e.g. correcting, reminding, reporting, etc.) are intrinsically threatening to a physician's professional identity and sense of self worth.... [T]he pharmacist must manage his/her own identity (i.e. appear professional, be helpful if necessary, assert own authority, etc.) and guard against offending the physician....[238]

Sexton and colleagues similarly reported that communicating errors within the team is impeded because of personal reputation (76%), threat of job security (63%), and the egos of other team members (60%).[239]

---

234. Helmreich, Culture, Threat, and Error: Assessing System Safety 1998,3.

235. Powell et al 2005, 3.

236. Sexton et al 2000, 745.

237. "Bringing Surgeons Down to Earth: New Programs Aim to Curb Fear That Prevents Nurses From Flagging Problems." *Wall Street Journal, November 16, 2005, D1. [WSJ 2005]*

238. Bruce L. Lambert. "Directness and Deference in Pharmacy Students' Messages to Physicians," *Social Science & Medicine*, 1995 Vol. 40, No. 4, 545-555, 546.

Another previously cited study on implementing technology for MICS cardiac surgery noted that:

> Encouraging low-status OR team members to speak up and challenge high-status surgeons went against the grain of the cultural and structural context of cardiac surgery.[240]

This same point was made in an Edmonson study, which referred to a cardiac surgeon who successfully adopted the interdisciplinary team training necessary to perform MICS. That surgeon said team training represented "a paradigm shift in how we do surgery." The customary model was "surgeons barking orders down from on high;" MICS required surgeons "to become a partner not a dictator.... This is a complete restructuring of the OR and how it works."[241] From a nurse's perspective:

> Disruptive physician behavior, with its negative consequences for both nurses and their patients, continues to be an ingrained problem and needs to be creatively and decisively addressed. It is not just a matter of nurses feeling good about where they work—research has shown that nurse-physician communication is one of the strongest predictors of patient outcomes.[242, 243]

Similar to the unsteady advent of MICS, it was advancing technology in aviation that first triggered questions about what Helmreich has called the "stereotype of the lone aviator battling

---

239. Sexton et al 2000, 747.

240. Edmonson, Bohmer, and Pisano 2001,710.

241. Amy C. Edmonson. "Speaking Up in the Operating Room: How Team Leaders Promote Learning in Interdisciplinary Action Teams." *Journal of Management Studies,* September 2003, Vol. 40, No. 6:1419-1452, 1439-1440.

242. Alan H. Rosenstein, MD, MBA; "Nurse-Physician Relationships: Impact on Nurse Satisfaction and Retention." *The American Journal of Nursing (AJN),* June 2002, Vol. 102, No. 6: 26-34.

the elements with no need for the support of fellow crewmembers."[244] During World War II, aircraft designers recognized that this macho attitude hindered the design of sophisticated new aircraft: a single individual operating in a highly stressed, highly technical environment could not effectively operate all of the resources, and manage all of the inputs, that the new technologies would impose. Post-war research (as cited above) confirmed that at least 65% of air crashes were attributable to:

- Inadequacies in leadership, communication skills, crew coordination, and decision making.

- Inadequate management and use of the various resources available to the crew.[245]

These hard lessons planted the seeds for CRM.

Applying the historical lessons to the present context, experience and hard data have proved that at some point in the chain of progress, whether the individuals involved in any high-risk industry have the "right stuff" is beside the point. "Right stuff" and best intentions do not—and cannot—guarantee

---

243. It is unfair to single physicians out for disruptive behavior. A 2004 survey of VHA hospitals across the country with more than 1,500 participants, published in *The American Journal of Nursing (AJN)*, reflected that nurses behaved disruptively almost as frequently as physicians. The survey also indicates that disruptive behavior represents another impediment to improved safety; disruptive behavior was perceived by the survey participants "as having negative or worsening effects, in both nurses and physicians, on stress, frustration, concentration, communication, collaboration, information transfer, and workplace relationships." According to *AJN*, "even more disturbing" was the belief among participants that disruptive behavior had "negative or worsening effects on adverse events, medical errors, patient safety, patient mortality, the quality of care, and patient satisfaction," therefore radiating "far beyond nurses' job satisfaction and morale, affecting communication and collaboration among clinicians, which may well, in turn, have a negative impact on clinical outcomes." (Rosenstein and O'Daniel January 2005, 55)

244. Helmreich, NTNU.

245. See, for example, NQF 2007, 37-38.

positive outcomes. Echoing the World War II aircraft designers, some surgeons have themselves observed:

- Health care has become so complex, with so much advanced technology and equipment and more specialization, that physicians can't know everything.[246]

- Medicine is ever-more complex, and the 80-hour duty week for trainees demonstrates daily that the old guardrails are not sufficient.[247]

Deadly human error, we have learned, surfaces from many sources unrelated to admirable individuality or technical skill, including poor communication, poor management, poor leadership, loss of situational awareness, automation-induced reverie, and overwork. This, in fact, underscores why CRM was developed. It filled an identified performance gap.[248]

The above exposition reveals that the traditional culture-driven—and relatively unchallenged—logic is flawed. Traditional logic actually *inhibits* learning:

> [P]eople in organizational hierarchies systematically suppress mistakes and deny responsibility. Hierarchical structures thus discourage the kind of systematic analysis of mistakes and transfer of valid data that would allow people to better design systems to prevent them.[249]

---

246. Teresa Carter, vice president of surgical services for two Novant Health hospitals in the Winston-Salem, N.C., region, as quoted in WSJ 2005.

247. Altpeter et al 2007, 531.

248. "Does CRM Need A New Name?"*Air Safety Week*, February 28, 2005.

249. Edmonson March 2004, 68.

In fact, one report observed the following:

> Regarding quality and safety of medical care, medical professionals have long used their professional power to resist proposals for measurement and systematic improvement efforts.[250]

These observations, however, are not intended to blame physicians or to ignore that significant progress, as noted above, has been made (with clinicians' active participation) in improving patient safety through CRM-based team training.[251] Rather, they explain why and how, in the vastly complex health care universe, an entrenched, positive professional culture has been overtaken by complexity and overwhelmed by the sheer magnitude and frequency of adverse events. In relation to the breadth and depth of system-wide need, the available research reflects that overall progress in patient safety has been slow and has occurred in discrete pockets, and that

> behaviors and attitudes in the operating rooms, emergency rooms, and intensive care units are similar in nature to attitudes that existed in cockpits before CRM.[252]

To be fair, there are cogent explanations on the other side. Even Helmreich has conceded that comparisons between health care and aviation not perfectly apt; he allows that health care in the managed care era is far more complicated.[253, 254] Along those lines, Singer and Tucker, who have aggregated and summarized other research relevant to improving safety in HCOs, reported that:

---

250. Singer and Tucker 2005, 8.

251. Therefore, Helmreich's above-noted comment that a certain professional mindset is "universal" seems an intentional exaggeration to make a salient point.

252. Powell et al 2005, 3.

253. Helmreich, as quoted in *WSJ 2005.*

Institutional and organizational factors in hospitals differ substantially from those of other hazardous industries. Particularly important in hospitals is the role of the medical professions. Professionals are indispensable to hospitals, yet many are governed more by external professional norms than by immediate administrative systems. Most hospitals operate with a bifurcated power structure to accommodate conflicting demands of administrators and physicians.[255]

Other institutional factors that may be detrimental to quality and safety in hospitals include (1) clinical training that promotes professional hierarchies and individual responsibility and accountability rather than non-punitive, team-based learning; (2) compensation policies that pay for mistakes rather than reporting and improvement; and (3) a tort system that promotes fear of malpractice and deters providers from discussing and learning from mistakes.[256]

---

254. On the other hand, Classen and Kilbridge (2002, 964) observed:

> It is often thought that health care is a far more complex field than other industries and therefore unable to achieve such low defect rates. However, deaths from anesthesia have fallen dramatically over the last two decades, from rates of 25 to 50 deaths per million anesthesia inductions to a rate of only 3.4 deaths per million inductions. Clearly, some parts of the health care system are performing at safety levels on par with the best in other industries; the challenge is to create this level of safety throughout all areas of health care.

> Anesthesia is, as mentioned previously, a "shining example" of what can be accomplished through CRM training to both improve performance and reduce malpractice premiums. Surgeons, however, have been generally slow to recognize this, focusing instead "on poor and worsening reimbursement and rising professional liability premiums." (Altpeter et al 2007, 530)

255. Singer and Tucker, 2005, 7.

256. Singer and Tucker, 2005, 7-8.

The Physician's Perspective on Change

The physician's perspective has been articulated in depth by David Classen and Peter Kilbridge in their 2002 report, "The Roles and Responsibility of Physicians to Improve Patient Safety within Health Care Delivery Systems." Although they recognize the need to improve patient safety and the possibility of doing so despite the complexity, there are many reasons why physicians may be averse to change.[257]

Unrealistic Expectations and Burdens

"First, do no harm": as already stated, the aboriginal credo is the very foundation of medical education and how physicians view themselves and the culture in which they work. For any student who hopes to survive medical school and actually treat patients, perfection is the performance standard. In this environment, mistakes are not tolerated; they are considered personal defects to be eliminated. Partly because of the intense focus on personal achievement and responsibility, the medical profession attracts perfectionists who become more so as they move through the hazing of medical training.[258]

The above text has mentioned that physicians have often exhibited autocratic, at times intimidating, behavior. But the ritualized milieu in which physicians are expected to achieve

---

257. David C. Classen, MD, MS, and Peter M. Kilbridge, MD. "The Roles and Responsibility of Physicians to Improve Patient Safety within Health Care Delivery Systems." *Academic Medicine*, October 2002 Vol. 44, No. 10: 963-972 [Classen and Kilbrige 2002]. Except as otherwise indicated, the following paragraphs were distilled or excerpted from this article.

258. In support of the notion that physicians are products of an entrenched culture, *Time Magazine* noted the following:

Centering clinical learning on patients is a fairly radical concept for a medical-education system that is notoriously resistant to change. Medical schools operate largely on principles established in 1910. (Teaching Doctors to Care, 2006)

perfection and bear responsibility for mistakes as personal failures represents its own culture of intimidation.

Intimidated Physicians Bury Mistakes

Traditionally, in the presence of peers and colleagues, clinicians and students are often singled out and vilified for their mistakes. Errors can keep a medical student from getting licensed. Errors can get a practicing physician barred from practice or sued for malpractice.

In addition, the emphasis on individual physician accountability has been expanded to cover all things related to safety. Regardless of the actual cause of a mistake, the physician is ultimately responsible for it. State scope-of-practice laws, for example, tend to place responsibility on the physician and not the overall care team. The focus on individual "name, blame, shame" is further institutionalized in morbidity and mortality conferences and by credentialing and peer-review bodies, which customarily seek to assign blame for mistakes rather than learning from them. All of this perpetuates the counterproductive belief that mistakes are caused by individual physicians rather than by systems.

Given this painful but common, recurring, and intimidating experience and the perfectionistic personalities of many physicians to begin with, it is understandable that most aspiring or practicing physicians have little interest in either advertising their own mistakes or in reporting or investigating those of others. Sexton and colleagues have confirmed this idea, observing that a third of intensive care staff did not acknowledge that they make errors, and more than half reported reluctance to discuss mistakes.[259]

---

259. Sexton et al 2000, 1.

Specialization: At Odds With Teamwork?

Regulatory oversight at the local and national levels tends to be specialty-driven, which further isolates the physician at the sharp end as the sole source of responsibility. This isolation reinforces the reluctance to share or relinquish power and creates resistance to fully accepting or participating in team-based care—despite the compelling evidence that team-based care can lead to better and safer outcomes. Further hardening this stance is the fact, already mentioned, that in some cases, even when physicians have participated in team-based training and have transferred some care roles to other health care professionals, their legal liability has actually *increased*.

Lack of Trust

Many physicians simply mistrust HCOs' motivations for engaging physicians in quality improvement programs, believing that HCOs care more about saving or making money than helping patients. In some cases, when physician integration efforts have failed to yield the expected economic benefits, team-building initiatives have unraveled.

On the flip side, physicians face accelerating downward pressure on their practice revenues[260] and in some markets, directly compete with hospitals. Without demonstrable economic benefit to physicians—or if it, in effect, *costs* physicians to participate—HCOs will have difficulty convincing physicians that process improvement matters to them. Simply reducing length of stay or hospital cost is not enough to enlist physician support; incentives between physicians and HCOs must be aligned.

---

260. Classen and Kilbrige 2002, 964.

Lack of Uniformity, Autonomy, Training, and Time

Other hurdles to engaging physicians in patient safety initiatives include:

- The bewildering complexity for creating a patient safety model among their various and often simultaneous relationships with integrated delivery networks (IDNs), hospitals, management service organizations, physician-hospital organizations, independent practice associations, and IDN-owned insurance companies.

- The fear that pressure to reduce variations in care will compromise physicians' flexibility in caring for individual patients. One study noted that this "perceived loss of autonomy" was a common thread for organizations encountering difficulty gaining physician interest and participation in safety initiatives.[261]

- Physicians' lack of training in quality improvement, team leadership, and general management, making them less comfortable and competent than they would like in these roles.[262, 263]

- Lack of time, and a natural disinclination to take on more work or responsibility.

---

261. Marshall 2007, 1002.

262. Singer and Tucker, 2005, 7-8.

263. On this theme, research suggests that even when doctors embrace this role, they need training to do it well. For example, doctors perceive teamwork and communication to be better than other team members. In the OR, other team members (nurses, anesthetists, and support staff) reported high levels of team effectiveness only 40% of the time whereas surgeons reported high levels of team effectiveness 77% of the time (Powell et al 2005, 3).

   This example underscores the need for physician training in CRM-based skills.

On the last point, and as Edmonson has observed, physicians in general are already over-burdened. Bombarded with proliferating advancements in medical science and technology, they must somehow digest it all to maintain their expertise, their individual contributions, and their livelihood. Despite the undisputed need to manage errors and improve patient safety, the attendant fundamental—and disrupting—cultural and behavioral changes represent an additional burden not easily embraced. And to make the prospect even less palatable, it requires physicians not only to give up clinical authority while possibly retaining legal liability, but also to become skilled and sensitized team leaders who can manage a patient safety project and create an environment that nurtures team learning.[264]

The Evolutionary Divide

Echoing how pilots reacted to early CRM programs, physicians have tended to resist team-based training as an unproven methodology that exalts "psychobabble" and diverts time and energy from their "real" work. As the director of a CRM program at VHA hospitals has said,

> Surgeons didn't want to talk about culture—they think it is touchy-feely and a waste of time.[265]

The evolutionary divide between aviation and health care can be summarized as follows:

> We [have] learned to teach co-pilots, for instance, that even if God himself is in the left seat, they still have to speak up instantly when something is wrong. Instead of the autocratic leader who needed and accepted no advice,

---

264. Edmonson, Bohmer, and Pisano 2001, 712.

265. Kathy Irvin, former surgical nurse and director of VHA's Transformation Program, as quoted in WSJ 2005.

we've redefined leadership by creating strong captains who know how to create a team to help them make better, safer decisions. In other words, we built exactly what health care is now struggling to create: a cooperative, collegial system accepting of its human weaknesses and completely opposite to the traditional hierarchical medical structure that assumes no physician can make a critical error.[266]

To bridge the divide and recalibrate the professional culture, the health care community needs a revised definition of the term "competence," consisting of a standardized "cluster of related knowledge, skills, and attitudes" that (1) affect a major part of one's job (one or more key roles or responsibilities); (2) correlate with successful job performance; (3) can be measured against accepted standards; and (4) can be improved through training and development.[267]

Conclusions About Barriers to Change

The analysis in this chapter reflects that the professional culture in medicine is simultaneously entrenched, complex, and "fragile," making it difficult to implement patient safety programs.[268] As one trauma surgeon said:

Staff members who have been here for a long time really need to be convinced that there is an advantage in doing this. It's going to take years.[269]

---

266. Aviation's Gift to Health Care: Human Lessons Paid for in Blood 2005.

267. Baker et al 2005, 263.

268. Peter Plantes, a physician and vice president at VHA, as quoted in WSJ 2005.

269. Marshall 2007, 1006.

Moreover, as some have glibly noted, unlike airline pilots and their hundreds of passengers, physicians are not going down with the ship.

However convenient it may be to blame physicians both for the patient safety problem and their resistance to its recognized CRM-driven resolution, this is unfair and misguided: they are, after all, products of their training and culture. Also, overcoming the barriers at the sharp end is only part of a larger mosaic of change throughout all of the cultural streams described above. As Helmreich instructs, all of the cultural layers must be in harmony in order for CRM to be accepted and flourish. Simply put, what an HCO says and does must match what it purports to teach.

In order for that match to occur and to engage physicians, organization-wide leadership, communication, and teamwork must be brought to bear. The following sections will detail how this can be accomplished.

Chapter 9

Charting the Course to High Reliability with Collaborative Care

Key Points in this Chapter

- Unless the recognized barriers to change are surmounted, sustainable safe health care and high reliability performance cannot be achieved.

- A successful journey to high reliability requires intelligent planning and execution. Senior leaders must recognize from the beginning that success depends on effective leadership, communication, and teamwork.

- Top-end leadership is indispensable to instilling a safety culture and achieving high reliability. However, lack of executive leadership has been reported in many cases.

- For a senior leader to get started, a step-wise approach is recommended. The first step is a candid self-assessment of the organization's current safety culture. The second step is to engage physicians and other key players early on.

- According to one prominent authority, the second step—connecting with clinicians—represents a "bottom up" approach that offers the best channel to medical culture change.

- Engaging clinicians involves answering their WIIFM, producing tangible benefits, and gaining their trust. Perhaps the best way to gain their trust is to assure shared enterprise liability.

- The term "leadership" as used in this book refers to leadership in the executive suite and in the clinic. While executive leadership lays the groundwork for high reliability, team leaders give the vision life.

The Confluence of Three Formidable Rivers

The above analysis is preamble to this conclusion: unless the recognized barriers to change are surmounted, sustainable safe health care and high reliability performance cannot be achieved. This statement, perhaps obvious, nevertheless implies a formidable passage.

A successful journey to high reliability requires intelligent planning and solid execution. The planning must be informed by an early recognition that success depends on an organization mastering the following three domains:

- Leadership (both at the top end and the team level).

- Communication.

- Teamwork.

Metaphorically, the organization is compared to a vessel, and the three domains to powerful rivers, because—as the following analysis will show—they are fluid, flow concurrently and perpetually, and in the end flow together to propel and sustain organizational improvement.

Leadership

Notwithstanding the myriad challenges, documented success with CRM programs has demonstrated that effective leaders can drive and ultimately achieve the transition to high reliability, flattening traditional hierarchies and establishing a blame-free environment in which physicians, nurses, pharmacists, technicians, and other staff actively participate.

Leadership and Patient Safety

What patient safety leaders recognize today is that culture drives quality and safety.[270] Culture and attitude are at the core of creating safer systems of care....Unless everyone is completely clear about the tasks that must be done, exactly who should be doing them, and just how they should be performed, the potential for error will always be high.[271]

As a manager...you're only going to be as good as your people's performance....It's also about embracing the idea that they—and the department they're heading—are part of a larger organization. You need to open up the world view of how they fit it into the total picture.[272]

[The extensive] literature on high performance work systems tends to speak to the systemic, complementary nature of the various management practices required to provide an environment that produces innovation, discretionary effort, and high levels of performance and service.[273]

Even though individual clinicians may champion specific quality improvement projects, change is rarely achieved without strong leadership. Leadership is needed throughout the process, from the initial identification of a target to the evaluative phase. A successful leader needs to dedicate time and commitment for the program to succeed....Quality improvement is also a continuous journey rather than a discrete, time-limited project.[274]

Leadership structures and systems must be established to ensure that there is organization-wide awareness of patient safety performance gaps, that there is direct accountability of leaders for those gaps, that an adequate investment is made in performance improvement abilities, and that actions are taken to assure the safe care of every patient served.[275]

Thus, in order to instill a non-punitive safety culture in any HCO, top-down commitment and leadership are essential. But according to some commentators, although considerable

270. Peirce 2005; Vol. 8, No. 1: 1-3,1

271. Spear 2005, 3, 5.

272. Anne Field. "Moving Managers from 'Me' to 'We'." *Harvard Management Update*, April 2006, Vol. 11, No.4, 1-4, 1-2,4; includes quotations from Susan Howington (Senior Vice president and Managing Director, Lee Hecht Harrison) and Hal Leavitt (Kilpatrick Professor of Organizational Behavior at the Stanford Graduate School of Business).

273. Pfeffer 2007.

274. J. Randall Curtis, et al. January 2006, 213.

275. NQF 2007, 1.

attention has been directed to how the professional culture of physicians presents barriers to patient safety efforts, "many problems" relating to current CRM programs "seem to be associated with weak leadership and the abdication of authority."[276] The National Quality Forum similarly noted that the barriers to improving health care safety include "a lack of leadership regarding safety,"[277] and that

> Leadership by trustees, chief executive officers (CEOs), physicians, and other leaders across all departments and services is the single most important factor in turning the barriers to awareness, accountability, ability, and action into accelerators of performance improvement and transformation.[278]

Yet, credible research has indicated that even when leaders understand the need to create a strong safety culture and their crucial role in doing so, "few hospital Chief Executive Officers (CEOs) devote sufficient time or resources to patient safety."[279]

If physicians need to be engaged, and their attitudes and behaviors shifted "from order giver to team member,"[280] then hospital leaders must take foundation-building steps to make that happen. Senior leaders therefore need—but according to the research generally lack—specific mechanisms to create a strong safety culture in their organizations.[281]

Notwithstanding the myriad challenges, documented success with CRM programs has demonstrated that effective leaders can drive and ultimately achieve the transition to high reliability.

276. Powell et al 2005, 7.

277. NQF 2007, 37.

278. NQF, 39.

279. Singer and Tucker 2005, 2.

280. Edmonson, Bohmer, and Pisano 2001, 699.

281. Singer and Tucker 2005, 2-3.

Getting Started: A Step-Wise Approach

The research assembled for this book, including research contributed by sharp-end clinicians, recommends a step-wise approach for establishing patient safety/CRM programs and specific projects within the overall program.

The step-wise approach[282] enables senior management to overcome several crucial hurdles to the program's success, because:

- It divides what at first may seem an overwhelming enterprise-wide prospect into customized, digestible, and cost and resource effective segments.

- It optimizes the chances for early successes that can be learned from, built on, and used as templates for other projects.

- It is most likely to engage the support of physicians. In light of the previous chapter on the culture of medicine, this point cannot be over-emphasized. Physicians will in most cases be team leaders, and in any case, their participation and behaviors will likely determine whether the patient safety program ultimately succeeds.

Step One: Candid Self-Assessment

Edmonson has observed that an appropriate "organizational context" is a prerequisite for a health care organization to become a high reliability organization.[283] To gain that

---

282. The "Plan-Do-Study-Act" model is considered a key component of improving the quality of health care. (See, for example, Antonino Gullo November 9–11, 2007.)

283. Edmonson September 2003, 1425, Figure 1.

perspective, senior leaders must first candidly assess their organization's commitment to safety and their current safety culture.[284]

Step Two: Engaging Champions

As noted above, engaging physicians and other key personnel is one of the main barriers to improved patient safety in general and CRM in particular. After all, individual attitudes and behaviors must be aligned or changed. Therefore, quality improvement leaders must engage key players early on, offering them a "compelling rationale for change"[285] or "to portray their program in terms that are meaningful to diverse stakeholders within and outside of the [unit]."[286]

Other researchers have expressed this threshold challenge more pointedly. Top-end leaders must find and deliver convincing answers to the inevitable but natural question previewed above: "What's in it for me?" Chapter 7 of this book has already suggested some persuasive responses to WIIFM. Here are additional tips, distilled from the assembled research, for appealing to, engaging, and motivating the various constituents at the outset: [287]

---

284. See, for example:

  J. Randall Curtis, MD, MPH; Deborah J. Cook, MD; Richard J. Wall, MD, MPH;Derek C. Angus, MD, MPH, FRCP; Julian Bion, FRCP, FRCA, MD; Robert Kacmarek, PhD, RRT;Sandra L. Kane-Gill, PharmD, MSc; Karin T. Kirchhoff, RN, PhD, FAAN; Mitchell Levy, MD; Pamela H. Mitchell, PhD, CNRN; Rui Moreno, MD, PhD; Peter Pronovost, MD, PhD; Kathleen Puntillo RN, DNSc, FAAN "Intensive care unit quality improvement: a 'how-to' guide for the interdisciplinary team." *Critical Care Medicine*, January 2006, Vol. 34, No. 1: 211-218, 214. [J. Randall Curtis, et al. January 2006]. Although the article is directed at improving quality in the ICU, the principles and guidance have direct, "first-steps" safety culture relevance to senior HCO leaders, and are referred to throughout this section of the book.

  Stephen M. Powell 2005, 3.

285. Edmonson September 2003, 1428. Similarly, Singer and Tucker, 1, 28.

286. J. Randall Curtis, et al. January 2006, 216.

- For hospital administrators: the opportunity to elevate reputation in the region based on improved outcomes and thereby to increase market penetration.

- For program managers and division chiefs: the promise of better outcomes.

- For clinicians: [288]

  - Improving patient care; tangible benefits help ensure physicians stay engaged.[289] As one team member convinced to embrace MICS said, "We all think our job is to help the patient."[290] According to Classen and Kilbridge, "simply reducing length of stay or cost to the hospital is not enough to garner ongoing physician support."[291]

  - Inviting them to lead or participate in the quality improvement movement:

    ...[P]hysicians are more likely to respond to quality initiatives if they lead them rather than if they have them imposed from the outside, regardless of their relationships with the delivery system.[292]

Use local baseline data to establish that a problem exists and, ideally, demonstrate that the proposed patient safety/CRM project will correct an identified problem:[293]

---

287. CRM—by design and in practice—has taken these considerations in account and given its high-profile, proven track record, the prospective adoption of CRM can actually be used to help align these otherwise divergent interests.

288. Many (if not most) of executive leadership principles described here also apply downstream, to individual team leadership (see Chapter 9). This makes perfect sense, since the organization-wide messaging and motivation required to improve patient safety and achieve high reliability status must be aligned at both the top end *and* the sharp end.

289. J. Randall Curtis, et al. January 2006, 216.

290. Edmonson September 2003, Vol. 40, No. 6, 1438.

291. David C. Classen and Peter M. Kilbridge 2002, 966.

292. David C. Classen and Peter M. Kilbridge 2002, 965.

The problem is that because of their skill, talent and knowledge, physicians generally are even more resistant to change than the general population....Persuading physicians and staff to adopt new ideas can be challenging, but collecting data and seeking help in decision-making can aid the process.[294]

Expanding on the above points and relating them to CRM, even when a positive organizational orientation exists, more granular considerations must be addressed to engage physicians at the outset and more broadly, to produce the changes needed for any quality improvement project to work. These considerations have informed the very development and evolution of CRM and its related tools and skills and reinforce CRM's suitability as the solution to this threshold barrier. On this theme:

> Physicians respond to patient-centered, team-based education that emphasizes evidence-based practice, recognized and standardized quality improvement approaches, and informatics. However, even if the deployed approaches work, physicians will resist them unless "the overwhelming and often fragmented amount of information regarding medical injury prevention is condensed to a focused, organized product the hospitals can easily understand and use," and if they do not add to their existing workload.[295] The worry here is that the management efforts and proposed "solutions" to prevent errors "may instead increase complexity and the likelihood of an accident."[296]

293. J. Randall Curtis, et al. January 2006, 216.

294. American Medical Association. "Agent for change: Doctors must buy into shifts in practice." *Admednews.com*, April 3, 2006. http://www.ebiconsult.com/downloads/AMAnewsarticle.pdf (accessed July 22, 2009).

295. John R. Meurer, et al. 2005, 239, 240, 242.

296. Singer and Tucker, 5.

According to Curtis and colleagues:

> Dissemination of mailed educational materials and conferences are least likely to change behavior. Audit and feedback of recent performance are the backbone of successful quality improvement initiatives but are insufficient by themselves. Informal discussions and formal presentations by local opinion leaders on the quality improvement team are crucial adjuncts to help change behavior, but reminders and prompts (such as preprinted orders) along with periodic interactive educational interventions are most useful for inducing and sustaining change. The most powerful behavior change strategies (and often the only strategies that are successful) are multifaceted rather single approaches, are adapted to the local setting, and address documented barriers in the environment.[297]

Langford is yet more granular: to "encourage physicians" she suggests: [298]

- Offering training after regular office hours, on Saturday mornings, or with a meal.

- Bringing in a respected outside physician champion to provide the training or a motivational presentation identifying the benefits of CRM-based teamwork training.

The figure below presents an algorithm summarizing the main features of a patient safety initiative that have been shown to resonate with clinicians, which may help suggest how to bring them on board early on.

---

297. J. Randall Curtis, et al. January 2006, 215.

298. Vinette Langford 2007, 3.

Patient Safety Solution Algorithm

Source: Adapted from John R. Meurer 2005, 240 (Figure 1).

According to Leonard and colleagues, the "bottom up" approach, based on connecting with clinicians, is the best way—the essential way—to approach medical culture change.[299]

However, with respect to the "bottom up" approach, and as a caution to senior leaders, a cautionary reminder is warranted. Specifically, a leader's formative efforts will likely prove futile unless clinicians trust the process; part of engaging them is cultivating their trust. In the optimal patient safety culture, quality improvement programs aim at improving quality, not placing blame; their success depends on collaboration and transparent disclosure—without fear of reprisal—of information that affects quality.

To reprise Classen and Kilbride, in some instances where team-oriented care has been implemented and physicians shared power and authority with other health care professionals, the

---

299. M. Leonard 2004, i89.

physicians' legal liability actually increased.[300] It therefore follows that perhaps the most powerful inducement that senior leaders can offer at the outset to fully engage physicians in this culture-changing venture and to motivate them to share their sharp-end power and authority is the assurance of shared liability:[301]

> What is clear...is the overwhelming importance physicians place on shared decision making and power sharing.
>
> *Without these, physicians are much less likely to cooperate in any initiatives, quality or otherwise* [emphasis added].[302]

Team Leadership – The Fundamentals

Team leaders, who are usually physicians, play a pivotal role in the success of patient safety/CRM programs.[303] This makes sense, since the organization-wide messaging and motivation required to improve patient safety and achieve high reliability status must be aligned at both the top end (as just discussed) and the sharp end. Team leaders are the champions, cheerleaders, and ambassadors of their organization's patient safety mindset. And more pointedly, high reliability teamwork cannot be achieved without team leadership.

That said, team leadership entails more than tacit buy-in and participation. This is because even when a senior leader has made all the right moves and deployed a well-designed and well-received patient safety program, the individual attitudes and behaviors of team leaders can dictate team outcomes.[304]

---

300. David C. Classen and Peter M. Kilbridge 2002, 965.

301. David C. Classen and Peter M. Kilbridge 2002, 970.

302. David C. Classen and Peter M. Kilbridge 2002, 965.

303. Edmonson September 2003,1443.

Edmonson has published several studies illuminating the characteristics of effective team leadership:

- Effective team leaders convey their organization's compelling case for change and have the opportunity to engage team members early on. In one study, surgeons took the lead in motivating the OR team members to accept MICS, emphasizing the benefits of MICS to patients (such as shorter hospital stays) and the excitement of innovation; one surgeon "went out of his way to communicate" in advance to team members.[305]

- Effective team leaders also communicate with others in the organization about the changes.[306]

- The high status of team leaders represents both a blessing and a curse. It made other team members afraid to speak up unless explicitly encouraged to do so, but it contributed to building excitement and courage when others perceived the invitation for change as genuine. In the end, the determinant of successfully adapting to fundamental change was not "greater skill, superior organizational resources, top management support, or more past experience as drivers of innovation," but face-to-face team leadership and teamwork.[307]

- Team leaders affect, if not shape, team psychology through "specific interpersonal moves."[308] Team leaders can directly influence intra-team communication and ultimately, successful

---

304. Edmonson September 2003, 1443-1444.

305. Edmonson September 2003, 1438, 1443, 1444; Edmonson, Bohmer, and Pisano 2001, 712; Amy C. Edmonson. "Group and Organizational Influences on the Detection and Correction of Human Error." *The Journal of Applied Behavioral Science*, March 2004 Vol. 40 No. 1:66-90 [Edmonson March 2004], 71, 86.

306. Edmonson September 2003, 1446.

307. Edmonson, Bohmer, and Pisano 2001, 712.

308. Edmonson September 2003, 1440.

implementation of patient safety initiatives via non-threatening leadership that downplays power differences within the team and emphasizes the importance of others' input (explicitly inviting them to speak up).

Speaking up is particularly important. In one of her studies, Edmonson observed that nurse manager leadership behaviors create and continually reinforce openness or fear about discussing errors and that team members' willingness to openly discuss mistakes is a primary influence on the rate of detected errors.

Therefore, a team leader's "interpersonal moves...create psychological conditions of meaningfulness and safety," and promote "team learning as an ensemble effort." This in turn enables customized adjustments to team routines.[309]

Team Leaders and Changing Routines

The last statement about a team leader's potential influence on changing routines is significant. Previous allusion has been made to the power of routines—both positive and negative. As Reason and Edmonson respectively have noted, ingrained inertia will arrest improvement:

> [F]ar from being random, mishaps tend to fall into recurrent patterns. The same set of circumstances can provoke similar errors, regardless of the people involved. The pursuit of greater safety is seriously impeded by an approach that does not seek out and remove the error provoking properties within the system at large.[310]

---

309. Edmonson September 2003, 1440-1444, 1446.

310. Reason 2000, 769.

> Routines...provide a source of resistance to organizational change, inhibiting the active search for new alternatives.[311]

Through interpersonal moves, team leaders can motivate team members to embrace change and speak up freely, thereby promoting the degree of team learning necessary to change harmful routines. This "bottom up" process is essential for propelling the organizational change necessary to improve safety and performance.

Despite the ingrained bias toward the stability of routines, research on organizations reflects that routines *can* change, albeit slowly, through evolutionary processes. Routines are most amenable to change when "exceptional mismatches" occur between current routines and environmental conditions. According to Edmonson, "routines can change when groups spend time reflecting on outcomes of previous iterations of the routines."[312]

The "exceptional mismatch" of which she speaks exists in the current health care milieu. Traditional patient safety practices and behaviors are apparently disconnected from the reality that preventable events are harming patients in unacceptable numbers. All of this amplifies the need for changed routines and the vital role that team leaders play in promoting positive changes through teamwork and team learning.

In the broader context of this book, this "exceptional mismatch" defines the very gap that CRM has been developed to bridge. CRM by design takes into account the extent to which team leaders can make or break any program; CRM training, in fact, concentrates on team "leadership-followership" so that all

---

311. Edmonson, Bohmer, and Pisano 2001, 685, 687.

312. Edmonson, Bohmer, and Pisano 2001, 687.

team members understand their place on the team and the need for active, respectful collaboration.[313]

However, a previously raised qualification merits repeating. Although CRM contemplates and values the input of all team members, it does not imply or advocate an amorphous free-for-all. CRM calls for team members to freely share input with the team leader, but requires the team leader, armed with a full array of relevant information, to decide the final course of action. Therefore CRM offers a sharp-end operating philosophy that promotes team member input while preserving authority.

Leadership in Perspective

The term "leadership" as used in this book applies to leadership in the executive suite and in the clinic. Both classes of leaders are essential to improving patient safety:

- Executive leaders must not only lay the groundwork for high reliability, but must also make sure the organization lives up to what it seeks, promoting it, nurturing it, and infusing it throughout the organization as part of its genome.

- Team leaders give the corporate vision life, performing the same nourishing functions within their teams.

However, leadership alone will not produce success; it is but one of the three rivers. Effective communication and teamwork—top-down and bottom-up, instilled from the time of each person's hire—are equally indispensable. Without both of these elements, neither executive nor team leaders will pass on the full complement of "genetic" information.

---

313. Leadership-followership is covered in more detail in Chapter 11.

Communication

Communication failures are the primary cause of inadvertent harm to patients (see Figure 9.2). In the operating room, avoidable surgical errors stem from communication breakdowns between hospital support staff and surgeons.[314, 315] In the perinatal setting, The Joint Commission reported in 2007 that 72% of injuries were related to poor communications.[316]

Fortunately, the mantra of "everyone in the same movie, and no surprises" is both effective and easy to teach.

Leonard and colleagues have advocated the "bottom up" approach to culture change.   However, given the inherent complexity of health care, coupled with the inherent limitations of human performance, they have also advocated that the approach be grounded in "standardized communication tools" so that team members have a "common mental model," and everyone gets "in the same movie."[317]   Standardized communication tools comprise a common "critical language"; without it, clinicians are less able to "predict and monitor what is supposed to happen...[or] alert team members to unsafe situations."

---

314. M. Leonard 2004, i85; Bringing Surgeons Down to Earth, 2005.

315. In "Bringing Surgeons Down to Earth: New Programs Aim to Curb Fear That Prevents Nurses From Flagging Problems," *The Wall Street Journal* echoed several themes consistent with this analysis. Communication problems included nurses failing to notify a surgeon of a change in a patient's color or respiration because, as reflected in a VHA survey of 20 hospitals, most of them were afraid to speak up and challenge the surgeon. The same survey found that surgeons often do not perceive a problem with communication and "were surprised to hear that staffers are afraid to challenge them." *(November 16, 2005, D1)*

316. Vinette Langford 2007, 3.

317. This concept, as previously noted, fits into the larger canopy of organizational culture: "...[H]ow work is carried out shapes the way members of an organization relate to each other and to the outside world. The levels of employee motivation and empowerment—and how conflict is resolved—both shape and are a measure of organizational cultures." (Westcott 2006, 2, 18)

Fortunately, Leonard notes,

> The mantra of "everyone in the same movie,
> and no surprises" is an effective one that is
> easy to teach.[318]

Not surprisingly, the barriers to effective communication (and ultimately teamwork) in the clinic are the same human factors—cognitive, environmental, and cultural—that increase the risk of adverse events overall. For example, a study of communication failures in one UK operating theater refers to

> ...three preventable causes of communication
> failures: increase in cognitive load,
> interruption of routine, and increase in tension.
> Broadly, these can be seen as effects of
> dysfunctional cognition, activity, and affect.[319]

Leonard and colleagues also point to those barriers to communication—and a common mental model—that are attributable to individual personality and training. For example, doctors and nurses typically have divergent perceptions because they

> ...are trained to communicate quite differently.
> Nurses are taught to be very broad and
> narrative in their descriptions of clinical
> situations ("paint the big picture"), whereas
> physicians learn to be very concise, and get to
> the "headlines" quite quickly. Nurses often
> relate being told during their educational
> process that they "don't make diagnoses."
> This leads to nurses telephoning physicians
> and being very broad and narrative in their

---

318. M. Leonard 2004, i86.

319. Jon Allard, Alan Bleakley, Adrian Hobbs, and Tina Vinnell. "Who's on the team today?": The status of briefing amongst operating theatre practitioners in one UK hospital. Journal of Interprofessional Care, March 2007 Vol. 21, No. 2: 189-206, 191-192. (Jon Allard March 2007)

descriptions, with the doctors impatiently "waiting to find out what they want."[320]

Communication principles and practices specifically related to CRM are analyzed in Chapter 13.

Teamwork

To improve patient safety and achieve high reliability performance, leadership and communication are essential but, again, not sufficient. Equally indispensable attention must be paid to the third "river": the work groups, the teams, that actually deliver health care to patients. This, according to Edmonson, is "...the point where organizational and cognitive effects meet and play out in enabling or preventing errors."[321] Therefore, it is what really matters.

At the end of the day, the patients' experiences of the entire continuum of care is the only real measure of quality.

Langford and the National Quality Forum echo this theme, stating that teamwork and teamwork training are "imperative to patient safety,"[322] and "central to transformational culture change."[323] Teamwork and team training bridge the gap between (1) the autonomous decision-making characteristic of the prevailing professional culture of physicians, which has been an asset in the clinic but "has typically downplayed teamwork and empowerment,"[324] and (2) the reality that in today's complex health care universe, care is delivered to patients by interdisciplinary and interdependent teams and that each team member plays an essential role in ensuring positive results and

---

320. M. Leonard 2004, i85.

321. Edmonson, Bohmer and Pisano, 685.

322. Vinette Langford 2007, 1.

323. NQF 2007, 39.

324. Singer and Tucker, 25.

reducing errors and patient safety risks.[325] For this reason, CRM principles recognize that each team member, and his or her contribution, is valuable. At the end of the day,

> [t]he patients' experiences of the entire continuum of care is the only real measure of quality, and every player, even the attending surgeon, is a cog in the wheel. Some cogs are clearly bigger than others, but if they don't mesh together, there will always be problems....Teamwork means caring for and about people. Intelligent caring takes enormous energy and the ability to share knowledge, communicate effectively and monitor performance. "[Y]ou can't have quality care without coordination of care."[326]

Members of effective teams rely on each other to help catch mistakes and correct them before they become life-threatening.

CRM fosters teamwork, but draws an important distinction between work *groups* and work *teams*. Teams are not "loosely coordinated groups of caregivers and support staff," but formally established and organized units composed of the trained physicians, nurses, and technicians assigned to work together for a shift. From larger teams, *ad hoc* teams can be formed to respond to emergencies (such as resuscitations).[327]

In the clinic, any work group that fails to perform as a team is doomed to fail.

This focus on teams and teamwork leads to another essential, refined point made by The National Quality Forum:

---

325. *WHO Surgical Safety Checklist (First Edition); Safe Surgery Saves Lives.* World Alliance For Patient Safety Implementation Manual, Geneva Switzerland: World Health Organization, May 2008; NQF 2007, 87.

326. Fostering Teamwork Between Sterile Processing and the OR 2003; includes quote from Jane Brock, MD, MSPH, associate medical director at Colorado Foundation for Medical Care (CFMC) in Aurora, Colorado.

327. John C. Morey December 2002, 1555.

Although teamwork is central to transformational culture change, more than teamwork training is needed.[328]

More precisely, teamwork is not an accident or the "automatic consequence of placing people together in the same room; it depends on a willingness to cooperate toward shared goals."[329] Thus, team skills are required for each team member. Sustainable teamwork is the result of learned skills rather than permanent assignments; performance is not degraded despite day-to-day changes in team composition. [330] Putting it another way, if each person learns team skills, he or she can be assigned where needed most and can interact with others effectively and appropriately, enabling HCOs to allocate resources more efficiently.

Fusing Teamwork and Communication

As consistently emphasized above, instilling a positive safety culture and improving patient safety require that team members share a common mental model, communicate, and ultimately, collaborate. If true collaboration is the prerequisite to change, then teamwork and communication do not subsist as isolated filaments, but as a fused compound (see Figure 9.2). Leonard says:

> *Effective communication and teamwork is essential for the delivery of high quality, safe patient care* [emphasis added].... Other high reliability domains, such as commercial aviation, have shown that the adoption of standardised tools and behaviours is a very

---

328. NQF 2007, 39.

329. Baker et al 2005, 253.

330. John C. Morey December 2002, 1555.

effective strategy in enhancing teamwork and reducing risk.[331]

His use of the singular verb "is" in the first line embodies the idea of fusion.

Unless a fused, standardized approach is employed, team performance will vary (as Leonard reported[332]) with individual personality and custom. This variation can, according to Edmonson,

> make those teams that most need improvement least likely to surface errors—the data that fuel improvement efforts.[333]

CRM and Collaboration

CRM theory and practice pursue and nourish collaboration—the fusion of good teamwork and effective communication—through standardized communication. To support this point:

- As observed in Allard's study of one UK hospital, the individualized barriers to collaborative and effective teamwork were overcome by adopting CRM and one of its standardized communication staples: team briefing from a relatively simple, standard checklist. This study recalls the similar result, and enormous potential, reported by *The New England Journal of Medicine* for a "simple" surgical checklist.

---

331. M. Leonard 2004, i85, i86.

332. M. Leonard 2004, i85, i86.

333. Edmonson, March 2004, 86-87.

- In the Leonard study, the CRM-based SBAR[334] briefing model proved "very effective in bridging this difference in communication styles and helping to 'get everyone in the same movie.'"

Non-technical advances such as these help stimulate the culture change that is the antecedent of high reliability performance. As Allard also wrote:

> Surgical culture itself is changing, for example, through increased recognition of the value of non-technical skills.... Surgeons who do not embrace such developments are likely to be challenged in the future by more enlightened colleagues.[335]

Conclusions

CRM-based patient safety initiatives are coupled to the well-documented reality just described. More specifically, human error and medical error cannot be productively addressed by technology or technical acumen alone. The solution depends, at its nucleus, on nontechnical—cognitive and social—skills.

- Communication failures account for the majority of mistakes and adverse events in the delivery of patient care.

- Human limitations, when coupled with the complexity of today's technology and care processes, ensures that errors will occur; the key is mitigation.

---

334. SBAR stands for Situation, Background, Assessment and Recommendation. This briefing model, developed by the United States military to facilitate concise, structured communication, is integral to CRM and is discussed in detail in Chapter 13.

335. Jon Allard March 2007, 203.

- Threat identification and error trapping can help prevent errors from ever reaching the patient.

- Effective teamwork and communication will help create a collaborative culture that promotes patient safety.

- Standardized tools and procedures will embed reliability into care units and teams to bridge communication gaps and style differences.

The assembled research demonstrates that CRM methodology can pull all of this together, promoting a culture of safety and improved performance "through improving interprofessional collaboration."[336] Moreover, CRM training also teaches "leadership-followership" so all members understand their place on the team and the need for mutual respect.[337] CRM training has succeeded in transforming groups that work together into teams that "problem solve jointly."[338]

---

336. Mitchell, Robins and Schaad 2005, 304-5.

337. More exposition on leadership-followership appears in Chapter 11.

338. Mitchell, Robins and Schaad 2005, 301.

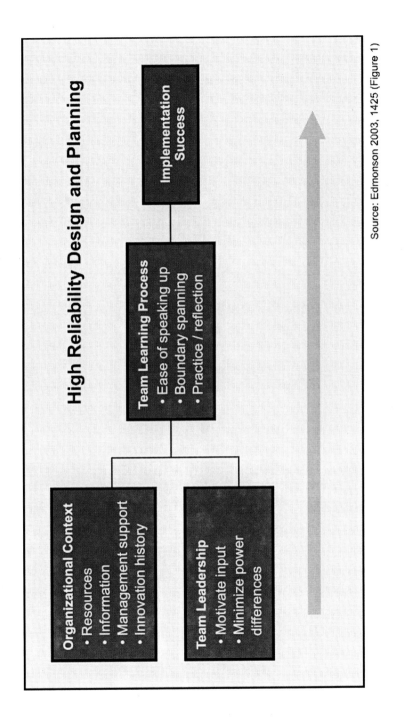

High Reliability Design and Planning

Implementation Success

Team Learning Process
• Ease of speaking up
• Boundary spanning
• Practice / reflection

Organizational Context
• Resources
• Information
• Management support
• Innovation history

Team Leadership
• Motivate input
• Minimize power differences

Source: Edmonson 2003, 1425 (Figure 1)

Chapter 10

Implementing a Successful CRM Program in Six Steps

Key Points in this Chapter

- To implement and institutionalize a successful and sustainable CRM program, the senior leader must follow six discrete steps: Plan; Test; Revise; Execute; Sustain; Improve.

- The Plan phase involves: Gathering relevant organization data; Identifying improvement opportunities, resources, and potential barriers; Engaging champions; Developing a detailed project plan, budget parameters, time lines, and metrics for measurement; and Building organization awareness and support.

- To give the overall program the best chance to succeed, the program should first be implemented on a small scale. To that end, in the Test/Simulate phase, the project is tested before it is formally rolled out. This phase includes classroom training, hands-on simulation, and perhaps a trial run in the clinic.

- In the Revise phase, the information gleaned from the Test/Simulate phase is used to make modifications before the project is introduced on a large scale.

- The planned, tested and revised project is formally launched in the Execute phase with appropriate organization-wide fanfare, and CRM team training formally begins. After training, the project moves into the clinic.

- Sustaining a CRM initiative is essential for institutionalizing safety-culture- driven high reliability. This step entails consistent refreshing (including CME), monitoring, measuring, and reporting. Top-end leaders must remain visibly and actively involved.

Step 1: Plan

Armed with self-assessments, guidance, and principles described in previous chapters, top-end leaders can begin their CRM-based safety improvement game plan. The planning should include the following component activities.

Prioritize and Choose Initial Project(s)[339]

- Assess safety/quality culture as described above.

- Gather available information and data on specific structures, processes, or outcomes, including patient flow, command, leadership, communication, decision making, resource management, and workload management.[340] Several validated tools are available to help both overall and unit-specific assessments and to identify areas of concern.[341]

- Identify opportunities for improvement, available resources for improvement initiatives, and potential barriers (including necessary changes in attitude or behavior). As Curtis and colleagues have stated:

> A major barrier to any quality improvement initiative is the individuals or groups who believe they do not need to improve. They may not believe in the process or they may feel threatened by it.[342]

---

339. J. Randall Curtis, et al. January 2006, 213, 214, 216.

340. Stephen M. Powell 2005,3.

341. These tools include the Patient Safety Climate Survey (an on-line survey developed to evaluate the corporate safety climate of the U.S. Army Medical Department) and the Safety Climate Scale. To assess ICU safety specifically, the Society for Critical Care Medicine offers the SCCM ICU Index. (See, respectively: (1) Lynne M. Connelly 2005, 415-428; (2) Mary A. Blegen 2005, 429-443; and (3) J. Randall Curtis, et al. January 2006, 214.)

342. J. Randall Curtis, et al. January 2006, 216.

- Consider beginning with a single, concrete project that is feasible and likely to succeed. This will help ensure that (i) quality improvement becomes routine and integral to the chosen unit, (ii) organization or unit specific refinements can readily be made, and (iii) the initial success can be publicized and replicated.

Pre-wire for success

- Identify and consult with potential clinical champions and leaders (nurses and physicians). Failure to do so early on is, according to Langford and Rollins, a common stumbling block:

> Making sure that the right individuals and groups are part of the change team is a key step. In order to model the multidisciplinary, collaborative environment that is the goal of teamwork training, it is important that both nurses and physicians are on the initial change team.[343]

Classen has also emphasized this step from a physician's perspective, noting that physicians are most likely to be engaged—and can help elevate an HCO to HRO status—when those "at the front line of care" are leading efforts to first identify and then redesign high-risk clinical processes.[344]

On this same theme, Curtis and colleagues wrote that one strategy for overcoming physician resistance is to seek "constructive ideas for how to improve the process...by engaging them....[I]nvite them to participate in the quality improvement process."[345]

---

343. Vinette Langford 2007, 3.

344. David C. Classen and Peter M. Kilbridge 2002, 970.

345. J. Randall Curtis, et al. January 2006, 216.

- Develop a basic project or business plan for the chosen project that includes:

  - A concise statement of the clear, compelling, and unified vision underlying the planned initiative.

  - An itemized list of each incremental task.

  - Budget parameters.

  - Time lines.[346]

  - Goals and objectives, including (to the extent possible) safety performance metrics with baselines and targets (see Item 1.4 below).[347]

  - CRM-based strategies and tactics to engage clinicians and change their behavior.

  - A method for creating, or using the current data collection system to create accurate baseline data and future data that will enable clinicians and other stakeholders to better understand the initial problem and to monitor and measure subsequent improvements—recognizing that human factors, and therefore non-technical markers, will be involved.[348, 349]

---

346. Although time lines will be unique to each organization, leaders should anticipate 6 to 12 months to implement a CRM program (Stephen M. Powell 2005, 3).

347. David C. Classen and Peter M. Kilbridge 2002, 969 (Table 1); Stephen M. Powell 2005, 3.

348. Powell and Hill January 2006, 198.

349. For example, anesthetists—who were among the first practitioners to embrace and notably improve using CRM—also embraced non-technical performance markers in their training by creating a list of Anesthetists Non-Technical Skills (ANTS). Two of the five skills listed involve teamwork and decision making. For decision making, the markers to evaluate performance included the individual and team ability to identify options; to balance risks and select options; and to reevaluate, monitor, and cross-check. (Powell and Hill January 2006, 198)

- Ascertain the extent of/enlist senior support: in successful initiatives, CEOs, other senior leaders, and governing boards expressly support the hospital's patient safety efforts and signal their importance.[350] This effort might be supported by showing off a well thought-out plan.

- Publicize: build organization awareness and support for the pilot project(s).[351] Also consider whether early organization-wide communications should include safety goals and objectives for the program or the first project(s).[352]

- Design the project elements: standardized tactics and tools and standardized CRM-skills training that can be adapted for use throughout the organization and are customized, based on the organization's unique business and clinical requirements.

Step 2: Test / Simulate

After general awareness has been established and the outlines of a pilot project designed, the project should be tested before it is formally rolled out. That test involves classroom training, but perhaps more important, hands-on simulation with role play.[353]

Simulation is an essential feature of CRM training, both at the outset of any program and consistently thereafter, to reinforce basic lessons, refresh and practice skills and methods, and evaluate progress.[354] Simulation has long been integral to CRM in aviation (particularly LOFT training) and has been

---

350. Singer and Tucker, 16.

351. Singer and Tucker, 1.

352. David C. Classen and Peter M. Kilbridge 2002, 969 (Table 1).

353. For ease of reference, the word "simulation" used here will also include "testing."

recognized as effective. At first, the adaptability of simulation to health care was intuitively presumed. But over time—despite little hard data directly linking CRM simulation to improved outcomes[355]—accumulating evidence nevertheless indicates that simulation is (1) feasible, useful, and valuable, and (2) well received by physicians and nurses.[356] Moreover, simulation in health care has been advocated by the Institute of Medicine (in 1999),[357] the National Academies, the Agency for Healthcare Research and Quality, and the Institute for Healthcare Improvement.[358] The National Quality Forum has indicated that simulation-based training reduces errors.[359]

Testing new processes before implementing them is a marker of a high reliability HCO committed to patient safety: simulation-based training reduces errors.

Musson and colleagues, citing the pioneering work of Gaba and Helmreich in the use of CRM-based simulation in anesthesiology, have indicated that "realistic role play is essential for acquisition of new skills."[360] Moreover, such prominent authorities as Classen and Gaba have expressly asserted that simulation "to test new processes before implementation" is a key marker of a high reliability health care

---

354. In aviation, special training in simulation is also required for those charged with evaluating and certifying flight crews (Helmreich, Merrit and Wilhelm 1999, 5).

355. David P. Baker, Sigrid Gustafson, J. Mathew Beaubien, Eduardo Salas, Paul Barach. "Medical Team Training Programs in Health Care." In: Henriksen K, Battles JB, Marks ES, Lewin DI (eds). *Advances in Patient Safety: from Research to Implementation*, Vol. 4, Programs, tools and concepts. AHRQ: Rockville MD Feb 2005. AHRQ Publication No. 05-0021-2, 256. (Baker et al, February 2005)

356. See, for example: Baker et al, February 2005, 256; M. J. Shapiro 2004, 420; M. Leonard 2004, i87-i88.

357. "Teamwork Takes Hold to Improve Patient Safety." *The Risk Management Reporter*, February 2005, Vol. 24, No. 1, 6. (Risk Management Reporter, February 2005)

358. What Pilots Can Teach Hospitals About Patient Safety 2006.

359. National Quality Forum 2007, 35, 57.

360. David M. Musson Spring 2004, 34.

organization committed to patient safety.[361,362] Gaba has further stated that "simulation ensures readiness; HROs recognize that ...simulation and drills pays off."[363] Despite these positive indicators, Shapiro and Musson respectively have observed as follows:

> Medicine is one of the few high risk, high stakes industries that has not yet embraced the importance of simulation in primary and continuing education of healthcare providers.[364]

> Currently exemplified by a number of leaders in this area, most notably in anesthesia, medicine needs to expand virtual and simulated training opportunities to enhance not only technical skills, but also interpersonal, small group, and interdisciplinary skills.[365]

For any CRM project, early simulation has several benefits. Generally, role-play simulation allows an interdisciplinary group of doctors, nurses, technicians and other staff to learn, understand and practice—with immediate feedback and debriefing—the various task and team-related skills (such as the use of checklists and briefing) and potential high-risks situations (such as handoffs, shift changes, and red flags) that will apply to their day-to-day work[366] while "no patients are at

---

361. David C. Classen and Peter M. Kilbridge 2002, 968 (Table 1) , 970 (List 1).

362. David M. Gaba, MD. "Safety first: Ensuring quality care in the intensely productive environment –The HRO model." *The Anesthesia Patient Safety Foundation [APSF] Newsletter*, 2003 Vol. 18, No. 1:1-4, Table (1).

363. David M. Gaba, MD. "Safety first: Ensuring quality care in the intensely productive environment –The HRO model." *The Anesthesia Patient Safety Foundation [APSF] Newsletter*, 2003 Vol. 18, No. 1:1-4, Table (1).

364. M. J. Shapiro 2004, 420.

365. David M. Musson Spring 2004, 34.

366. See, for example: Baker et al, February 2005, 256; Health Care at the Crossroads: Strategies for Improving the Medical Liability System and Preventing Patient Injury 2005, 17.; Risk Management Reporter, February 2005, 6.

risk for exposure to novice caregivers or unproven technologies."[367]

A trial run can also have other notable benefits:

- Edmonson noted that thorough dry-run practice sessions have "emerged as an important influence on ease of speaking up," helping to "launch a new way of relating to each other, experimenting with ideas and possibilities, and practicing alternative moves." Being able to speak up in practice makes it easier to do so on the job.[368]

- A trial run can also help identify "change agents...who have strong communication and team-building skills" to become champions, advocates, or perhaps CRM trainers.[369]

- Senior leaders can get an early gauge on the program, and potentially an early win that can catalyze the program throughout the enterprise.

For all of these reasons, Dunn and colleagues, in *The Joint Commission Journal on Quality and Patient Safety* (June 2007), wrote:

> We emphasize testing the adoption of team practices on a very small scale, with one team working in a clinical unit and with modifications to fit the local environment before any attempt at implementation on a larger scale.[370]

367. Health Care at the Crossroads: Strategies for Improving the Medical Liability System and Preventing Patient Injury 2005, 17.

368. Edmonson September 2003, 1436.

369. Stephen M. Powell 2005, 3.

Step 3: Revise

This is an extension of Step 2 (Test / Simulate). Armed with the information gleaned from the trial run, customized modifications are made before the project is formally introduced on a large scale.

As revisions are considered, it is important that consensus is built around key concepts early and often. Without building support among key stakeholders, efforts can quickly stall out at this phase. Be sure to set milestones and cutoff dates to ensure progress and momentum.

Step 4: Execute

The planned, tested, and revised project is formally launched, with appropriate organization-wide fanfare.

CRM team training formally begins. The training consists of (1) classroom work, including moderator-led discussions of actual adverse event case studies[371] and (2) targeted, job-specific, interactive exercises and simulations for newly formed teams. The interactive sessions feature immediate instructor feedback and afterwards, thorough debriefing.

After training, the project moves into the clinic. Actual work teams use CRM at the sharp end. Their skills are monitored and measured in real time, via debriefs following medical procedures.

---

370. Edward J. Dunn, M.D., M.P.H.; Peter D. Mills, Ph.D.; Julia Neily, R.N., M.P.H., P.M; Michael D. Crittenden, M.D.; Amy L. Carmack, M.A.; James P. Bagian, M.D., P.E. "Medical Team Training: Applying Crew Resource Management in the Veterans Health Administration." *The Joint Commission Journal on Quality and Patient Safety*, June 2007, Vol. 33 No. 6: 317-325, 323.

371. Some organizations also utilize on-line learning sessions.

**Safer Healthcare's CRM Program Design Model
for Hospitals and Patient Care Settings**

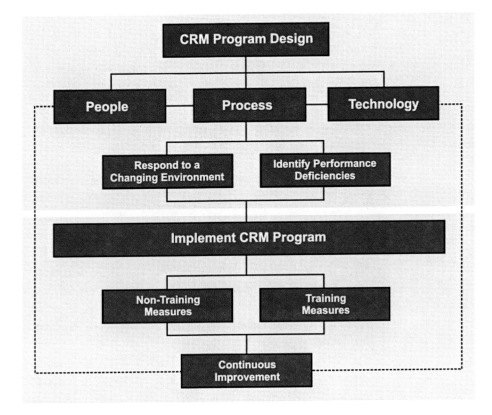

Safer Healthcare's CRM programming is specifically designed to improve team coordination and communication, develop associated behavioral models, and facilitate the development of instructive feedback models to review performance and correct deficiencies. It is built upon the analysis and targeted improvement of three key organizational elements: People, Process and Technology.

Step 5: Sustain

This step merits particular attention.

Sustaining any CRM initiative is essential for transforming and reinforcing an organization's safety culture, institutionalizing high reliability, and accumulating improvements. On the sharp end, this means consistent coaching, refreshing, monitoring, and measuring:

- Future training and refresher training is planned as part of a regular training cycle.

- Safety issues and lessons learned are incorporated into all physician education activities, including CME.[372]

- On the organizational end, this means:

- After the initial project is well-established, identifying other units or groups for CRM training.

- "Changing leads" and "maintaining momentum," as emphasized by Langford. Changing leads means ensuring continuity despite the inevitable personnel attrition, absences, and substitutions by developing and training a reserve of new team leaders. Maintaining momentum is critical because "changing behavior takes time." Some organizations maintain momentum by imposing time lines for initial training, data collection, and implementation.[373]

- Developing the in-house capability to create and execute CRM projects through train-the-trainer programs. [374]

---

372. See, for example: Stephen M. Powell 2005, 3; David C. Classen and Peter M. Kilbridge, 968 (Table 1) , 970 (List 1).

373. See, for example: Bringing Surgeons Down to Earth, 2005; Singer and Tucker, 1, 14, 28; J. Randall Curtis, et al. January 2006, 212 (Table 2); Vinette Langford 2007.

- Encouraging and receiving dissenting opinions and clinician feedback, and implementing viable suggestions.[375]

- Rewarding safety and reliability.[376]

- Constantly learning from both successes and failures.

- In addition to ongoing training and informal reinforcement, sustaining any CRM-based performance improvement program requires scientifically sound performance measures. In other words, the quality improvement program itself should be subjected to a quality improvement process. Without formal evaluation of a quality improvement program, it is impossible to judge whether it is successful and sustainable.[377]

Step 6: Improve

Gauging performance to identify opportunities for improvement involves:

- Regularly reporting and analyzing errors, events, near misses, and outcomes.

- Gathering that data via a standardized, robust IT-based system.

- Regularly comparing the program data to project metrics to (1) track performance and improvement, and (2) monitor physician participation, analyzing the

---

374. Stephen M. Powell 2005, 3.; David C. Classen and Peter M. Kilbridge, 968 (Table 1) , 970 (List 1).

375. Singer and Tucker, 14.

376. Id.

377. J. Randall Curtis, et al. January 2006, 215.

data to decide if modifications to strategies or tactics are warranted.[378]

- Regularly reporting and sharing data regarding performance in relation to safety metrics.[379] This, according to Singer and Tucker, is a primary trait of leaders in HROs.[380]

These elements, taken together, point to an abiding principle. In order to sustain any culture-changing CRM initiative, the top-end leaders must remain visibly and actively involved and must lead by example. This is no casual statement. Without continuous senior involvement and encouragement, simple and consistent messaging, and consensus building—all aimed at helping "personnel to take ownership of the system and implementation"—the essential trust will not be established,[381] and the entire initiative will probably lose momentum, unravel, and ultimately flounder.[382]

Senior leaders can demonstrate and help cement their organization's safety culture through executive rounds: regular, informal, and face-to-face meetings with clinical teams in each department (including radiology, pharmacy, and laboratories).[383] Curtis recommends that senior leaders make executive rounds several times each month[384] to:

---

378. See, for example: Vinette Langford 2007, 3; David C. Classen and Peter M. Kilbridge, 970.

379. David C. Classen and Peter M. Kilbridge, 970.

380. Singer and Tucker, 14.

381. Helmreich, Culture, Threat, and Error: Assessing System Safety 1998, 11.

382. See, for example: Bringing Surgeons Down to Earth, 2005; Singer and Tucker, 1, 14, 28; J. Randall Curtis, et al. January 2006, 212 (Table 2); Vinette Langford 2007.

383. If the hospital has a formal quality improvement committee or department, executive rounds can effectively integrate those personnel into each improvement project.

384. J. Randall Curtis, et al. January 2006, 215.

- Reinforce, directly with front-line staff, key messages about communication, teamwork, patient safety, and reporting errors.

- Praise and encourage.

- Talk up the project's overall progress and successes.

- Discuss previous feedback with clinicians and give them the opportunity for real time, direct feedback.

- Gauge first-hand if interdisciplinary team leadership remains appropriately engaged in using CRM methods and skills, encouraging speaking up and freely reporting problems, errors, and near-misses.

- Research has indicated that leaders who focus solely on safety during informal rounds are more successful at creating and sustaining a culture of safety than those who do not.[385]

Executive rounds are part of what should, in effect, become a consistently pursued public relations effort to promote and sustain the patient safety program, characterized by broad reach and frequency. This can be accomplished, in addition to the face-to-face rounds mentioned above, via regular corporate communications such as intranets and newsletters. Senior leaders should celebrate the successes of each project not just with the teams involved, but organization-wide (including other hospital executives and the hospital board) and with the public.[386]

---

385. Institute for Healthcare Improvement Idealized Design Group and Allan Frankel, MD. "Patient Safety Leadership WalkRounds™." *Institute for Healthcare Improvement (IHI.org)*.

386. J. Randall Curtis, et al. January 2006, 216.

Steps 1 through 6 have been informed by the aggregated body of research on safety culture and CRM. That research also demonstrates that improved performance and patient safety are the natural outgrowth of following Steps 1 through 6.

If an HCO follows those steps, in concert with an eye toward continuous process improvement, it will be positioned to establish a self-sustaining culture of safety, constant self-examination and learning, and continuous evolution and improvement, all leading to high reliability performance. For patients, this translates into safer hospitals that deliver "intelligent caring."[387]

With the foundation of a detailed project plan in place, the next chapter will detail the specific methods, tools, and skills of a CRM program.

---

387. Fostering Teamwork Between Sterile Processing and the OR 2003; includes quote from Jane Brock, MD, MSPH, associate medical director at Colorado Foundation for Medical Care (CFMC) in Aurora, Colorado.

Part Four

The Six Essential CRM Skills

Recap and Introduction to Part Four

The preceding content in this book is prologue. It provides the historical and conceptual backdrop for understanding the nature and extent of the current patient safety challenge, the impediments to meeting it, and the basics for going about it through CRM methodology. This part of the book will describe the specific core CRM skills which, if instilled, will propel an HCO toward high reliability performance.

To summarize and reset, CRM methodology and its implementing skills grew out of two core principles:

- All human beings are fallible and susceptible to error. Therefore, mistakes will inevitably be made, even by the most proficient and well-intentioned professionals. Preventable human error is the main cause of deadly and costly medical mistakes.

- In the clinic, the rich diversity of individuals—their personalities, cultural backgrounds, talents, and skills—can manifest mindsets and behaviors that impede communication, and therefore threaten the safety of patients.

Patient safety—and how to manage the human factors that can threaten it—have been intensely debated. Beyond debate, however, is the proposition that patient safety is a problem and something *must* be done to improve it. Historically, failure or defect rates between 2% to 5% have been the tolerated norm in health care, but this rate is much too high compared with other high risk industries. In fact, even 99% error-free performance is grossly insufficient.

Improving patient safety by reducing preventable errors improves quality and also reduces costs.

CRM has succeeded in reducing error and improving safety in aviation and is now being used successfully in other complex, high-risk industries, including health care. By design, CRM is a flexible, systemic method for optimizing human performance and increasing safety, by:

- Recognizing the human factors that are the root causes of preventable error.

- Recognizing that in complex, high-risk settings, teams rather than individuals are the most effective operating units.

- Instilling practices that use all available resources to reduce the adverse impacts of human error.

CRM is now recognized as an evidence-based "best practice" for improving patient safety and building and sustaining high reliability performance in delivering health care. On this point, research has shown that:

- Medical teams trained in CRM can perform more work at a lower cost while improving patient safety.

- Increasing patient safety is a "win-win" proposition for health care workers, associated with reduced risk/ fear of malpractice claims and increased morale/job satisfaction.

However, CRM is not (1) a quick fix to improve patient safety, (2) cook-book medicine, (3) a way for management to dictate clinician behavior, or (4) a scheme to undermine a team leader's authority.

CRM has evolved through five previous, carefully analyzed, generations. Current CRM theory recognizes that:

- The root causes of preventable errors are both organizational (systemic) and individual. These causes include interlaced organizational, professional, and individual cultural filters and roadblocks. First and foremost, organizations need to instill a positive safety culture.

- The term "error" is somewhat a misnomer. In the CRM/patient safety context, "errors" actually mean correctable shortfalls in leadership, team work, task allocation, communication, situational awareness, and decision making, which represent the recognized root causes of harm.

Therefore, CRM skills and methods focus on "threat management" to address these shortfalls and are designed not only to eliminate, trap or mitigate errors, but to identify systemic threats to safety.

There is no universal CRM training program. The method's inherent flexibility allows any organization to tailor programs to meet its own performance/improvement needs.

CRM protocols are also informed by the following basic precepts, grounded in credible research:

- The causes of human error are the same for all occupations.

- Despite the concentration on individual performance, recognizing and managing threats to patient safety is, quintessentially, a systemic pursuit. Individual "errors" can be more productively considered consequences of systemic factors rather than blameworthy personal defects. (That said, a "bottom up" approach, from sharp-end clinicians on up, offers the best pathway to medical culture change.)

Threats to patient safety can be active or latent:

- Active threats: the acts or omissions of individuals at the sharp end that can have immediate adverse consequences. Individual errors can result from both cognitive limitations (such as stress or fatigue) and behavioral limitations (such as lack of assertiveness or low morale).

- Latent threats: the systemic (including cultural) conditions that can breed unnecessary harm to patients.

AHRQ and The Joint Commission both acknowledge the value of teamwork in the professional medical environment. Team training is now becoming a standard for accreditation and for ongoing in-service staff education and training.

The five hallmarks of a positive safety culture and high reliability in an HCO are: (1) a fundamental acknowledgment that life-threatening human error is inevitable; (2) a willingness to direct resources toward improving safety; (3) a commitment to collaboration across ranks; (4) a blame-free environment; and (5) a commitment to constantly learn and improve. A successful transition to high reliability depends on effective (a) leadership, (b) communication, and (c) teamwork.

All of these principles—evidence-based "best practice" principles—have been incorporated into the specific tools and methods that comprise CRM practice. Recognizing that there is no universal CRM program, that CRM can be taught in a variety of ways,[388] and that the various dimensions of CRM intersect and overlap, the following chapters have been organized according to six essential skills.

---

388. See, for example, Dynamics Research Corporation 2004, 2-14.

The six essential CRM skills include:

- Teamwork and Team Leadership

- Situational awareness

- Standardized Communication

- Conflict Resolution

- Decision Making

- Briefing and Debriefing

Chapter 11

Teamwork and Leadership Skills

Key Points in this Chapter

- CRM team training is designed to transform work *groups* into work *teams* and to transform *group* work into *team*work.

- Teamwork involves an amalgam of attitudes, knowledge, and skills, focused on (1) how each individual performs as a member of the team, and (2) how the entire team performs as a unit.

- Any health care delivery group that fails to perform as a team will eventually cause harm to patients.

- To achieve high reliability team performance, each team member must have skills that are transferable, task to task and from team to team, unaffected by personal variables.

- CRM team training promotes teamwork and team performance by (1) encouraging participation from each individual in a work group; (2) developing the skills necessary for that individual to perform effectively as a member of the group; and (3) conducting full-team simulations that replicate actual clinical situations.

- The documented organizational benefits of effective teamwork include (1) improved quality, productivity, and patient satisfaction; (2) reduced turnover and absenteeism; and (3) reduced costs.

- Highly effective teams and highly effective team members exhibit 11 common traits (respectively detailed below). Being a good teammate also means being a good follower.

- CRM promotes emotionally intelligent situational leadership.

189

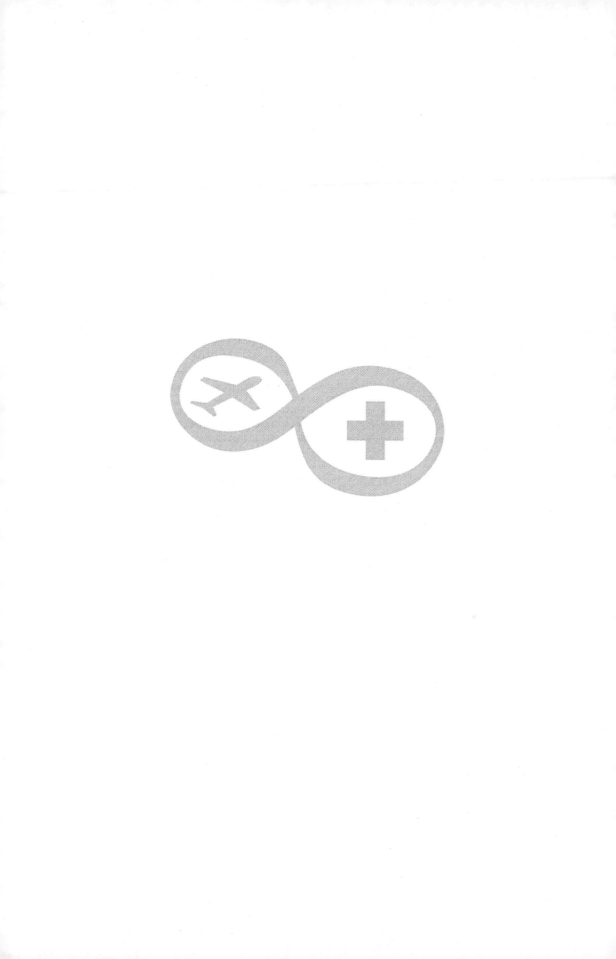

While evidence suggests that teamwork is crucial for better quality care, teaching of teamwork skills and team concepts is virtually nonexistent in nursing and medicine, where training is almost exclusively focused on individual technical skills. Our education, training, and testing seem based on the assumption that health care is delivered by individuals in isolation. And while providers are trained individually in their autonomous professions, on the job, they are always expected to perform as a team. But identifying a group of providers and calling them a team does not imply that they will perform well or at all as a team. Evidence suggests that effective teamwork does not arise spontaneously, but rather requires specific skills and development.[389]

What is a Team?

A "team" is a group of two or more individuals who must interact and adapt in order to achieve a common objective. In a hospital or any health care delivery setting—at the sharp end:

- The group is assembled according to the particular and specialized capabilities (the knowledge and skills) of its members.

- Based on those capabilities, each member is assigned a specific role or task.

- The group works in dynamic, complex, high stress, and time-constrained environments, often under heavy individual workload and information overload.

- In that difficult environment, the group faces rapidly evolving, ambiguous situations that nevertheless require multi-faceted decisions, with severe consequences for mistakes.

389. Amer Kaissi, Trista Johnson, Mark S. Kirschbaum. "Measuring Teamwork and Patient Safety Attitudes." *Nursing Economics,* 2003 Vol. 21, No. 5: 211-218, 211.

Work teams differ from work groups because the tasks of their individual members are inextricably interdependent and are subordinate to the ultimate mission: to help a patient. To accomplish that mission, coordination and collaboration among members—teamwork—is an absolute necessity.

What is Teamwork?

As previously noted, a group that works together is not automatically a team. To be considered a team, certain teamwork skills and characteristics must be evident in the group's day-to-day work.

Teamwork involves an amalgam of attitudes, knowledge, and skills,[390] focused on:

- How each individual performs as a member of the team.

- How the entire team performs as a unit.

Any health care delivery group that fails to perform as a team will eventually fail. In the present context, failure means causing harm to patients—and perhaps killing them. CRM training emphasizes team performance, focusing on "leadership-followership" so that all members understand their place on the team and the need for active participation and mutual respect.

Effective teams exhibit collective efficacy. They optimize their resources, self-correct, compensate for each other by providing back-up, and reallocate functions as necessary. Because effective team can coordinate without overt communication, they can respond efficiently in high-stress, time-restricted environments. Effective teams recognize

---

390. Id.

potential problems or dangerous circumstances and adjust their plans and actions accordingly.

In aviation, teamwork-related behaviors are called "threat and error management behaviors" because they have been shown to help manage threats and errors in commercial aviation cockpits. In health care, the term "behavioral markers" has been employed. Behavioral markers are observable, non-technical behaviors that contribute to performance in a work environment.

The Objectives and Value of Team Training

This book has described the various organizational, cultural, and individual factors that influence team performance. Hospital teams must be able to function as a unit, even if team composition changes from day to day. In addition, team members have individual personalities and moods and individual tasks that may vary from day to day. Therefore, to achieve high reliability team performance, each team member must have teamwork-related skills that can be easily transferred from task to task and from team to team, unaffected by personal variables.

CRM team training promotes teamwork and team performance by (a) encouraging participation from each individual in a work group; (b) developing the skills necessary for that individual to perform effectively as a member of the group; and (c) conducting full-team simulations that replicate actual clinical situations and feature real-time feedback and debriefing.

At the conclusion of a CRM team training session, it is expected that participants will be demonstrably proficient in:

- Understanding how teamwork and communication contribute to patient safety.

- Understanding and respecting personal communication styles.

- Describing techniques used for effective teamwork, situational awareness (SA), communication (including assertiveness), resolving conflict, and decision making.

- Using the SBAR technique.

- Designing and leading customized team briefings and debriefings.

- Developing strategies to integrate the learned teamwork and communication tools into their local work setting or department.

Of course, as previously noted in relation to top-end leadership, maintaining these CRM skills with existing staff and promptly teaching them to each new hire are critical for institutionalizing and sustaining any patient safety initiative. Therefore, mandatory regular training or refresher courses, either stand-alone or as part of CME, are a must. Moreover, these follow-up courses can introduce customized refinements in process or procedure dictated by previous program results, advances in medicine, and newly identified best practices.

CRM Team Training

Teams improve as the individuals in them improve. This book has previously detailed how an HCO can benefit from instilling, enterprise-wide, CRM-based team skills and consistent and sustainable teamwork models. Those organizational benefits are "well documented in the literature,"[391] and include:

- Increased commitment to organizational mission.
- Increased ownership and stewardship.
- Enhanced cross-functional understanding.
- Collaborative, interdisciplinary process design and problem solving.
- Objective analysis of opportunities, problems, and solutions.
- More innovation.
- More flexible response to change.
- Improved quality, productivity, and patient satisfaction.[392]
- Improved morale, and reduced turnover and absenteeism.[393]
- Reduced operating costs.

Although each team member must focus primarily on team goals and team success, the reality is that teams improve as the individuals in them improve. Therefore, well-tuned individual skills are vital. CRM team training teaches individual skills that promote personal growth, ultimately translating into improved job performance.

---

391. Id.

392. Id.

393. Id.

The individual benefits of CRM, as previewed above, include:

- Better problem-solving skills.

- Increased knowledge of, and ability to confidently handle, interpersonal dynamics.

- Skills for future leadership roles.

- Broader knowledge of business processes.

- Feelings of commitment and satisfaction.

- A sense of being part of something greater than one's self.

- Lower stress[394] and increased quality of work life.

11 Common Traits of Highly Effective Teams

The following key elements are characteristic of high reliability health care teams and organizations. All of them inform the design of, and reflect the skills cultivated by, CRM training.

Team Trait No. 1
Clear unity of purpose

Everyone is watching the same movie: each team member is committed to patient safety and understands and accepts that he or she is responsible for safety.

Team Trait No. 2
Clear objectives and expectations

The members, as a group, openly discuss how the group will function to achieve its stated objectives. Everyone participates. The group produces a clear, detailed, and mutually

---

394. Id.

agreed approach, including norms, processes, rules, and expectations. Performance goals are stated as clear, concrete milestones against which the team measures itself. The group defines and achieves a continuous series of "small wins" ascending to larger goals.

Team Trait No. 3
Open and frequent self-assessment

As a normal part of its work routine, the group will stop to examine and discuss how well it is doing, as well as any impediments to effective performance. Problems are openly discussed until a solution is found.

Team Trait No. 4
Practice

Teams simulate actual scenarios and prepare for the unexpected.

Team Trait No. 5
Vigilance

Team members have situational awareness and are on alert for normalization of deviance—the gradual, inertial drift from performance standards that ultimately causes sub-standard performance to become the norm (as happened with the *Challenger* disaster).

Team Trait No. 6
Positive work atmosphere

The work atmosphere is informal, comfortable, and relaxed. There is no detectable acrimony. All members are respected, engaged, and involved.

Team Trait No. 7
Free expression

The members freely express feelings and ideas and listen to each other. Every idea is given a hearing. People are not afraid to float a creative idea even if it seems extreme. If a discussion goes off track, someone brings it back in short order.

Team Trait No. 8
Healthy disagreement

The rationale for each group action is carefully analyzed and open to discussion and dissent. Dissenters do not stifle their opposition despite apparent consensus. The group seeks to amicably resolve disagreements rather than dominate the dissenter. Conversely, dissenters do not try to dominate the group and express a legitimate difference of opinion. If disagreements are not resolved, the group devises a way to live with them without degrading performance.

Team Trait No. 9
Constructive criticism

All criticism is constructive and positive in tone and is aimed at removing a group obstacle to high reliability performance.

Team Trait No. 10
Genuine consensus

Although group members recognize that the group leader has ultimate responsibility and authority for decisions, an autocratic edict or simple majority is not generally accepted as a basis for action.

Team Trait No. 11
Respect for the group

Members arrive punctually to team meetings, prepared and ready to participate. When action is taken, clear assignments are made (who, what, when). Each member willingly accepts and completes the assignment on time.

11 Traits of Highly Effective Team Members

Each team member is part of, and integral to, the team mosaic: high reliability teams are composed of highly effective team members. Here are their key individual traits, all consistent with or mirroring the team traits listed above.

Team Member Trait No. 1
Team focus

The member has a highly attuned sense of belonging and loyalty to the team and desires to complete team tasks efficiently and effectively. He or she encourages and demonstrates team spirit and mutual respect among team members.

Team Member Trait No. 2
Respect for the group

He or she arrives punctually to team meetings, prepared and ready to participate. When action is taken, and an assignment is made, he or she willingly accepts and completes the assignment on time.

Team Member Trait No. 3
Individual growth and development

The team member is keenly interested in self-development and promoting self-development and self-confidence of teammates. He or she strives to improve the team/organization as a whole by developing and fostering good relationships and individual and team/organizational skills.

Team Member Trait No. 4
Big Picture awareness

The team member understands the big picture—the work-related roles, duties, and expectations of others with the group and the organization, and how they interplay.

Team Member Trait No. 5
Understanding human diversity and limitations

He or she accepts that people have different attitudes, opinions, prejudices, personalities, stressors, and emotional and intellectual bandwidth, all of which affect the ability to perform effectively under pressure. He or she also recognizes that these differences may pose barriers to communication, situational awareness, decision making, and teamwork, and therefore create threats to patient safety.

Team Member Trait No. 6
Open and receptive communication/consensus building

The team member encourages consultation and the free exchange of ideas, soliciting comments and opinions from others. He or she is willing to listen, encouraging work colleagues to share common goals and reach consensus solutions.

Team Member Trait No. 7
Situational awareness

He or she spots barriers and red flags that inhibit or threaten safety and performance and takes appropriate steps to neutralize their negative effect.

Team Member Trait No. 8
Pitching in

He or she recognizes when a teammate needs help and offers it.

Team Member Trait No. 9
Readiness to seek help

He or she is modest enough to ask for help from others to solve problems, without feeling inferior.

Team Member Trait No. 10
Managing conflict

The member is able to anticipate potential areas of conflict, technical or personal, and acts assertively and rationally to resolve them in order to eliminate or minimize the potential adverse effects on the team or the organization.

Team Member Trait No. 11
Giving and requesting criticism and feedback

He or she is willing and able to give and accept constructive criticism. He or she is willing and able to analyze information and provide appropriate feedback to the initiator of the information. He or she willingly requests feedback after performing a task, to understand or confirm its success/failure/ outcome.

Team Leadership and Followership

In light of the above exposition on teams and teamwork, it is apparent that leadership and followership are inseparable sides of the same coin, and accordingly, both are essential ingredients in CRM team training.[395]

Underlying that training module is the real-world principle that even when team members share a common mental model and a genuine commitment to the organization and its patient safety mission, the sharp-end skills and behaviors of team leaders often dictate the team's success or failure. These skills are the non-technical "soft skills" often derided by pilots in the early days of CRM and since then, by physicians.

---

395. Chapters 9 and 10 have explained at length the need for, indicia of, and suggestions for top-end HCO leadership in establishing a safety culture and navigating toward high reliability performance through CRM. This section concentrates on team leadership.

Hierarchy, or status-derived power distance, is a primary risk factor for impeding team performance because it often inhibits people from speaking up.

As previously noted, hierarchy, or status-derived power distance, is a primary risk factor for impeding team performance because it often inhibits people from speaking up. Effective leaders flatten the hierarchy and create an atmosphere of comfort and security that empowers and motivates team members to participate, perform, and speak up. Authoritarian leaders create or perpetuate unnecessary and avoidable threats to patient safety.

Team Leadership Do's and Don'ts

Abundant information is available, both scientific (formal) and empirical (informal),[396] about leadership in general and the traits of good and bad team leaders in particular.[397] A treatise on

---

396. For example, John Wooden, architect and coach of the storied UCLA basketball dynasty, has devised a Pyramid of Success, which has been adopted by many organizations and businesses. A graphic of the pyramid can be viewed as part of the following article: *"John Wooden's Pyramid Still Standing."* Entrepreneur.com. March 27. 2007. http://www.entrepreneur.com/management/leadership/article176282.html (accessed April 17, 2009).

397. The mass of information is so vast that it is often difficult to determine primary sources. Therefore, relatively few citations appear in this section. The general concepts and characteristics herein have been distilled from multiple sources that say essentially the same thing and are considered a consensus view.

leadership is beyond the scope of this book. That said, while recognizing that no single leadership trait or style fits all in all circumstances, in the CRM/health care teamwork context, a "wish list" of key leadership traits and skills[398] can nevertheless be suggested.

Many of these traits and skills are the same as, or overlap with, those mentioned previously for effective teams and team members.[399] Following are "the Do's," the 20 Key Traits and Skills of Highly Effective Team Leaders

Leaders are not necessarily born. But they can be cultivated, through CRM training, with the appropriate mindset, attitude, and behavior.

Trait No. 1
Champion

Mirrors, champions, and is a good will ambassador for the organization's commitment to a patient-centric, high-reliability safety culture.

Trait No. 2
Big Picture

Understands the relationship between organizational objectives (including profitability) and team performance.[400]

---

398. The word "leadership" as used here reflects the apparent contemporary blurring, as indicated in the research, of the differences between "leaders" and "managers." Traditionally, "leaders" have focused on big picture relationships, and managers on discrete functions. In the patient safety/CRM context, a flexible blend of both is required of team leaders. CRM training by design incorporates these blended sharp-end roles and skills.

399. This follows because the team leader is also a team member.

400. A. J. Schuler, PhD. *"Are You A Leader? Part II: Leadership Self Test Answers and Discussion."* 2003. http://www.schulersolutions.com/leadership_self_test_answers.html (accessed April 17, 2009).

Trait No. 3
Safety focus

Is constantly alert for threats to safety in planning and implementing tasks.

Trait No. 4
Commitment to excellence

Is unwaveringly committed to excellence in all aspects of the workplace and in delivering care to patients.

Trait No. 5
Intelligent adherence

Follows prescribed processes and procedures, but not blindly, in order to stay alert (maintain situational awareness) and adapt to unique circumstances.

Trait No. 6
Team orientation

Recognizes that more can be accomplished by empowering others than by ruling them. Fosters team cohesion by creating adult/adult, rather than adult/child relationships with colleagues. Avoids making himself/herself comfortable at the expense of others; avoids using rank or status for personal advantage over others.[401]

Trait No. 7
Flexibility

Accepts and adapts to necessary change. Recognizes and accepts alternative ways of accomplishing a task. Adapts to new conditions, teams, team members, and tasks. Is receptive to new ideas or opinions.

---

401. This is one of the 14 leadership traits specified in the United States Marine *Corps' Guidebook for Marines,* 1984 (Marine Guidebook). A list of these traits is available at http://www.6mcd.usmc.mil/ftl_site/Handbook/ marinecorpsleadershiptraits.htm (accessed April 17, 2009). In the Marine Guidebook, the trait described in this sentence is called "Unselfishness".

Trait No. 8
Stability

Maintains mission and task focus during change. Completes assigned tasks even when unique circumstances require deviations from standard processes and procedures.

Trait No. 9
Bearing [402]

Maintains a confident and assertive—but not overbearing—leadership presence. Maintains poise and performs effectively under stress. Is resilient, recovering and learning from prior mistakes or failures. Accepts criticism.

Trait No. 10
Self-Awareness/Assessment

Understands his or her own limits and fallibility and those of other team members. Is conscious of the environmental and human factors that influence individual and team actions and decisions. Is self-analytical and willing to admit mistakes and imperfections in performance.

Trait No. 11
Respect

Respects others and their diversity. Welcomes different perspectives in the group. Is fair and consistent. Can agree to disagree, respecting the rights of others to dissent while adhering to his or her decision-making role as leader.

Trait No. 12
Sharing/Teaching

Recognizes the need to improve the knowledge of others and shares his or her knowledge and experience to accomplish this.

---

402. This is also one of the 14 leadership traits listed in the Marine Guidebook.

Trait No. 13
Communicating

Effective team leadership depends on effective communication, which is addressed in greater detail below, but includes the following:

- Interpersonal Communication: the leader is a good listener. Asks questions and welcomes them. Is sensitive to cultural differences and to non-verbal communication. Exercises tact[403] to maintain good relations, but is polite, calm, appropriately firm, and decisive.

- Gives feedback and criticism in constructive tone.

- Group dynamics: understands and manages group discussions.

- Well-reasoned persuasion: imparts solid reasoning for each decision.

- Praises, encourages, and motivates others. Shows appreciation and gives (or shares) credit where merited. Encourages speaking up and constructive input from team members.

Trait No. 14
Planning and organizing

Plans and organizes tasks effectively to achieve stated goals.

Trait No. 15
Delegating

Shares out work by assigning tasks to others.

---

403. One of the 14 traits listed in the Marine Guidebook.

Trait No. 16
Dealing with uncertainty and the unexpected

Recognizes and deals promptly with ambiguous, uncertain, or unexpected situations.

Trait No. 17
Observing

Observes/monitors team activities, without hovering, to confirm they are functioning as intended.

Trait No. 18:
Resolving conflict

Recognizes and resolves conflict while dissipating hostility.

Trait No. 19:
Solving problems/making decisions

Spots problems, identifies their sources, and effectively decides how to resolve them, even in the face of uncertainty and time pressure. To that end, understands how and when to use available technical and team resources to gather information, consulting with others as necessary. Announces decisions clearly and professionally.

Trait No. 20
Reporting

Understands the organization's need for data and other actionable information, and appropriately reports not only adverse events and near misses but also the team's successes in avoiding or mitigating error.

Situational Leadership

Overall, the genus of team leadership called for here, and what CRM promotes, is situational leadership: more precisely, *emotionally intelligent* situational leadership. Achieving this plateau involves applying skills that can readily be taught. [404]

The traits referred to above are not intended as a cookie-cutter checklist, but a list of general indicators and direction finders. There are, in fact, numerous leadership styles, each of which can be effective if matched appropriately to the circumstances. On the other hand, the analysis in this book points to the caveat that the so-called "autocratic" or "transactional" styles—based on power and status—are misaligned with the increased intra-team interaction and communication required to improve patient safety.

Emotional intelligence has been touched on previously and is further discussed below. "Situational leadership" refers to a still-evolving model originally developed by Kenneth Blanchard and Paul Hersey in the late 1960s.[405] Over time, the model has been accepted by hundreds of enterprises and has been adopted by all branches of the United States military,[406] because it is not only customizable and effective but is easy to understand and use. Equally important, successful use of the model, which is aligned with CRM practice, involves applying behavior skills that can readily be taught through training.

The situational model recognizes that leadership styles vary based on individual personalities, but also with the situation.

---

404. For a brief summary consistent with that below, see Bernard L. Erven. "Becoming an Effective Leader Through Situational Leadership." Department of Agricultural, Environmental and Development Economics, Ohio State University Extension July 2001. http://aede.osu.edu/people/erven.1/HRM/ Situaltional_Leadership.pdf, accessed April 17, 2009.

405. Hersey has, in fact, trademarked the concept: Situational Leadership®.

406. See, for example, Major George W. Yeakey, U.S. Army, Retired. "Situational Leadership." *Military Review*, January-February 2002.

Therefore, versatility is critical to effective leadership. The model holds that depending on the situation, different styles must be used in directing and supporting followers. The model identifies four styles—directing, coaching, supporting, and delegating—arranged in a matrix. Effective leaders move around the matrix as the situation dictates and adapt their style according to the development level of the followers and their diagnosed need for direction or support, based on their experience, competence, commitment, confidence, and motivation.

One study, by Baker and Brown, emphasizes skills over styles. In their view, successful situational leadership "relies on effectiveness in four communication components: communicating expectations, listening, delegating, and providing feedback"[407]—all of which are imbedded in CRM training.

11 Traits Associated With Team Failure

Poor leaders and good ones share many of the same traits. But it can take only one difference to derail a team.

Trait No. 1
Failing to face reality

Failing to acknowledge that patient safety is a problem and that the traditional, culture-ingrained attitudes and behaviors of clinicians are part of it.

---

407. Nicole A. Brown and Randolph T. Barker. "Analysis of the Communication Components Found Within the Situational Leadership Model: Toward Integration of Communication and the Model." *Journal of Technical Writing and Communication*, 2001. Vol. 31, No. 2: 135-157.

Trait No. 2
Forgetting the Big Picture

Losing sight of the organization's safety culture and patient safety objectives, and going off track.

Trait No. 3
Rigidity

Although competent, the leader is unable or unwilling to adapt to new ideas, new information, or changing times.

Trait No. 4
Leading by instilling fear

Emphasizing title or status instead of expertise and experience.

Trait No. 5
Invulnerability / macho[408]

Invulnerability is a false sense that one is impervious or unable to make errors. This can also be called being "macho."

Trait No. 6
Imbalance

The leader is a workaholic or lacks self-knowledge. Imbalance skews perspective and impedes decision making.[409]

Trait No. 7
Poor or unclear communications

Important messages are lost or garbled.

---

408. Invulnerability and macho are two of the five "hazardous attitudes" of pilots identified by the Federal Aviation Administration. (U.S. Department of Transportation, Federal Aviation Administration 1991, Chapter 3, Paragraph 13, 11)

409. Bill George. *Authentic Leadership: Rediscovering the Secrets to Creating Lasting Value*. San Francisco: Jossey-Bass, 2003, 46.

Trait No. 8
Intemperance

The leader is impulsive. He or she lacks professional bearing and self-control, enabled by followers who are unwilling or unable to intervene appropriately.

Trait No. 9
Callousness[410]

The leader ignores or discounts the organization's mission and objectives or the wants, needs, and value of team members (especially subordinates).

Trait No. 10
Integrity slip

What the leader says does not match what he or she does. Is unwilling to do what he or she demands others to do.

Trait No. 11
Power play

Fails to collaborate, share power, or share credit.

Followership

The traits listed above of highly effective team members are also the foundation for effective followership. More to the point, one cannot be a good follower unless he or she is first an effective team member. In fact, effective leaders are also followers and can seemlessly integrate into various power-sharing situations.

---

410. Rigidity, intemperance, and callousness are three of the seven traits of bad leadership isolated by Barbara Kellerman in her 2004 book, *Bad Leadership: What It Is, How It Happens, Why It Matters* (Harvard Business School Press).

Followers are mission critical to any team-centered endeavor, representing the power that permits work groups and organizations to achieve their stated goals. Moreover, because all team members (even team leaders) must answer to someone, all of them are also followers and need to be good followers.

Good followership skills include positive behaviors, aligned with effective communication, that emanate from (1) a positive baseline mindset, and (2) keen situational awareness—the second essential CRM skill.

Chapter 12

Situational Awareness Skills

Key Points in this Chapter

- Situational awareness (SA)[411] is arguably the most important factor affecting patient safety. When situational awareness is lost, communication suffers and the potential for human error—and harm to patients—increases.

- SA represents a mindset rather than a specific behavior or procedure. An SA mindset enables clinicians to spot potential threats and initiate effective protocols to eliminate them. Good SA has proved directly related to effective team performance.

- SA is a critical skill that can be taught and acquired via CRM methodology.

- SA has been extensively studied and variously defined, but essentially it means clinicians know what is going on around them and use that information to anticipate what will happen next and, consequently, communicate effectively and make good decisions.

- It is not easy to turn good SA into effective performance. Today's sophisticated systems and technologies are both blessing and curse; instead of getting the right information, a clinician may end up with too much information. Moreover, the information that compromises SA comes from various sources: written, verbal, and non-verbal. Discerning what information is important for the task at hand requires a high level of cognition based on a combination of reasoning, intuition, and perception.

---

411. In practice and in research, the terms "situational awareness" and "situation awareness" are used interchangeably. Although the latter is more correct in style and usage, the former is much more prevalent. Both terms are also referred to as "SA." All three terms are used in this chapter.

- CRM team training is vital to SA. CRM imparts skills that build a collective mindset—a "shared mental model"—that is prophylactic against and compensates for (1) individual foibles and cognitive limitations and (2) data overload.

- In the clinic, circumstances can change rapidly. Preserving SA requires consistent peer-monitoring to spot "red flags"—signals that safety is threatened. "Red flags" include lack of attention; ambiguous information or instructions; confusion; distraction; fixation; lack of leadership; poor communication; and overwork, stress, and fatigue.

- The "See It, Say It, Fix It" communication model is a useful and straightforward tool for maintaining SA or getting it back on track once derailed.

- SA is crucial to the CRM tenet of utilizing all available resources to solve problems. To achieve and preserve team SA in the clinic, all team members must actively pay attention and share information with the team through effective communication. When this happens, SA guides the process and the process also enhances SA.

Situational Awareness: An Introduction

Several experts, including Helmreich, have classified the various individual and performance (or systems) factors that impact team performance and, in turn, patient safety.[412] As the previous chapters have indicated:

- The individual factors include aptitude, physical environment, and culture (professional, organizational, and national).

- The performance/systems factors include team formation and management, standard routines, and organization-wide and intra-team communications.[413]

However, the performance/systems factors command equal if not primary emphasis, since harmful patient events "are largely grounded in systems errors (communication, teamwork and situational awareness) rather than technical mistakes."[414]

Situational awareness is arguably the most important performance factor affecting patient safety, because SA is central to effective communication. When situational awareness is lost, communication suffers and the potential for human error—and harm to patients—increases.

Among all of the performance/systems factors that affect patient safety, situational awareness is arguably the most important. [415, 416] SA is "central" to effective communication:[417] when situational awareness is lost, communication suffers and thus the potential for human error—and harm to patients—increases.[418, 419]

---

412. These factors are addressed in detail throughout this book.

413. Pizzi, Goldfarb, and Nash 2001, 505.

414. Jon Allard March 2007, 190.

415. Alfred Cuschieri, MD. "Nature of Human Error: Implications for Surgical Practice." *Annals of Surgery*, November 2006, Vol. 244, No. 5: 642–648, 644. (Alfred Cuschieri November 2006)

Situational awareness (SA) is central to effective communication and patient safety because SA represents a mindset rather than a specific behavior or procedure:[420]

> An individual's understanding and classification of the situation he or she is in forms the basis for all subsequent decision making and performance. Even the best trained people will perform poorly if their situational awareness is incorrect or insufficient.[421,422]

An attuned SA mindset enables clinicians to spot potential threats and initiate effective protocols to eliminate them. SA, in fact, is part of AHRQ's "standard competency nomenclature" of skills that previous investigations have proved "directly related to effective team performance."[423] That SA is considered a "skill" is significant; skills can be readily taught and acquired, in this instance via CRM methodology.[424]

---

416. In his article about human error in the OR, Dr. Alfred Cuschieri differentiates (1) "limelight" (newsworthy) errors, such as wrong site surgeries, leaving instruments in patients, and technical operating errors, from (2) "Cinderella" errors, which include prophylaxis errors and loss of situation awareness. He observes that

   Cinderella errors...in the context of health care safety are probably more important because of their greater relative frequency (although data are not available). The concern in this context is that defense measures and protocols are rightfully used against limelight errors, but defense systems against Cinderella errors may be less robust. (Alfred Cuschieri, November 2006, 644)

417. John C. Morey, Robert Simon, Gregory D. Jay, Robert L. Wears, Mary Salisbury, Kimberly A. Dukes, and Scott D. Berns. "Error Reduction and Performance Improvement in the Emergency Department through Formal Teamwork Training: Evaluation Results of the MedTeams Project." *Health Services Research,* December 2002, Vol. 37, No. 6: 1553-1581, 1577. (Morey, et al. December 2002)

418. Teamwork Takes Hold to Improve Patient Safety February 2005, 5.

419. International Association of Fire Chiefs 2003, 19.

420. Alfred Cuschieri November 2006, 643.

421. Morey, et al. December 2002, 1577.

422. This excerpt from Morey also goes on to note: "One study of aircraft accidents found that as many as 88% of all accidents attributed to human error had an underlying problem with situational awareness."

Situational Awareness: Definitions

Situational awareness has been variously defined (concisely and otherwise) as follows:[425]

- Situational awareness occurs when a common team appraisal of the internal and external environment is developed to apply to current task strategies and help anticipate future situations.[426]

- A general definition of SA that has been found to be applicable across a wide variety of domains describes SA as the perception of the elements in the environment within a volume of time and space, the comprehension of their meaning, and the projection of their status in the near future.[427]

- Recognizing that human beings are prone to error, situational awareness is a concept that addresses the need to maintain attentiveness to an event, being alert and oriented.[428]

- SA is an adaptive, externally directed consciousness.[429]

---

423. AHRQ 2008, 14.

424. Avoiding error, as previously suggested, is the highest aspiration of CRM training. One of the main thrusts of this book is that medical teams can be trained through CRM to avoid error, and can actively practice doing so, by (1) maintaining a high level of proficiency; (2) following SOPs; (3) minimizing distractions; (4) planning ahead; (5) maintaining situational awareness; and (6) effectively using all resources. (International Association of Fire Chiefs 2003, 21)

425. Quotation marks have been omitted from this bulleted list. Generally, and except as otherwise indicated, the bullet text has been excerpted verbatim to underline the variety of SA definitions.

426. Powell and Hill January 2006, 188.

427. Mica R. Endsley. "Theoretical Underpinnings of Situation Awareness: A Critical Review." In *Situation Awareness and Analysis Measurement* by M. R Endsley and D.J. Garland (Eds.). Mahwah, NJ: Lawrence Erlbaum Associates, 2000, 3. (M. R. Endsley 2000)

428. International Association of Fire Chiefs 2003, 5.

429. M. R. Endsley 2000, 14.

- Situational awareness refers to the care team maintaining the "big picture" and thinking ahead to plan and discuss contingencies. This ongoing dialogue, which keeps members of the team up to date with what is happening and how they will respond if the situation changes, is a key factor in safety.[430]

- The term "situational awareness," derived from aviation, refers to knowing the conditions that can affect one's work,[431] or the work of one's team.[432] In the team context:

  - Situational awareness refers to the extent to which team members are aware of the status of a particular clinical event impacting the team; e.g., in-patient bed availability.[433]

  - Positive patient outcomes rely on the ability of the team to establish and maintain SA throughout the life of the team.[434]

  - Loss of situational awareness means you can't see the forest for the trees.[435]

- Simply stated, situational awareness is knowing what is going on around you.[436]

- Situational awareness means pilots and other crew members have a good sense of where the plane is and what the conditions are:

---

430. M. Leonard 2004, i87.

431. Susan Mann 2006, 2-3.

432. Dynamics Research Corporation. *MedTeams ® Emergency Team Coordination Course® Student Guide.* 2004, 1-7.

433. Dynamics Research Corporation 2004, 3-3.

434. Dynamics Research Corporation. *MedTeams ® Emergency Team Coordination Course® Student Guide.* 2004, 1-7.

435. Steven J. Henkind and J. Christopher Sinnett October 8, 2008, 1692.

436. Endsley 2000, 2.

"If the humans do have appropriate situational awareness, they make the right decisions," Allen [John Allen, deputy director of flight standards at the FAA] said. "But if things start breaking down, you have an accident or an incident."[437]

- Situational awareness refers to the cognitive processes involved in forming and changing mind-set. In the medical context, situational awareness involves the identification of an evolving situation, which may lead to an adverse event unless abortive or corrective action is taken.[438]

Situational Awareness: Three Levels

As the above list of definitions implies, situational awareness has been extensively studied. Two eminent authorities in this arena are Mica R. Endsley and John C. Morey. Both analyze situational awareness on an ascending scale of three levels:

Level One: Perception

Perceiving critical factors in the environment. Endsley calls this a fundamental "perception of cues," without which "the odds of forming an incorrect picture of the situation increase dramatically."[439]

437. Sarah Vos. "In Aviation, Human Factors Are An Entire Field Of Study." *McClatchy Newspapers,* September 25, 2006. http://www.comairflight5191crash.com/source/news/mcclatchy_092506.html (accessed December 26, 2008).

438. Alfred Cuschieri November 2006, 643.

439. M. R. Endsley 2000, 3.

Level Two: Comprehension

Going beyond mere perception; understanding what environmental cues mean, particularly their relevance to a decision maker's goals. In Endsley's words, "This is analogous to having a high level of reading comprehension as compared to just reading words."[440]

Level Three: Expert Application

The highest level of SA: the capability to use perceived and comprehended current events and dynamics to forecast or anticipate what will happen next.[441] As Endsley notes, this "is the mark of a skilled expert."

Endsley also describes the "temporal aspects" to SA, which are key subsets of SA Levels 2 and 3. Temporal aspects relate to how much time is available to make assessments and decisions and take action to solve problems: How immediate is the threat? How long before it becomes reality? How quickly is the current situation changing?[442]

Both Endsley and Morey support the idea that situational awareness is a foundational mindset from which all effective communications, decisions, and acts flow (see Endsley's diagram in Figure 7.1) This idea tilts toward at a general conclusion that the higher the level of any individual's situational awareness, the more effectively he or she will perform.

Endsley rejects that conclusion. He argues that even though situational awareness is strongly linked to sound decision making and performance, SA is nevertheless separate from both.[443]

---

440. M. R. Endsley 2000, 4

441. Morey, et al. December 2002, 1577; M. R. Endsley 2000, 4.

442. M. R. Endsley 2000, 4; see also Alfred Cuschieri November 2006, 643.

> Situational awareness is depicted as the operator's internal model of the state of the environment. Based on that representation, operators can decide what to do about the situation and carry out any necessary actions. Situational awareness therefore is represented as the main precursor to decision making....[444]

Thus there is much more underlying the three levels of SA, and much more to "turning good situational awareness into successful performance."[445] First, as Endsley points out, today's systems and technologies are extremely sophisticated and complex. This is both blessing and curse. On the one hand, as Cuschieri notes,

> It seems obvious that access to health information technology at the coal face of medical practice is of value in improving quality of care and patient safety....The 3 benefits identified [are] increased adherence to guideline based care (evidence-based practice), enhanced surveillance and monitoring, and decreased medication errors.[446]

On the other hand is Endsley's observation that clinicians are bombarded with, and must somehow...

> ...comprehend a dazzling array of data which is often changing very rapidly....The problem with today's systems is not a lack of information, but finding what is needed when it is needed....It is becoming widely recognized that more data does not equal more information....Unfortunately, in the face of

---

443. Endsley writes: "SA is not decision making and decision making is not SA." (2000,5. He repeats this theme on page 18.)

444. M. R. Endsley 2000, 4.

445. M. R. Endsley 2000, 5.

446. Alfred Cuschieri November 2006, 643.

this torrent of data, many operators may be even less informed than ever before. This is because there is a huge gap between the tons of data being produced and disseminated and people's ability to find the bits that are needed and process them together with the other bits to arrive at the actual information that is required for their decisions....Issues of automation and "intelligent systems" have frequently only exacerbated the problem, rather than aided it.[447]

Sound SA, therefore, inherently involves discerning what is important for the task at hand.[448] For example: a surgeon may be aware that her teammate is wearing blue sneakers or that the air conditioning isn't working right, but neither data byte will help the patient lying at the tip of her scalpel.

Second, as Endsley also points out, people with perfect SA still make bad decisions. For example, organizational or technical factors (such as outdated equipment) may limit the available options; the decision maker may lack experience or training or be an inveterate risk taker.[449] A 1995 study, in fact, reported that 26.6% of aviation accidents were attributable to poor decisions despite apparently adequate situational awareness.[450]

This all suggests that the "perception" and "comprehension" necessary to achieve high-acuity situational awareness represent an elevated plateau of cognition based on an essential, but scientifically imprecise, amalgam of reasoning, intuition,[451] and perception. After all, to achieve high reliability

---

447. M. R. Endsley 2000, 1.

448. M. R. Endsley 2000, 2.

449. Endsley also concedes that good decisions can be made with poor SA, even "if only by luck." (M. R. Endsley 2000, 5)

450. M. R. Endsley 2000, 5, 18.

performance, a clinician's individual perception must closely match the objective clinical reality.[452, 453]

In the SA context, CRM team training is pivotal. CRM team training imparts skills that build a collective perception that is prophylactic against—and compensates for—individual foibles, cognitive limitations and mismatches, and data and sensory overload.

The Shared Mental Model

For medical teams, good situational awareness requires a "shared mental model." This equates to Leonard's image of "being in the same movie." Along these lines, Morey has observed as follows:

> Effective situational awareness depends on team members developing accurate expectations for team performance by drawing on a common knowledge base. This concept, known as maintaining a "Shared Mental Model," allows team members to effectively perform the following:

---

451. Gary Klein embraces and champions the power of intuition, but Endsley appears to consciously avoid the term. That said, what Endsley refers to as "long term memory stores" is consistent with the idea that intuition plays a role in SA:

    ...SA is a unique product of external information acquired, working memory processes and the internal long-term memory stores activated and brought to bear on the formation of the internal representation. (M. R. Endsley 2000,10)

    More exposition on the nature of intuition, and its role in decision making, appears in Chapter 15.

452. International Association of Fire Chiefs 2003, 19.

453. On the other hand, sound decisions promote but cannot guarantee high reliability performance. Timely and proper execution of sound decisions yields high reliability, and as previously observed, many organizational and individual factors can derail execution. (See, for example, M. R. Endsley 2000,5,18.)

- Anticipate the needs of other team members;

- Predict the needs of other team members;

- Adapt to task demands efficiently.

> In other words...[a]ll the team members share an understanding of the objective and mission to be accomplished.[454]

Others have a slightly different perspective on the shared mental model:

> A mental model is a mental picture or sketch of the relevant facts and relationships defining an event, situation, or problem. A mental model held by members of a team is referred to as a shared mental model. A mental model becomes shared by team members through the processes of planning, team decision making, and vocalizing; and is maintained through situational awareness and communication.[455]

> Communication handoffs are critically important in creating a shared mental model around the patient's condition.[456]

Thus, some believe that a shared mental model is a predicate to situational awareness. Others seem to emphasize the reverse. Either way, as Endsley notes, there is "a strong relationship between SA and mental models." [457, 458] Endsley also articulates, as the work of others implies, that this strong relationship has a transitive property; although SA does not

---

454. Morey, et al. December 2002, 1577.

455. Dynamics Research Corporation 2004, 2-9, referring to (but not citing) the work of Gary A. Klein. However, this same language appears in many other sources, and therefore definitive attribution is unclear.

456. Haig, Sutton, and Whittington, March 2006, 167.

457. M. R. Endsley 2000, 5.

equate to decision making, "decisions are formed by SA and SA is formed by decisions."

Regardless of the theoretical construct, shared mental models are a "vital mechanism" for forming and maintaining SA under very challenging conditions.[459] Mental models help overcome the limitations of a person's working memory. Mental models help direct and focus a clinician's attention to the most relevant aspects of a situation, enabling that clinician to perceive, assimilate, and understand information, and to project future developments. [460]

Three Essentials for Shared Mental Models

Endsley's work, as cited extensively in this section, refers to both organization-derived (top-down) and individually employed (bottom-up) mental models, which nevertheless seem influenced if not shaped by top-down modeling. His observations also predominate toward individual rather than team SA and are not specifically tailored to medicine. However, his observations on mental models, their essential ingredients, and their relationship to SA are nevertheless illuminating and relevant to—and plainly support—the patient safety-centered CRM team training principles described throughout this book.

---

458. According to Endsley, true situation awareness represents a snap shot—the current state of the mental model. He uses the example of a running car engine. One can have an overall mental model of how the engine works, but the actual situation model (SA) is its current state (for example, its temperature and fuel level). This situational model embraces not only the car's relevant current values, but an understanding of how they project. For example, if the temperature is too high, the car will overheat; if the fuel is low, it will run out of gas. (M. R. Endsley 2000, 5, 13)

459. M. R. Endsley 2000, 12, 13.

460. Id.

Endsley posits three essentials relating to shared mental models: [461]

- Goals
- Preconceptions/Expectations
- Automaticity

Each of these three areas is described in more detail below.

Goals

Active goals are central to developing shared mental models and ultimately, situational awareness. Goals, provided they are clearly articulated, represent a top-down driver of focus and attention across the organization and inside the clinic. The clinician actively seeks the relevant information needed to attain those goals, and simultaneously, the goals act as a filter to distill that information. Therefore, SA, despite its classification as a mindset, also involves active, purposeful behavior directed toward achieving an articulated goal in a specific environment.[462]

Active goals also drive mental models from the bottom up:

- The goal to diagnose an illness based on certain symptoms will activate the mental model associated with that diagnostic behavior.

---

461. Most of the theoretical information or background in this "essentials" portion, including the quoted (and block quoted) text, is distilled or extracted from M. R. Endsley 2000, 13-16.

462. It is recognized, however, that in the real world, clinicians typically have multiple—if not competing—goals that shift in importance. At any one time, only a subset of those goals may be actively pursued. For example, while a clinician may be busily engaged elsewhere, when a code is called, a new goal will be triggered, which then activates a new mental model and new locus of attention. In short, goals must be juggled. (M. R. Endsley 2000, 14)

- That goal and its associated mental model direct attention in gathering and distilling information from the clinical environment. For this reason, selecting the correct goal is extremely critical for achieving SA: if the clinician is pursing the wrong goal (or a less important goal), critical information may be missed or ignored.

- Goals and their associated mental models help to integrate and interpret information to attain comprehension. As Endsley puts it, "The goal determines the 'so what' of the information."[463] For example, an elevated blood sugar level can only be interpreted in comparison to the goal: the desired level. Selecting the wrong mental model may lead to misinterpreting the information.

For these reasons, "dynamic switching" between top-down and bottom-up goal processing is an underlying key to SA. Endsley says:

> I feel a recognition of goals is key to understanding SA. Without understanding operator goals, the information in the environment has no meaning.[464]

The above analysis on goals meshes with the safety culture themes stressed in this book. The organization's overall commitment to patient safety leads to developing an organization-wide vision (mental model) and goals in support of it. CRM team training is activated to help impart the vision in the clinic and achieve those goals. In microcosm, at the sharp end (what Cuschieri calls the "coal face"), CRM team training cultivates team leaders with an understanding of the top-down organizational vision and goals and empowers subordinates, from the bottom up, to actively contribute.

---

463. M. R. Endsley 2000, 14.

464. Id.

Preconceptions/Expectations

Situational awareness is also impacted by preconceptions and expectations. In any situation, people tend to see or hear what they expect. What they expect can, as previously detailed, be shaped and colored by individual variables (including personal biases), or by systemic factors such as ingrained mental models or specific instructions; nurses, for example, may develop strong expectation based on a team pre-op briefing. In any event, expectations influence where and how people direct their attention and how they perceive the data they take in.

Expectations are a double-edged sword. On the positive side, expectations imply preparedness: they help clinicians filter diverse data into actionable subsets.[465] On the negative side, studies have shown that teams given "a well-developed set of expectations based on a pre-mission video briefing tended to fall into traps easily when events and situations did not unfold as expected." This trap is a risk even for teams composed of highly experienced individuals and results in mismatching and misinterpreting information.[466] Especially significant for patient safety and high reliability health care, those studies also showed that the teams overly influenced by expectations had not developed strong group skills for active problem solving.

This section echoes this book's previous text on the benefits and dangers of routine and SOPs. The *Challenger* and *Columbia* disasters graphically demonstrate that a judicious balance must be struck to avoid traps and complacency.

---

465. The concepts in this section and the next on automaticity are related to heuristics, all of which are further analyzed as part of Chapter 15 (Decision Making).

466. Endsley writes that "even highly experienced air traffic controllers developed quite elaborate stories to explain away conflicting information that was inconsistent with the mental model created by earlier information."

Automaticity

Pattern matching is essential for using mental models to develop and maintain SA. Clinicians must be able to match critical cues in the environment to corresponding elements of the mental model.[467, 468] Predictably, experience and training play a central role; experts are generally better at contextual pattern matching than novices and can do so almost instantly.[469]

However, as was the case with expectations, pattern matching can be risky because it can lead to virtually automatic decision making. The entire sequence thus "can become highly routinized."[470] This mechanism works well when a low attention is required in familiar situations: those who like to read an engrossing novel outdoors will unconsciously shoo away insects; people who commute by the same route every day may not consciously recall how they got home; a professional basketball player pivots and jumps to block an opponent's shot. In these examples, automaticity is a positive because it reduces demand on our limited capacity to pay attention. But as with expectations, automaticity of cognitive processes can reduce or preclude responsiveness to novel yet crucial stimuli outside the routine.

Endsley recognizes and accepts the benefits of a "fair degree of automaticity," but sternly cautions that in "highly cognitive, complex systems"—such as contemporary medicine—"the need for SA remains."

---

467. M. R. Endsley 2000, 11.

468. Endsley also refers to "schema" as an associated, similar construct relating to pattern matching of "prototypical system states." Experienced operators match critical cues in the environment to the schema, enabling them to instantly classify and comprehend situations, and thereby simplify decision making. (M. R. Endsley 2000,11)

469. M. R. Endsley 2000, 12.

470. M. R. Endsley 2000, 15.

In most real-world domains, people must perform based on more than just stimulus-response. They need to combine information and anticipate events that are beyond their experience. They must be proactive, not just reactive. They must be goal driven and not just data driven. These aspects of successful performance require SA and are at odds with automaticity of cognitive behaviors.[471]

Achieving and Maintaining SA

Based on the above analysis and following the principles espoused in this book, the optimal SA continuum presents as follows:

- Once the appropriate group mindset and shared mental model are in place, situational awareness is monitored, maintained, and enhanced by team members continuously and consistently sharing information.[472]

- That information is shared effectively and appropriately via CRM-based communication methods and tools.

- Based on a full array of relevant information, sound decisions can be made.

As previously noted, the various threads of information that constitute situational awareness come from various sources. Information is delivered in writing, verbally, and non-verbally. Information cues can therefore be overt or quite subtle and is sometimes registered subconsciously.

---

471. Id.

472. Dynamics Research Corporation. *MedTeams® Emergency Team Coordination Course® Student Guide.* 2004, 1-7, 3-3. [Dynamics Research Corporation 2004]

But Endsley has already imparted the key to achieving team SA in the clinic, regardless of the type or source of information. Specifically, in order to receive and utilize all available resources to solve problems—a core commandment of CRM—all team members must actively pay attention,[473] "keep their brains turned on," and share information with the team through effective communication methods. Reiterating the transitive properties of SA, when team members actively participate and rely on each other, SA guides the process and the process yields SA.

To recap, CRM training teaches the tools and techniques to develop and maintain the shared mental model that flows from a top-down cultural commitment to patient safety and allows the concerted pursuit and achievement of common goals. It also teaches ways for clinicians to communicate effectively in pursuit of those goals. Therefore, assuming appropriate CRM team training and regular reinforcement (through CME and in practice), can SA be reduced to a grade school teacher's admonition to "pay attention?"

Arguably so. Endsley notes that "much can be said about the importance of attention on SA," and points to several confirming studies, one of them his own, which "found that the single most frequent causal factor associated with SA errors involved situations where all the needed information was present, but was not attended to by the operator (35% of total SA errors)."[474]

Again, experienced operators are not immune.

> Good SA requires enough awareness of what is going on across a wide range of SA requirements (global SA) to be able to

---

473. See, for example, M. R. Endsley 2000, 9; International Association of Fire Chiefs 2003,9.

474. M. R. Endsley 2000, 9; see also Alfred Cuschieri November 2006, 643.

determine where to best focus one's attention
for more detailed information (local SA).[475]

As one might suspect, and as previous examples have amply
demonstrated, most attention errors are attributable to
distractions and cognitive overload (including juggling too
many competing tasks, information deluge, and fatigue).
Consequently, those at the sharp end can fail to respond timely
or appropriately to rapidly changing developments.

The next part of this chapter will address how to maintain
situational awareness in the clinic, and how to spot threats that
can undermine SA.

Peer Monitoring or "Check Back"

The high-stakes, fluid environment in the clinic means, as
suggested by the earlier "snap shot" metaphor, that situational
awareness is also fluid. Hence, all team members must remain
alert, and situational awareness must be constantly and
consistently updated by applying CRM-trained communications
tools.[476]

The latter activity, interchangeably referred to as "situation
monitoring," [477] "peer monitoring,"[478] "cross checking,"[479]
"cross monitoring,"[480] "teamwork monitoring,"[481] or "check

---

475. See, for example, M. R. Endsley 2000, 9; International Association of Fire
Chiefs 2003,9.

476. International Association of Fire Chiefs 2003, 19.

477. Susan Mann January 1, 2006, 2-3.

478. Agency for Healthcare Research and Quality (AHRQ) 2001, 505.

479. TeamSTEPPS™. "Strategies and Tools to Enhance Performance and Patient
Safety: Implementing a Teamwork Initiative." *New York State Dept of Health,
Patient Safety Conference*. May 21-22, 2007. http://www.health.state.ny.us/
professionals/patients/patient_safety/conference/2007/docs/teamstepps-
implementing_a_teamwork_initiative.pdf (accessed July 27, 2009).

480. Dynamics Research Corporation 2004.

back," is recognized by AHRQ as another fundamental of CRM.[482] Along these lines, AHRQ has stated that

> Along with his or her clinical responsibilities, each team member undertakes the intermittent process of peer monitoring or "check" actions, engaging in this check cycle as frequently as possible. The teamwork check cycle begins with each team member monitoring his or her own situational awareness and cross monitoring the actions of other teammates. If during the monitoring mode the monitoring teammate observes a suspected error in progress, that individual intervenes with a direct question or offer of information. The erring teammate may then acknowledge the lapse, correct it and continue working. Alternatively, the monitoring teammate may have lost situational awareness.
>
> The non-erring monitored colleague can then provide feedback to correct the peer's situational awareness. If team members are in strong disagreement about how patient care should proceed, advocacy, assertion and perhaps third-party involvement may be used to resolve the situation.[483]
>
> Over time, the check cycle becomes habitual, resulting in hundreds of team checks daily, all with the potential to break the error chain.[484]

Grogan and colleagues condense cross-checking into four components:

---

481. Id.

482. Agency for Healthcare Research and Quality (AHRQ) 2001, 505.

483. Thus, the peer monitoring cycle also integrally involves the CRM communication tools referred in this book.

484. Pizzi, Goldfarb and Nash 2001, 505.

- Monitor the situation.

- Recognize red flags.

- Communicate red flags precisely.

- Follow up with feedback.

To communicate precisely, clinicians would, using the SBAR technique, make effective assertive statements— statements that command attention, convey concern, state the problem, and propose a solution.[485]

From the Susan Mann article cited above, here is a real-world clinical example of situation monitoring in an L&D unit, which is closely linked to a shared mental model:[486]

> Once an L&D unit has established a shared mental model that takes into account the acuity of the patients, the workload of the entire unit, and patient care plans, situational monitoring is possible. Situational monitoring occurs when providers scan the environment for potentially unsafe conditions or practices. A team member can then intervene to prevent or mitigate adverse events.

> Let's use the second stage of labor as an example of situation monitoring: Physicians and nurses can lose perspective on the progress of fetal descent or the severity of fetal heart rate abnormalities. Situation monitoring would allow another provider to raise concerns regarding a patient's FHR tracing displayed on a central monitor. This action allows the patient's care team to regain perspective and reassess the plan for the patient.

---

485. Eric L. Grogan 2004, 845.

486. Susan Mann January 1, 2006, 4.

The team members' shared responsibility for vigilant cross-monitoring and maintaining SA also includes routine updates of relevant essential information.[487]

The cross-monitoring cycle quite naturally implicates and involves other essential CRM communication techniques, including assertion, advocacy, and the "Two-Challenge Rule," all discussed in greater detail in the following chapter.

Losing Situational Awareness

Because situational awareness is the primary determinant of a hospital team's capability to spot and address threats to patient safety, the same factors that undermine patient safety also by definition undermine situational awareness. And because the presence of any of these factors—commonly referred to as "red flags"—may signal an imminent threat to a patient,[488] they merit reinforcing in relation to SA.

Red Flags

The factors that undermine situational awareness and signal threats include the following:

- Not knowing the plan.[489]

- Lack of attention.

- Ambiguity.

  Conflicting inputs cloud meaning. For example, in 2006 two planes nearly collided in mid-air after a

487. Dynamics Research Corporation 2004, 3-3.

488. Eric L. Grogan 2004, 848.

489. Morey, et al. December 2002, 1577.

control tower command to "climb two five zero" was heard by a pilot as "climb to five zero."[490]

Ambiguity and confusion in the written word also undermine SA and threaten patient safety. For example, medication errors are often associated with illegible handwriting of orders, which often include abbreviations. A commonly reported error is misinterpreting the letter "U," intended to represent the word "units," as "0" (that is, "10U" is misread as "100" units).[491, 492] If not caught, this error would likely result in an inappropriate and potentially harmful dose.

- Preoccupation/distraction.

This and other ignored red flags contributed to the 2009 crash of Continental (Colgan) Flight 3407 in Buffalo.

- Fixation.

Focusing attention on one isolated issue to the exclusion of others is what happened to the crew of UA 173. They became so determined to deal with a

---

490. Cited in Jon Allard March 2007, 191.

491. Luigi Brunetti, Pharm.D. John P. Santell, M.S., R.Ph. Rodney W. Hicks, Ph.D., A.R.N.P. "The Impact of Abbreviations on Patient Safety." *The Joint Commission Journal on Quality and Patient Safety*, September 2007 Vol. 33, No. 9, 576-583, 576. [Luigi Brunetti September 2007]

492. Abbreviation errors are an all-too-common communication lapse, responsible for nearly 5% of all medication errors between 2004 and 2006. Of those, 78.5% originated from medical staff, 15.1% from nursing, and 4.2% from pharmacy. Moreover, approximately 30% of all handwritten prescriptions required clarification and correction by a pharmacist to prevent an error.

Therefore, because pharmacists and nurses are often charged with contacting the prescriber to resolve the problem, this problem also causes unnecessary and avoidable (1) drains on, and inefficient allocation of, human resources, and (2) friction and even conflict between the health care professions—which further deteriorate communication.

In response to this problem, The Joint Commission has developed as "Do Not Use" abbreviation list. (Luigi Brunetti September 2007)

landing gear warning light, the plane ran out of fuel and crashed. Fixation also afflicted the group of experts attending to Elaine Bromiley; they were so intent on reviving her that they lost track of how long her brain had been starved of oxygen.

- Lack of leadership: no one is "flying the plane."

- Poor communication.

As previously stated, the extent of situational awareness depends on effective and consistently updated communication.[493] The red flags that signal substandard communication include the following:

- Failure to share information with the team.

- Failure to request information from others.

- Failure to direct information to specific members of the team.

- Failure to include patients in communications involving their care.

- Unavailable or under-utilized white boards.

- Inconsistencies in utilizing automated systems.

- Poor documentation.

- Confusion or disorder.

- Unjustified deviations from policies or procedures.

- Unmet targets.

- Unresolved discrepancies or conflicts.

- Workload/overload.

- Just too busy or too rushed to stay on top of everything, or behind schedule.[494]

---

493. Morey, et al. December 2002, 1577.

- Boredom.

- Complacency.

- Trying something new under pressure.[495]

- Fatigue.

- Inordinate stress.

- A gut feeling that something is wrong.

As previously suggested, Klein and other experts consider this final red flag (a gut feeling that something is wrong) one of the most reliable because all people, and particularly seasoned clinicians, can sense threatening stimuli long before consciously putting them together. This is the same as, or certainly similar to, the "pattern matching" Endsley describes and, although he avoids the term, intuition.

Loss of situational awareness often occurs over time, usually leaving behind a retraceable trail of missed red flags.

Workload

Endsley and other authorities have noted the link between situational awareness and workload. As already mentioned, workload is a red flag threat to individual SA. SA can be compromised from overwork—"when workload demands exceed maximum human capacity"—but also from underwork, which impairs vigilance.[496] Either way, team performance will degrade and put patients at risk.

---

494. The effect of workload on SA is separately discussed in the next section.

495. Teamwork Takes Hold to Improve Patient Safety February 2005, 5.

496. M. R. Endsley 2000, 19.

The above analysis also teaches that workload is a team dynamic. Workload among team members can change markedly during a shift and therefore must—as an ingrained part of cross-checking—be monitored and reported throughout the shift.[497]

Therefore, managing workload is another balancing act. For highly tuned SA and optimum performance, one's work should be stimulating and challenging but not overwhelming. A moderate to high workload is generally consistent with this balance.[498]

Although Endsley recognizes the link between SA and workload, he carefully distinguishes them as "separate constructs." To do otherwise would obscure a wider operating reality: overwork skews the supply and demand of human resources available to care for patients. This is vital for CRM theory as well. Since CRM is about improving patient safety by efficiently using all resources, including people, time, and materials, any imbalance in or drain on those resources poses an inherent threat to patient safety.

To correct threatening workload imbalances, tasks must be delegated or re-assigned to other team members or to other teams entirely. This is a sharp-end activity, driven by overall situational awareness and situation monitoring to track team workload and available resources. That activity aligns with and promotes other bedrock themes detailed in this book:

---

497. Dynamics Research Corporation 2004, 3-5.

498. Dynamics Research Corporation 2004, 4-4, apparently referring to, but not fully citing, the following notable work on workload, performance, and decision making:

Huey B.M., Wickens C.D. *Workload Transition: Implications for Individual and Team Performance.* Washington, DC: National Academy Press, 1993.

Urban, Julie M., Bowers, Clint A., Monday, Susan D. and Morgan, Jr. Ben B. "Effects of Workload on Communication Processes in Decision Making Teams: An Empirical Study with Implications for Training." *Proceedings of the Human Factors and Ergonomics Society 37th Annual Meeting.* 1993. 1233-1237.

- A team's ability to self-correct—to monitor, analyze, and critique its own performance through instructive feedback (for example, via debriefing) and then correct deficiencies—is a marker of high reliability performance.

- A team's ability to gather information on the fly and adjust resources and activities accordingly are markers of the adaptability and flexibility characteristic of high reliability performance.

- Willingness to "pitch in" is characteristic of a good team mate and good followership.

A team's ability (1) to self-correct by monitoring and critiquing its own performance, and (2) to gather information on the fly and adjust resources and activities accordingly are markers of high reliability performance.

The distinction between SA and workload impacts the design and execution of particular CRM tools and techniques. This distinction is tethered to reality; people in the real world "make tradeoffs between the level of effort extended and how much they feel they need to know."[499]

In short, people may desire to improve SA but will resist working much harder to achieve it; in the clinical setting, they likely consider themselves burdened enough. This dose of reality circles back to the previous statements that the tools and techniques for CRM in general, and SA-enhancement in particular, must be relatively easy to learn, easy to remember, and easy to use. The rewards of achieving and maintaining SA must exceed the effort required to realize them; otherwise, the entire CRM program and initiative will *increase* workload and backfire.

---

499. M. R. Endsley 2000, 19.

See it. Say it. Fix it.

The "See It, Say It, Fix It" communication model is helpful once a task or operation has begun. It represents a straightforward tool for maintaining SA or getting it back on track once derailed.

Despite its surface simplicity, the "See It, Say It, Fix It" model works because it is based on a combination of interdependent, core CRM principles: situational awareness/ monitoring, effective communication via appropriate assertiveness, and collaborative decision making. In short, a threat to patient safety cannot be resolved unless it is first spotted and properly articulated.

The "See It" portion is shorthand for the situational awareness and monitoring components and skills detailed above. The "Say It" portion is equivalent to Edmonson's admonition to "speak up," which is fundamental for gathering all the relevant facts a clinical team needs to perform effectively, and links to the SBAR technique. "Say It" also implies the use of appropriate and timely assertiveness, critical language, and the other communication tools and techniques CRM imparts. The "Fix It" portion, while logically centered on decision making, also involves the tools and techniques detailed in this book for respectful communication, collaborating, and resolving conflict.

The "See It, Say It, Fix It" method can also be used, for example, to implant or reinforce a mental model or even as a "break the huddle" mantra to remind all team members that SA is a shared responsibility.

Final Reminders

There is no greater defense against the loss of situational awareness than perpetual vigilance.[500] And although, as Endsley notes

> ...[T]here is "no set threshold of SA that can guarantee a given level of performance...[and] a person with even a high level of SA will not always perform well...[;] in making such assessments, it is also fair to say that there is no such thing as too much SA. More SA is always better...and increases the likelihood of effective decision making and performance."[501, 502]

Finally, each team member has a responsibility for team situational awareness. This responsibility includes team briefings and debriefings (discussed in Chapter 16). To have maximum effect, these team interactions must be framed in the effective communication techniques described in the next chapter of this book, including appropriate advocacy, feedback, and closed-loop communications.

---

500. International Association of Fire Chiefs 2003, 5, 14.

501. M. R. Endsley 2000, 20.

502. Again, overload of information is not the same as, and actually impedes, SA. Endsely notes that although

> ...SA is operationally defined as that which one really needs to know...a person can have too much extraneous information that interferes with accessing and processing needed information [;] extraneous information, by definition, is not part of SA. (M. R. Endsley 2000, 20)

Chapter 13

Standardized Communication Skills

Key Points in this Chapter

- Poor communication among caregivers was the most frequently cited root cause of all sentinel events reported between 1995 and 2004.

- Therefore, effective communication is crucial to patient safety. Effective communication means transmitting messages that all team members can clearly understand. This in turn calls for messaging that is standardized in both structure and nomenclature in order to impart critical information among diverse personalities and cultures, even under duress.

- CRM team training has proved effective in instilling standardized communication techniques, which center on eight fundamental components: (1) the sender; (2) the receiver; (3) the message; (4) encoding; (5) the medium (including non-verbal communication); (6) decoding/response; (7) feedback; and (8) repetition.

- Impediments to effective team communication include (1) behavior-driven failures; (2) individual filters and roadblocks; (3) sender errors; and (4) receiver errors.

- The CRM communication skill boils down to respectfully and clearly conveying the intended message and confirming that the intended message has been received and understood. It involves the following five core subset skills: (1) inquiry; (2) listening; (3) advocacy/assertion; (4) resolving conflict; and (4) closing the loop.

- The SBAR (**S**ituation, **B**ackground, **A**ssessment, and **R**ecommendation) model, which is easy to learn, remember, and use, promotes effective communication in the clinic by enabling the concise delivery of critical information in a standardized, predictable format.

- SBAR has become a staple of CRM team training because it incorporates virtually all of the CRM-based fundamentals of effective communication and helps eliminate many of the recognized barriers to effective communication.

- Checklists have proved useful in reducing human error and are a fundamental tool in the CRM approach to standardized communication.

Effective communication, which is timely, accurate, complete, unambiguous, and understood by the recipient, reduces error and results in improved patient safety.

The Joint Commission
2008 National Patient Safety Goals

Communication—open communication—is crucial to high reliability performance and improved patient safety. But open communication alone is not enough. In the clinic, where lives are at stake, unstructured communication becomes dangerous cacophony. Therefore, the lynchpin of improved performance and patient safety is *effective* communication: messages conveying meaning that all clinical teammates can clearly understand.

Research bears this out. "Insufficient communication" among caregivers was the most frequently cited root cause of all sentinel events (including medication errors, delays in treatment, infant abductions, and wrong-site surgeries) reported to The Joint Commission between 1995 and 2004. In the OR specifically, poor communication was the root cause of more than 70% of reported sentinel events.[503] Moreover, ineffective team communication is all too common; according to one study, among 421 "communication events," 129—more than 30%—involved a "communication failure."[504, 505]

For these reasons, The Joint Commission's National Patient Safety Goals have consistently directed health care organizations to continuously improve the quality of communication among caregivers.

---

503. See for, example:

"2008 National Patient Safety Goals." Goal 2: 2. *The Joint Commission.* 2008. http://www.jointcommission.org/NR/rdonlyres/82B717D8-B16A-4442-AD00-CE3188C2F00A/0/08_HAP_NPSGs_Master.pdf (accessed April 27, 2009).

F. Jacob Seagull, MD; Gerald R. Moses, PhD; Adrian E. Park, MD. "Pillars of a Smart, Safe Operating Room." In Advances in Patient Safety: New Directions and Alternative Approaches, Vol. 3. Rockville, MD: U.S. Department of Health and Human Services, Agency for Healthcare Research and Quality (AHRQ). 2008, 7-8. (Seagull et al, 2008)

L. Lingard; S. Espin; S. Whyte; G. Regehr; G. R. Baker; R. Reznick; J. Bohnen; B. Orser; D.Doran; E. Grober. "Communication failures in the operating room: an observational classification of recurrent types and effects." Quality and Safety in Health Care. 2004, Vol. 13: 330-334, 330. (Lignard et al, 2004)

504. Lingard et al, 2004, 330.

The solution to this problem, and the key to effective communication among care givers in clinical settings, is improved interpersonal communication through standardized communication. Standardized communication means messaging that is formalized through process, procedure and nomenclature ("critical language").

The use of standardized communication to promote safety has been routinely dramatized in popular movies and television, and has long been a staple in the military and in global aviation.

NATO uses the familiar phonetic alphabet (Alpha for A, Bravo for B, Charlie for C) and standard responses (such as "Roger," or "copy" to confirm that a message has been received and understood) to ensure intelligible voice communications, even between persons with different native languages. The rules of communication also dictate that only one person speaks at a time and that the others listen.

The FAA imposes mandatory air traffic control rules regarding radio and telephone communications. Among them:

- **Authorized Transmissions**
  Transmit only those messages necessary for air traffic control or otherwise contributing to air safety.

- **False or Deceptive Communications**
  Take action to detect, prevent, and report false, deceptive, or phantom controller communications to an aircraft or controller. Correct false information.

---

505. In this study, which was part of a larger project to develop a team checklist for improving communication in the OR, a "communication failure" was defined as an event that was flawed in one or more of these dimensions: content, audience, purpose, and occasion of a communication exchange. Of the 129 communication failures analyzed, 45.7% were attributable to "occasion" (poor timing); 35.7% to "content" (information was missing or inaccurate); 24% to "purpose" (issues were not resolved); 20.9% to "audience" (key individuals were excluded). These failures had notable consequences; "a third of these [failures] resulted in effects which jeopardized patient safety by increasing cognitive load, interrupting routine, and increasing tension in the OR." (Lingard, et al. 2004, 330)

Broadcast an alert to aircraft operating on all frequencies within the area where deceptive or phantom transmissions have been received.[506]

Standardized communication techniques have established a reliable way to impart critical information even among diverse cultures and under unanticipated, high stress situations (see text box below). In the health care arena, Classen and Kilbridge have noted that "standardization of processes"—safe processes that are designed based on "knowledge gained from industry and organizational experience"—and customized "standard solutions" are indicia of a positive patient safety culture.[507] Linking these ideas to CRM, Lingard and colleagues have reported that team training has proved effective in instilling standardized communication techniques. Therefore, although there are several ways to teach CRM, standardized communication is an essential skill in all of them.

The Eight Components of Communication

CRM-based training on communication among clinical team members emphasizes sender-receiver interaction and generally includes the following eight fundamental elements:

Communication Component 1: The Sender

The sender is the person or organization initiating the communication to impart information. The sender should consider the actual (or perceived) source of the message; information sent through a hierarchical cascade can garble the

---

506. U.S. Department of Transportation, Federal Aviation Administration. Order JO 7110.65S, effective February 14, 2008 (last revised March 12, 2009), Paragraphs 2-4-5 and 2-4-6.

507. David C. Classen and Peter M. Kilbridge 2002, 968 (Table 1), 970 (List 1).

sender's identity, causing confusion and a failure to motivate the receiver.

Communication Component 2: The Receiver

The sender must know his or her audience and understand the motivating connection between the sender and the intended receiver. For example:

- Nurses and physicians are trained differently. As a result, and as previously noted, nurses tend to be narrative and descriptive, while physicians, who are trained to solve problems, tend to be interested in "just the facts" bullet points.

- Evidence suggests the target audience will receive the information more quickly and readily if they identify or have common ground with the sender. For example, it is more likely that a GP will adopt new guidelines on managing patients with dyspepsia if another GP is the source of the information.

- People respond and learn in different ways and at different paces.

Communication Component 3: The Message

This is the essential idea or information the sender intends to convey. It is the main point that is being transmitted between the parties involved in the process.

Communication Component 4: Encoding

The sender translates the message into content, tailoring it according to the intended purpose and audience.

Communication Component 5: The Medium

The content of the message and the way it is delivered are separate issues. The sender should identify the best method to deliver the message to the intended audience. For in-person verbal communications, the sender should also bear in mind that the encounter will also include verbal inflection, tone, and pitch (verbal cues) and *non-verbal* communication such as dress, gestures, and facial expressions ("body language").

This last point warrants special emphasis because, in fact, body language is the primary message conveyor, followed by verbal cues. Words, while important, are the third-ranked conveyor.

Communication Component 6: Decoding/Response

The receiver transforms the sender's message back into thought and reacts to what he or she just saw, heard, or read.

Communication Component 7: Feedback

The sender should request feedback to confirm the message has been received and has had the intended effect. The sender should also be aware, however, that the feedback provided may not be a complete representation of the receiver's actual reaction.

Communication Component 8: Repetition

Effective communicators recognize that their intended messages will not likely be received and understood after only one iteration, especially where, as here, fundamental changes are sought. For any CRM initiative to gain traction in an HCO, a 30% to 50% adoption rate may be needed at the sharp end; this alone implies that repetition and reinforcement will be essential.[508]

Impediments to Effective Communication

Communication problems exacerbate the risk of injury and death. These problems may be loosely organized into four overlapping categories:

- Behavior-driven failures.

- Filters and roadblocks.

- Sender errors.

- Receiver errors.

Behavior-driven Failures

Among team members, behavior-driven communication problems that increase the risk of harm to patients include:

- Failure to inform team members of a patient's problems.

- Failure to discuss alternative procedures.

- Failure to plan for and communicate contingencies.

- Failure to monitor situations and other team members' activities.

- Overt hostility and frustration which may result from stress, fatigue, complexity, or workload.

Filters and Roadblocks – The Top Twelve

All of us bring to the workplace filters and foibles that affect—and often impede—communication. They include, as previously suggested, genetic encoding, national or ethnic

---

508. In the marketing world, this is referred to as "impressions," or "reach and frequency."

culture, parental influence, and personal prejudices and life experiences. Awareness of these impediments is therefore vital to effective communication and may include the following (which may be behavior driven and therefore overlap with the problems just listed):

1. Resistance to change.

2. Defending against appearing foolish or stupid.

3. Arguing to support an opinion even when not supported by fact.

4. Blaming others when a message is misunderstood.

5. Withholding information that could benefit the group.

6. The "Halo Effect": considering a team member infallible.

7. The "Odd Man Out": failing to hear a team member because of tenure, race, or gender.

8. Complacency.

9. Fatigue.

10. Workload/complexity.

11. Distractions.

12. Recklessness: acting or speaking without first considering risks and benefits.

Common Sender Errors

"What do you mean?" is a good indicator that the receiver has missed the sender's message, but such an unvarnished response cannot always be expected. Messages get missed when, for example, the sender has:

- Not established a clear frame of reference; for effective communication, the receiver and the sender must be on the same page.

- Omitted essential details.

- Given biased or weighted information, including an opinion.

- Disregarded the power of non-verbal cues.

- Communicated disrespectfully.

- Failed to repeat. In the clinic, where distractions abound and team members can be preoccupied with their own thoughts, a single iteration of essential information will probably fail to penetrate.

Common Receiver Errors

Receiver errors that cause communication breakdowns generally fall into one of six types:

- Listening with a preconceived notion. The receiver already has his mind made up before the sender opens his or her mouth.

- Brain turned off. Receiving messages requires conscious effort and concentration.

- Thinking ahead of the sender. This includes, for example, extrapolating the sender's thoughts, finishing the sender's sentences, and formulating a response before the sender finishes. (One trigger for the receiver here is if the sender says, "Please hear me out.")

- Missing the non-verbal signals.

- Disrespectful response.

- Not asking for clarification. Failing to employ the old standby, "So what you are saying is ..." can thwart communication.

Core Communication Subskills

At the heart of CRM is the understanding that at the sharp end, errors are reduced, injuries are avoided, and performance is enhanced through clear and concise communication based on firm rules of conduct that are grounded in mutual respect and shared responsibility. Therefore, CRM-trained communication, in essence, boils down to this: respectfully and clearly conveying the intended message and confirming that the intended message has been received and understood.

Similar to the background presented in this chapter, CRM training first imparts an overview and team understanding of the attributes of, and impediments to, effective communication, and once this foundation is established, concentrates on teaching the following five core subset skills:

- Inquiry.

- Listening.

- Advocacy/Assertion.

- Resolving conflict.[509]

- Closing the loop.

CRM, because it is grounded in shared responsibility, not only empowers but *requires* that all team members respectfully speak up and, in effect, ask "Why?" whenever a discrepancy exists between what is happening and what should be happening. Along these lines, team members should:

- Assume nothing.

- Ask whenever in doubt.

- Question unclear instructions.

- Question uncertainty.

Active listening is a learned skill that involves more than just hearing. It means that the listener has situational awareness, is aware of and avoids the filters and roadblocks that impede communication, and is attuned to non-verbal indicators. A good active listener:

- Uses all senses to stay focused on the sender.

- Makes eye contact with the sender.

- Suppresses filters and roadblocks.

Appropriately assertive advocacy promotes situational awareness and enables team members to respectfully challenge team leaders. The five elements of assertive advocacy are:

---

509. Although "resolving conflict" is included this list of subskills, we found this topic so content-laden and of such vital importance that it has been broken out as one of the six primary CRM skills. It is addressed in the next chapter of this book.

- An opening statement, addressing the receiver by name.

- Stating a concern and owning it ("I think we may be heading for a problem.").

- Stating the problem ("It looks like…").

- Offering a solution ("I suggest that we…").

- Asking for response/obtaining agreement ("What do you think?" or "Do you agree?").

The Two Challenge Rule

The Two-Challenge Rule[510] was developed in aviation as a standardized communication tool for subordinates to challenge superiors. The idea behind the rule is that if any team member spots a potential safety risk and asserts a concern, but the concern is initially ignored, that team member is empowered to "stop the line." More specifically, the subordinate is required to challenge a questionable action by a superior twice, if necessary. In aviation:

> If no answers or if nonsensical answers are provided, the subordinate is empowered to take over the controls.[511]

---

510. See, for example:

Team STEPPS. "Mutual Support Training Module 5": 9,10. http://www.unmc.edu/rural/patient-safety/tool-time/TT10-120406-TeamSTEPPS-Part5/TS_Module5_MutualSupport_06_1.pdf (accessed July 27, 2009).

Robert Simon, EdD; May Pian-Smith, MD; Daniel Raemer, PhD. "Challenging Superiors in the Healthcare Environment: The Two-Challenge Rule." *Technology in Anesthesia: Meeting abstract from the 2005 International Meeting on Medical Simulation.* http://www.anestech.org/media/Publications/IMMS_2005/Simon.pdf (accessed July 27, 2009).

Institute for Safe Medication Practices. "Intimidation presents serious safety issues." *ISMP Quarterly Action Agenda*, October-December 2003. http://www.ismp.org/MSAarticles/A1Q04Action.htm (accessed July 27, 2009)

511. Simon, Pian-Smith and Raemer 2005.

After the second challenge, everything must stop until the safety issue is resolved, either by the team or up through the chain of command.

The Two-Challenge Rule, like most CRM practices, has been adopted from aviation and applied in the clinic. According to one authority:

> Many healthcare organizations have been promoting a high reliability organizational (HRO) culture. An important characteristic of HROs is that everyone has an obligation to independently stop an ongoing process when they believe there is an issue of safety or quality.[512]

A recent study[513] about teaching the Two-Challenge Rule to residents observed as follows:

> Residents train in a historically hierarchical system. They may be compelled to question their teachers if they do not understand or disagree with a clinical decision, have a patient safety concern, or when treatment plans are unclear.[514]

In the study, the Two-Challenge rule was used during simulated obstetric case debriefings in an atmosphere that emphasized (1) joint responsibility for safety and (2) "conversational technique that is assertive and collaborative (advocacy-inquiry)." The study concluded that this approach

> ...specifically improved the frequency and quality of challenges directed toward

---

512. Id.

513. May Pian-Smith, C.M. MD; Robert Simon, EdD; Rebecca D. Minehart, MD; Marjorie Podraza, MD; Jenny Rudolph, PhD; Toni Walzer, MD; Daniel Raemer, PhD. "Teaching Residents the Two-Challenge Rule: A Simulation-Based Approach to Improve Education and Patient Safety." *The Journal of the Society for Simulation in Healthcare*, Summer 2009, Vol. 4, No. 2:84-91.

514. Id., 84.

superordinate physicians... [and] speaking up by residents to other physicians. Providing increased opportunities for resident learning, sharing responsibility for patient safety, and overcoming communication barriers within the medical hierarchy may improve teamwork and patient safety.[515]

One of the key takeaways here is that subordinates, together with the power to speak up and, if necessary, stop the line, also have the responsibility, under the joint responsibility construct, to do so and make sure their concerns are heard.

SBAR as a Standard Communication Tool

The SBAR model has been shown to promote effective communication in the clinic by enabling the rapid and concise delivery of critically important information in a standardized, predictable format. For these reasons, and because it is easy to learn and use, SBAR has become a staple of CRM team training.

Because communication breakdowns in the clinic result in harm to patients, The Joint Commission has for years urged hospitals to develop standardized communication methods. This general admonition became particularly focused in 2006, after it was recognized that many, if not most, harmful communication breakdowns occur during patient handoffs.[516] According to *The Wall Street Journal*:

> ...For hospitals, the "hand-off" has long been the Bermuda Triangle of health care.[517]

---

515. Id.

516. A patient "handoff" occurs, for example, when a patient is moved from one unit to another or turned over to other clinicians during a shift change. Handoffs also occur at admission and discharge.

To address this persistent threat to safety, The Joint Commission has, since 2006, required that clinical facilities "implement a standardized approach to hand-off communications, including an opportunity to ask and respond to questions."[518] Kaiser Permanente, the largest non-profit health system in the United States, pioneered that effort by adopting from the military[519] and adapting to the clinic the "SBAR" method of standardized sender-receiver communication.[520,521]

SBAR stands for Situation, Background, Assessment, and Recommendation:

- **Situation: What's the problem?**
  The sender identifies himself or herself and identifies the patient. He or she concisely states the problem—specifically, what is happening with or to the patient.

- **Background: What's the context?**
  Through concise statements, the sender provides sufficient information to give the receiver the context for the problem.[522]

---

517. Laura Landro. "Hospitals Combat Errors at the 'Hand-Off'." *The Wall Street Journal*, June 28, 2006, D1-D3. (WSJ 2006)

518. Kathleen M. Haig, R.N.; Staci Sutton, R.N.; John Whittington, M.D. "National Patient Safety Goals/SBAR: A Shared Mental Model for Improving Communication Between Clinicians." *Joint Commission Journal on Quality and Patient Safety*, March 2006, Vol. 32, No. 3: 167-175, 167. (Haig, Sutton, and Whittington, March 2006)

519. SBAR had been used to brief personnel on nuclear submarines during a change in command (WSJ 2006).

520. Another SBAR pioneer, perhaps the first, was OSF St. Joseph Medical Center in Bloomington, Illinois, which began using SBAR in 2004—about two years before The Joint Commission's requirement. SBAR training was incorporated not only into team resource management training but into general staff orientation by handing out pocket cards and posting laminated "cheat sheets" at each phone. SBAR eventually became the standard communication method in all types of organizational reporting. (Haig, Sutton, and Whittington, March 2006, 167, 169)

521. A sample Kaiser Permanente SBAR tool is included in this chapter as Figure 13.2.

- **Assessment: What have you found or observed?**
  The sender summarizes what he or she has observed and his or her evaluation of the problem based on that observation.

- **Recommendation: What should we do next?**
  The sender makes an informed, specific suggestion as to how to fix the problem and requests feedback.

The SBAR technique has become a staple of standardized communication in CRM team training. This is so for many reasons:

- SBAR incorporates virtually all of the CRM-based fundamentals of effective communication.

- Through SBAR, senders and receivers (1) interact directly using standardized statements and language that are, by mutual advance agreement, considered respectful and appropriately assertive (that is, critical language)[523] and (2) expect feedback.[524]

- Because SBAR is by definition standardized and can be readily customized for any organization or team,[525] it promotes a common mental model, helping to put everyone—once again borrowing Leonard's phrase—"at the same movie." To reinforce what has been

---

522. The "Background" step implies that before initiating the communication, the sender has reviewed the chart (if time allows) or otherwise understands the clinical background or context for the communication, and has anticipated and is prepared to answer questions from the receiver.

523. For example, in Kaiser Permanente's perinatal unit, a nurse or midwife who becomes concerned about a patient can simply say to the physician, "I need you now," and the physician will respond in person "100% of the time." (M. Leonard 2004, i87)

524. Powell and Hill January 2006, 187; M. Leonard 2004, i85.

525. In this regard, Leonard has observed that SBAR "can be used in virtually any clinical domain, and has been widely applied in obstetrics, rapid response teams, ambulatory care, the ICU, cardiac arrests, and other areas." (M. Leonard 2004, i86)

previously stated, without a common mental model, situational awareness declines.

- SBAR effectively engages a leader's situational awareness "through the eyes of the bedside caregiver."[526]

- In addition, the standardized predictability of the SBAR model, by formalizing what is going to be communicated and how, helps eliminate many of the recognized barriers to effective communication. Owned as SOP by an entire team, SBAR eliminates the "hint and hope" (trial balloons) method of communication typical of power-and-distance diluted messages from subordinates to superiors and therefore helps "bridge the differences in communication style" (based on differences in traditional education) [527] and the "long-standing cultural barriers in the exchange of patient information"[528] between nurses and physicians."

- SBAR offers a straightforward outline for organizing thoughts. It requires that information be clarified and commonly understood. It de-personalizes the conversation, focusing non-judgmentally on the problem and the common goal, not the personalities; the SBAR method directs attention to *what* is right, not *who* is right. (This important theme is repeated later in this book.)

- SBAR is simple tool that is easy to learn, remember, and use—even under extreme duress.[529]

---

526. Haig, Sutton, and Whittington, March 2006, 174-175.

527. M. Leonard 2004, i90.

528. WSJ 2006.

529. Along these lines, Leonard has asserted that "Our experience has reinforced the belief that simple rules are best for managing complex environments." (M. Leonard 2004, i85)

Through the SBAR technique, crucial information is concisely shared. Also, as Leonard and colleagues have observed, SBAR organically infuses disciplined, critical thinking:

> The person initiating the communication knows that before they pick up the telephone that they need to provide an assessment of the problem and what they think an appropriate solution is.[530]

Even if the sender's recommendation is not the ultimate answer, there is inherent value in reporting the problem so that it can be appropriately addressed.

Because the SBAR technique directs focus and streamlines essential communication, it is often used as briefing tool.[531] However, those same attributes have made SBAR readily adaptable to many other hospital applications (see Figure 13.3).[532]

The Institute for Healthcare Improvement sums up the wide utility of the SBAR method as follows:

> SBAR is an easy-to-remember, concrete mechanism *useful for framing any conversation*, especially critical ones....It allows for an easy and focused way to set expectations for what will be communicated and how between members of the team, which is *essential for developing teamwork and fostering a culture of patient safety* [italics added].[533]

---

530. M. Leonard 2004, i86.

531. Briefing and debriefing, essential principles of CRM training, are discussed in more detail in Chapter 16.

532. Haig, Sutton, and Whittington, March 2006, 169.

Closing the Loop

As documented success in the military and in aviation suggests, "closed loop" ("repeat back" or "read back") communication is particularly effective in the clinic, regardless of whether the sender or receiver initiates the exchange.

Closing the loop allows senders and receivers to confirm they are "watching the same movie" and thus ensures comprehension. In fact, no communication interaction should be considered complete until the receiver expressly acknowledges—preferably repeats or reads back—the sender's message to confirm it has been received and understood. (In aviation, this is the analogue to "Roger Wilco": "message received and understood, will comply.")

Communication Aids

Communication aids and shortcuts include visual displays of essential information. Posted white boards, for example, offer "big picture" snapshots that are useful for adjusting schedules, coordinating resources, and assigning (or reassigning) staff and staff responsibilities where needed most.

Checklists

Checklists are used extensively in both medical and non-medical industries as aids to guide users through accurate task completion. A checklist functions as a support resource by

---

533. Institute for Healthcare Improvement. "SBAR Technique for Communication: A Situational Briefing Model." IHI.org. http://www.ihi.org/IHI/Topics/ PatientSafety/SafetyGeneral/Tools/ SBARTechniqueforCommunicationASituationalBriefingModel.htm (accessed May 13, 2009)

delineating and categorizing items as a list—a format that simplifies conceptualization and recall of information. Checklists have proven effective in performance improvement and error prevention and management.

Checklists are a fundamental tool in CRM's approach to standardized communication. Aviation has for decades used FAA-mandated checklists to reduce human error. In the health care realm, and as noted previously, checklists have been proved remarkably effective in high-intensity fields such as trauma, anesthesiology, and cardiology—in the last discipline (as previously cited), yielding as much as 55% improvement in some primary outcomes. Checklists are have also proved effective for organizing briefings and patient transfers, two other main concerns of CRM training.

Despite this positive evidence, the use of checklists in medicine has not been widely embraced as part of routine practice or mandated by any regulatory authority.[534,535] And once again, professional culture seems to have gotten in the way of positive change. Clinicians often believe that using checklists and similar memory aids "is an admission of weakness or lack of medical skill or knowledge. Furthermore, clinicians often view standardization, or the use of standardized tools such as

---

534. A.M.Wolff; S.A. Taylor; J.F. McCabe. "Using checklists and reminders in clinical pathways to improve hospital inpatient care." *The Medical Journal of Australia*. 2004, Vol. 181, No. 8: 428-431;Brigette M. Hales, MSc; Peter J. Pronovost, MD, PhD. "The checklist-a tool for error management and performance improvement." *Journal of Critical Care*. September 2006, Vol. 21. No. 3: 231-235. (Hales and Pronovost 2006)

535. In July 2004, The Joint Commission imposed a mandatory Universal Protocol for Preventing Wrong Site, Wrong Procedure, Wrong Person Surgery.™ The three elements of the protocol are (1) verifying the intended patient, procedure, and procedure site; (2) marking the intended site; and (3) conducting a "time-out" immediately before beginning the procedure, during which team members actively verify the details relating to the first two elements. Although the "time out" is mandatory, and The Joint Commission states that "preoperative verification checklist may be helpful," it stops short of expressly requiring a checklist. (Implementation Expectations for the Universal Protocol for Preventing Wrong Site, Wrong Procedure and Wrong Person Surgery™ 2003)

checklists, as a limitation to their clinical judgment and autonomous decision making."[536]

Simply put, CRM principles challenge and oppose this mindset as contrary to the vast weight of available evidence. CRM training integrates simple checklists as a "best practice" tool to eliminate error. There are three basic checklist types:

Read and verify

Clinicians do what they have been trained to do and then double check against the checklist.

Challenge and response

One team members asks questions, and another answers and verifies with closed loop responses.

Read and do

Generally, best used only in unusual situations. The checklist is read aloud by a team member not directly working on a patient, with each item verified by closed loop responses. Caution is advised: this approach is often derided as "cookbook medicine."

---

536. Hales and Pronovost 2006.

Chapter 14

Conflict Resolution Skills

Key Points in this Chapter

- Conflict is a normal, predictable, and inevitable by-product of group dynamics—especially in the clinic, where complexity, pressure, stress, and stakes are extremely high. The challenge, therefore, is to resolve conflicts productively and without rancor.

- Effective conflict resolution, a core CRM skill, is imperative because those who follow the CRM tenet to speak up must at times disagree and critique, thereby creating potential conflict.

- The guiding principle of CRM-trained conflict resolution—and CRM-trained leadership—is to arrive at *what* is right, not *who* is right.

- Conflict in the workplace, and particularly in the clinic, is complex. The substantive and procedural elements of a problem are complicated by ongoing relationships and by individual filters and roadblocks, feelings and emotions. These complications can cloud thinking and deflect genuine problem solving—in CRM parlance, representing the loss of situational awareness and failing to utilize all available resources.

- There are two general approaches to resolving conflict: the "conflict styles" approach and the "Interest-Based Relational" (IBR) approach. The effective use of either approach (or a blend thereof) requires awareness of one's own (1) filters and roadblocks and (2) preferred or instinctive response to conflict.

- There are five different conflict resolution styles, and all can be useful at times. Typically, however, the most effective style is dictated by the circumstances and involves collaboration.

- The IBR approach aligns with CRM's overarching safety culture and patient safety objectives and closely resembles the collaborating style of resolving conflict. IBR incorporates CRM's effective communication principles, including (1) active listening, (2) respectful, assertive advocacy, and (3) closing the loop.

- The CRM skills of situational awareness, standardized communication, and resolving conflict suggest that emotional intelligence (EI)—although often ignored in medicine—may be the most important baseline skill for acquiring the others. EI involves attaining sufficient self-awareness to (1) avoid the barriers to effective communication, (2) become a good listener, and (3) distinguish personality traits and behaviors from genuine problems. Studies have shown that EI is positively linked with team performance.

Although treated in this book as a separate topic, effective conflict resolution is a subset of effective, standardized communication and therefore is emphasized as a core competency in CRM team training.

Conflict is Normal

An extensive canon of material is available on resolving conflict, and an exhaustive analysis is beyond the scope of this book. Nevertheless, it is useful to highlight certain fundamentals that underlie and inform CRM skills training.[537]

First and foremost, conflict is a normal, predictable, and inevitable by-product of group dynamics, especially in the clinic where complexity, pressure, stress, and stakes are extremely high. The challenge, therefore, is to resolve conflicts productively and without rancor.

This is precisely what CRM training aims to accomplish. Repeating a previous theme, the guiding principle of CRM-trained conflict resolution—and CRM-trained leadership[538]—is to arrive at *what* is right, not *who* is right.[539] After all, the ultimate mission is to help patients by eliminating or mitigating human error. Appropriate and respectful conflict resolution builds mutual trust and confidence and promotes learning, professional and personal growth, greater situational awareness, team cohesion, and improved performance and patient safety.[540]

---

537. Relatively few citations appear in this section. The general concepts presented have been distilled from multiple sources that say essentially the same thing and are considered a consensus view.

538. This book has consistently asserted that effective leaders will support CRM standards by preserving a clear, genuine, and reliable channel for legitimate dissent, which includes actively listening to subordinates, encouraging constructive criticism, and asking questions, while respectfully reinforcing the functional necessity that final decisions rest with the leader.

This skill becomes doubly imperative for both leaders and followers because those who follow the CRM-trained tenet to speak up must at times disagree and critique, thereby creating friction and potential conflict.[541]

Conflict: Definitions and Clarifications

Conflicts are disagreements with more at stake: the parties involved perceive a threat—physical, emotional, power, or status—to their needs, interests, or concerns. For each person, the threat triggers a response, which may be cognitive (the "inner voice"), physical (rapid heartbeat, perspiration), or psychological and which may be manifested in thoughts, feelings, emotions, or behaviors.

As the above definition implies, perception is the subjective "reality" that drives conflict. A perceived threat may not be an actual, objective threat. Moreover, people who believe they are

---

539. Along these lines, here is an excerpt from the landmark and highly instructive book, *Difficult Conversations: How to Discuss What Matters Most*, by Douglas Stone, Bruce Patton, and Sheila Heen (Penguin Group (USA), 1999):

> As we argue vociferously for our view, we often fail to question one crucial assumption upon which our whole stance in the conversation is built: I am right, you are wrong. This simple assumption causes endless grief....What am I right about? I am right that you drive too fast. I am right that you are unable to mentor younger colleagues....I am right that the patient should have received more medication after such a painful operation....I am right that I deserve a raise....The point is this: difficult conversations are...about conflicting perceptions, interpretations, and values. They are not about what a contract states; they are about what a contract means. They are not about which child-rearing book is most popular; they are about which child-rearing book we should follow. They are not about what is true; they are about what is important....
>
> But the question remains: if feelings are the issue, what have you accomplished if you don't address them? ...[Y]ou may find that you no longer have a message to deliver, but rather some information to share and some questions to ask. Instead of wanting to persuade and get your way, you want to understand what has happened from the other person's point of view, explain your point of view, share and understand feelings, and work together to figure out a way to manage the problem going forward....
>
> We need to have a learning conversation.

involved in the fray may not be at all; others may be unaware that they are somehow caught up in it; some with nothing at stake simply jump in and take sides. Therefore, most conflict is attended by significant misunderstanding that often distorts and exaggerates the parties' differences. Constructively resolving conflict first involves understanding and clarifying the "true" threats—the actual issues about which the parties disagree and who is actually involved.

Conflict in the workplace, and particularly in the clinic, is complex. The substantive and procedural elements of a problem ("What's gone wrong with this patient? How do we solve it?") are complicated by ongoing relationships and by individual filters and roadblocks (previously discussed), feelings, and emotions. These complications can cloud thinking and deflect genuine problem solving. In CRM parlance, the former represents loss of situational awareness and the latter failing to utilize all available resources.

Resolving conflicts effectively, as promoted in CRM training, requires perspective, information gathering, and

---

540. The following sources offer useful, basic, and representative summaries of the concepts presented in this section:

MindTools™. Conflict Resolution: Resolving conflict rationally and effectively. http://www.mindtools.com/pages/article/newLDR_81.htm (accessed May 1, 2009). [MindTools]

University of Wisconsin-Madison, Office of Quality Improvement & Office of Human Resource Development. "What is Conflict? Definitions and Assumptions About Conflict." http://www.ohrd.wisc.edu/onlinetraining/ resolution/aboutwhatisit.htm (accessed May 1, 2009). [UWM-What is Conflict?]

University of Wisconsin-Madison, Office of Quality Improvement & Office of Human Resource Development. "Conflict Resolution Menu-8 Steps: Overview." http://www.ohrd.wisc.edu/onlinetraining/resolution/ stepsoverview.htm (accessed May 1, 2009).

International Women's Media Foundation. "My Big Fat Difficult Conversation." http://www.iwmf.org/article.aspx?c=larticles&id=417 (accessed May 1, 2009). [IWMF]

Ralph W. Kilmann. "Conflict Mode Instrument." http://www.kilmann.com/ conflict.html (accessed May 4, 2009).

understanding. This is achieved through predictable, reliable, and user-safe techniques.

Approaches and Styles Matter

Effective conflict resolution techniques are typically derived from one of two approaches (or a customized blend thereof): the "conflict styles" approach and the "Interest-Based Relational" (IBR) approach. The effective use of either approach requires an underlying self-awareness of one's own (1) filters and roadblocks and (2) preferred or instinctive approach and response to conflict. It should be kept in mind, however, that different situations may call for different styles; a style that works under relative calm may prove disastrous when facing genuine life-threatening emergencies.

Conflict Resolution: The Five Styles

Five main styles of resolving conflict have been identified.[542]

---

541. It is also recognized that although CRM training encourages team members to diplomatically question the actions and decisions of others, an over-zealous individual can misinterpret this as an unrestricted right to challenge all decisions under the CRM banner. This is an incorrect spin on CRM training, which in this context advocates a healthy questioning of authority to confirm or promote situation awareness.

542. Several constructs similar to the "five styles" model exist. One of the best-known was introduced in 1974 by Kenneth W. Thomas and Ralph H. Kilmann (Thomas and Kilmann 1974). According to Dr. Kilmann's website:

This instrument is designed to measure a person's behavior in conflict situations. "Conflict situations" are those in which the concerns of two people appear to be incompatible. In such situations, we can describe an individual's behavior along two basic dimensions: (1) assertiveness, the extent to which the person attempts to satisfy his own concerns, and (2) cooperativeness, the extent to which the person attempts to satisfy the other person's concerns. (http://www.kilmann.com/conflict.html, accessed May 4, 2009)

Style 1: Avoiding

This style seeks to evade conflict entirely. An avoider delegates difficult conversations and decisions, accepts default decisions, and doesn't want to hurt anyone's feelings, hoping "it will blow over." The avoider would rather give up important ground than risk unpleasant argument. This approach generally makes sense only when "when victory is impossible, when the controversy is trivial, or when someone else is in a better position to solve the problem."[543] Usually, however, because this approach does not address the root causes of the conflict or resolve it, and because genuine concerns go unexpressed, seeking to avoid conflict merely allows it to fester and postpones it.

Style 2: Competing/Controlling

In contrast to avoiders, competitors generally put themselves first, seem to know what they want, aim to win, and take firm stands. They often occupy positions of power, relying on status, rank, expertise, or persuasive ability. This style may be useful—or even imperative—in emergencies that demand quick decisions, when unpopular decisions must be made, or to protect the group from a member who has strayed in a way that threatens the group.

The competing style can be problematic, especially when routinely employed, because it:

- Tends to be characterized by aggressive communication, use of coercive power, and low regard for enduring relationships.[544]

---

543. MindTools.

544. UWM-What is Conflict?

- Tends to result in responses that increase the level of threat.[545]

Controllers typically seek control over a discussion, in both substance and ground rules.

Style 3: Accommodating

Accommodators are not assertive like competitors. They generally try to smooth things over via cooperation and diplomacy and allow the perceived needs of the group to displace their own, which may go unexpressed. The accommodator "often knows when to give in to others, but can be persuaded to surrender a position even when it is not warranted." [546]

The accommodation style may be appropriate when issues matter more to one person than another, when preserving peace is more important than winning debating points, or to air grievances after a negative event occurs.[547] Generally, however, accommodating is unlikely to yield optimum results in pursuing high reliability sharp end performance.

Style 4: Compromising

Compromisers seek solutions that, through give-and-take tradeoffs, will—albeit partially—satisfy everyone. To preserve relationships, compromisers settle for "mini-wins".[548]

Compromise can be the best available option for resolving a conflict when the cost of conflict is higher than the cost of losing ground, when equally strong opponents are at an impasse, or when a deadline looms.[549] On the other hand,

---

545. Id.

546. Id.

547. IWMF.

548. IWMF.

549. MindTools.

because compromising requires everyone to give up something, this approach is generally more satisfactory than satisfying. The underlying sources of the conflict usually stay buried, virtually guaranteeing that the pattern will repeat.

Although various conflict resolution styles must be employed and moderated as situations dictate, collaborating is best aligned with the highest aspirations of CRM training and is considered the most effective way to resolve conflict.

Style 5: Collaborating

The analysis in this book clearly points to the conclusion that although various styles must be employed and moderated as situations dictate, collaborating is best aligned with the highest aspirations of CRM training and is considered the most effective way to resolve conflict.

Collaborating in the conflict resolution sense entails pooling individual needs and goals to achieve a common goal. Often called "win-win problem-solving," collaboration requires assertive communication and cooperation in order to achieve a better solution than the individuals involved could have achieved alone. It offers the chance for consensus, the integration of needs, and the potential to exceed the "budget of possibilities" that previously limited our views of the conflict. It brings new time, energy, and ideas to resolve the dispute meaningfully.[550]

The Interest-Based Relational Approach

The IBR approach also aligns with CRM's overarching safety culture and patient safety objectives and closely resembles the collaborating style just described.

---

550. UWM-What is Conflict?

IBR theory is grounded in "keeping the eye on the ball": to improve patient safety, all team members have an interest in achieving common goals. And in pursuing those goals, IBR emphasizes respect for individuals and their differences (mutual respect) while averting intransigence.

Under the IBR approach, people and problems are consciously separated. This is actually a situational awareness tack, which concurrently:

- Guards against a reflexive reaction that someone is "just being difficult,"

- Permits receptivity to the prospect that genuine, rational concerns need surfacing and debate.

- Focuses effort on identifying the source of the problem and solving it.

- Helps diffuse the emotional charges that attend disagreements and often mutate honest differences into unfocused ill will that undermines performance.

The IBR approach, echoing the above-described "good listener" and "assertive advocacy" principles, offers a five-step process for resolving conflict, summarized below.

Step One: Set the Scene

Using a professional, assertive (that is, not submissive or disrespectful) style:

- Establish the mindset that the conflict may represent a mutual problem best resolved through discussion and negotiation.

- Emphasize that the initiator is presenting his or her perception of the problem.

- Use active listening skills to understand each participant's positions and perceptions. Hear them out before responding.

- Be aware of non-verbal signals from each participant.

- Restate, paraphrase, and summarize (the previously mentioned "repeat back" idea).

Step Two: Gather Information

This step is intended to gain objective understanding of the conflict and get at its root cause by understanding the other person's underlying interests, needs, concerns, motivations, and goals, and also understanding how one's own actions might be impacting them—while leaving emotions and personalities out of the equation. This step involves:

- Soliciting the other person's opinion, confirming respect for it, and expressing the need for his or her cooperation to solve the problem.

- Seeing the conflict objectively, noting how it may be disrupting the team and affecting performance.

- Considering the conflict from the other person's point of view.

Step Three: Agree on the Problem

Clarify each person's perceptions and explicitly state the problem(s) that needs solving. Identifying the problem is the first step to solving it.

Step Four: Brainstorm Solutions

Seek and receive input from all involved, staying open to all proposed options. From a CRM perspective, this is part of utilizing available resources.

Step Five: Negotiate a Solution

By this time, the conflict may have in effect resolved itself: a mutually satisfactory solution may have surfaced through the very process of exploring each person's position. If not, seek a "win-win" collaborative, or at least compromised, resolution.[551]

State the resolution clearly and concisely, and close the loop with repeat backs.

Emotional Intelligence

Several earlier mentions have been made of "emotional intelligence" (EI). This concept is generally disparaged, ignored, or dismissed in society at large and in medicine in particular. However, this section on resolving conflict and the associated CRM-related compass points of situational awareness and standardized communication suggest that EI may be the most important baseline skill for acquiring the other skills needed to improve patient safety and achieve high reliability. EI enables the self-awareness necessary (1) to cut through the filters and roadblocks to effective communication, (2) to become a good listener, and (3) to distinguish personality traits from genuine, negotiable problems.

The scholarly sources cited earlier also strongly indicate that emotional intelligence, and the other "soft skills" on which

---

551. Under certain circumstances, "agreeing to disagree" may be the best available result.

CRM relies, goes beyond what is often dismissed as "pop psychology." Some studies have begun, in fact, to link EI to effective conflict resolution.[552] For example, one scientific study has noted that:

> The influence of emotional intelligence on team performance is of particular interest to researchers and practitioners as teamwork becomes more prevalent in organizations. [553]

That study, designed to "examine the utility of emotional intelligence for predicting individual performance, team performance, and conflict resolution styles," analyzed 350 respondents working in 108 teams. The study found that

> emotional intelligence indicators were positively linked with team performance and were differentially linked to conflict resolution methods.[554]

This study follows another by the same authors relating to nurses and how they resolve conflicts.[555] In that study, the authors wrote:

> How nurses maintain relationships and resolve conflict in the workplace is considered an important skill in the nursing profession....In this paper we explore the utility of emotional intelligence in predicting an individual's

---

552. Other sources state this in the converse: effective conflict resolution is one of the skills that comprise, and is a marker of, emotional intelligence. See, for example, HelpGuide.org. "Managing And Resolving Conflict: Conflict Resolution Skills." http://www.helpguide.org/mental/ eq8_conflict_resolution.htm (accessed May 4, 2009), 4.

553. Peter J. Jordan and Ashlea C. Troth. "Managing Emotions During Team Problem Solving: Emotional Intelligence and Conflict Resolution." *Human Performance*, 2004, Vol. 17, No. 2:195-218, 195.

554. Id.

555. Peter J. Jordan and Ashlea C. Troth. "Emotional intelligence and conflict resolution in nursing." *Contemporary Nurse*, August 2002, Vol. 13, No. 1:94-100, 94.

preferred style of conflict resolution. Theorists such as Goleman have proposed a strong link between emotional intelligence and successful conflict resolution. A preliminary analysis of our empirical study indicates that individuals with high emotional intelligence prefer to seek collaborative solutions when confronted with conflict.

Chapter 15

Decision Making
Skills

Key Points in this Chapter

- Decision making in the clinic is a vital link in the patient safety chain. It is a complicated endeavor, depending on proper situational awareness and situation assessment—each of which involves other component tasks.

- Decision making is a practical skill that can be taught as part of CRM training. However, decision making cannot be considered in isolation from other CRM skills, because the factors that affect patient safety—and the CRM approaches that aid improvement—interrelate.

- Excessive workload degrades individual SA and therefore also jeopardizes decision making and performance. That said, safety threats can arise from underwork as well as overwork.

- Decision-making theory is generally divided into two schools: the analytical or classical model (CDT) and the Naturalistic Decision Making (NDM) model. Although debate continues about the relative merits of each, the CDT model has been nearly supplanted in recent years by the NDM model, which attempts to describe how clinicians *actually* make decisions (employing intuitive and nearly automatic pattern matching) rather than how they *should* make decisions.

- Recognition-primed decision making (RPD) is a type of NDM well-suited to the clinic. The RPD model holds that in almost any situation, an expert decision maker will pick up ingrained cues that he or she recognizes as a matching pattern (that is, a mental model), thereby priming a decision—a course of action—to achieve the desired outcome. Research has shown that use of RPD enhances clinical effectiveness.

- RPD involves both rational and intuitive thought processes and a rapid succession of pattern matches and mental simulations to arrive at the best decision under the circumstances. Performing this activity effectively requires metacognition: awareness of one's own cognitive processes and thoughts and the factors that influence them, including one's own biases and limitations. This concept is related to situational awareness and emotional intelligence—which aligns it with CRM principles—and is another teachable CRM skill.

- In the same way that a mental model supports SA and individual decision making, a *shared* mental model supports team SA and team decision making.

- Heuristics, simple decision-making rules developed through experience, can help guide rapid decisions in the face of complexity or uncertainty. However, like most "simple" guides, heuristics can also *mis*guide.

- Despite the asserted primacy of NDM, CDT continues to play a useful role in the pursuit of safety. Mnemonic decision-making aids such as IMSAFE and DECIDE, which are uniform and easy to learn and incorporate into clinical practice, have proved valuable and remain a valid part of CRM training.

- CRM theory and practice have, in effect, taken into account and adapted to the strengths and weaknesses of both the CDT and the NDM approaches. While CRM supports the use of tools such as checklists and mnemonic aids to standardize safe practices and reinforce or create shared mental models, CRM rejects blind adherence to them. CRM recognizes the indispensable value of hands-on clinical judgment as the situation dictates.

Making good decisions in the interest of patient safety requires clarity of purpose, clarity of mind, and a concise and accurate array of relevant information.

Decision making is another vital link in the patient safety chain. Although treated separately in this book, some experts consider decision making a subset of situational awareness. That approach is perfectly appropriate because of the recognized integral relationship between the two.[556] The relationship is quite organic. Situational awareness involves recognizing potential threats and gathering and assimilating all information relevant to deciding what to do next.[557] In the team context, this is a shared responsibility and a collaborative activity,[558] thus reinforcing the value of investing teams with a shared mental model.

Some experts worry about collaborative decision making, concerned that it may take too much time when an emergent situation demands a split second decision. After all, "an untimely decision can often be just as devastating as an inaccurate one."[559] This concern is addressed in greater detail below.

Making good decisions requires clarity of purpose, clarity of mind, and a concise and accurate array of relevant information. Anything that constricts or contaminates any of these ingredients jeopardizes decision making and therefore threatens patient safety. Urban and colleagues identify four classes of interacting individual and group dynamics—"team input variables"—that "demonstrate the complexity of the determinants of team performance" and influence decision

---

556. See, for example, M. R. Endsley 2000, 5.

557. Although as previously mentioned, Endsley recognizes this relationship and agrees that "decisions are formed by SA" (and vice versa), he nevertheless asserts that "it is important to recognize that SA and decision making need not be coupled as one process and in practice frequently are not." He inserts this caution because even given adequate SA, the decision maker "has conscious choice in the decision to implement the [learned] linked recognition-primed decision action plan or to devise a new one." (Endsley 2000, 5)

558. Morey, et al. December 2002, 1577.

559. Urban 1993, 12.

making relating to any task.[560] The four classes, and how each threatens decision making, include:

- **Task characteristics**
  Threat: Increased stress

- **Work characteristics**
  Threats: Hierarchies, poor safety culture, lack of patient safety awareness, poor working conditions

- **Individual characteristics**
  Lack of individual experience or acumen, filters, biases, cultural differences

- **Team characteristics**
  Inability to adapt to changes, degradation of SA, lack of diversity

Workload and Decision Making

As previously noted, excessive workload can degrade individual situational awareness and, by extension, also jeopardize decision making and performance.[561,562] In the team context, "membership in a team alone" and the "coordination demanded by team tasks" can actually *increase* workload.[563]

Managing workload is a balancing act. Overlap among team members helps, but Urban and colleagues present the following related challenge:

> ...under low and moderate levels of workload, more task overlap resulted in better performance. Under high workload, however,

---

560. Urban 1993, 11.

561. See, for example, Urban 1993, 12-13.

562. Although in 1993, Urban (13) did not definitively conclude that this cascade also applies in the team setting, the research cited in this book clearly does.

563. Urban 1993, 13-14.

partial task overlap was associated with the best team performance….[U]nder high workload, a high degree of overlap overwhelms team members with too much information to be assimilated. Hence, partial overlap allows for the best possible performance in this situation.[564]

In the clinic, high workload is all but unavoidable.[565] The challenge is about managing workload to maintain or improve performance.

Overall, and as the thrust of this book reflects (for example, the "three rivers" metaphor), the various factors that affect patient safety and the CRM tools and techniques that can improve it closely interrelate and form a multi-threaded tapestry. On that point, Salas and Klein

> …have found that we cannot study decision making in isolation from other processes, such as situational awareness, problem solving, planning, uncertainty management, and the development of expertise.[566]

The challenge of managing workload to preserve decision-making capability and the respectful assertiveness emphasized in CRM training are examples of dependency upon interrelationship. Because of the need to make quick and timely decisions in emergencies, research suggests that "teams should be trained to make requests spontaneously, and to provide necessary information in a timely manner rather than wait for team members to ask for needed information."[567] Doing so certainly requires respectful assertiveness (as advocated

---

564. Urban 1993, 20.

565. Urban 1993, 74.

566. Eduardo Salas, Gary Klein. *Linking Expertise and Naturalistic Decision Making*. Mahwah, New Jersey: Lawrence Erlbaum Associates, 2001, 3.

567. Urban 1993, 74-75 [citing the research of others].

earlier), but with respect to situational awareness and workload, even more nuanced skill is called for:

> In addition, in order to avoid overwhelming the team's communication channels, they [teams] should be trained to present information and requests in a timely fashion at an appropriate pace....[A]s workload increases, teams should avoid a possible tendency to ask more questions or to rely more heavily on question and answer sequences to transmit needed information and coordinate activity within the team. Training should sensitize team members to the fact that such a strategy will likely not offset the effects of increased workload and may even degrade the team's performance under stress. Finally, team training should also emphasize the development of adaptability such that in high workload conditions, teams will be flexible enough to use communication strategies that are different from those used in low workload conditions.[568]

Decision Making and Situational Awareness

As already stated, Endsley recognizes the relationship between situational awareness and decision making, but draws a subtle yet important distinction between the two:

> Just as there may be a disconnect between the processes used and the resultant situational awareness, there may also be a disconnect between situational awareness and the decisions made. With high levels of expertise in well-understood environments, there may be a direct situational awareness-decision link,

---

568. Urban 1993, 74-75 [citing the research of others].

whereby understanding what the situation is leads directly to selection of an appropriate action from memory. This is not always the case, however. Individuals can still make poor decisions with good situational awareness. The relation between situational awareness and performance, therefore, can be viewed as a probabilistic link. Good situational awareness should increase the probability of good decisions and good performance, but does not guarantee it. Conversely, poor situation awareness increases the probability of poor performance. For instance, being disoriented in an aircraft is more likely to lead to an accident when flying at low altitude than when flying at high altitude. Lack of situational awareness about one's opponent in a fighter aircraft may not be a problem if the opponent also lacks situational awareness.[569]

Decision Making Theory and Terminology

Current theory on decision making, particularly in highly pressurized situations, has evolved amid significant academic upheaval that began in the 1980s. As a result of that upheaval, the previous decision-making paradigm—called the "analytical," "rational," or "classical" model—has been nearly supplanted by the "Naturalistic Decision Making" (NDM) model.

Naturalistic Decision Making

The NDM model was impelled by watershed research that revealed a fundamental and profound difference between

---

569. Endsley 2000, 25-26.

making decisions under normal conditions and in emergencies. More specifically, the new research showed that:

- Under time pressure, analytical decision-making strategies deteriorate.

- Even under low time pressure, analytical strategies "require extensive work and lack flexibility."[570]

In contrast, NDM theory concentrates on the real world: how people *actually* make decisions rather than how they *should* make decisions.[571] NDM theory also holds that decision making in emergencies involves a measure of intuition. However, intuition is not entirely innate; to make good decisions, training and experience must be brought to bear and can, in effect, create intuition.[572]

Recognition-Primed Decision Making

Recognition-primed decision making (RPD) is a prime example of naturalistic decision making that is well-suited for the clinic.[573] The RPD model, first described by Klein and his colleagues in the 1980s—and which they have ever since powerfully and persuasively advocated—led to development of

---

570. Simpson January 2001, 1.

571. See for example, Dédale Asia Pacific March 31, 2006, 44; Simpson January 2001, 4.

572. Dédale Asia Pacific March 31, 2006, 94 (Table 8.8);

573. See, for example:

Caroline E. Zsambok, Gary A. Klein. *Naturalisitc decision making*. Mahwah, New Jersey: Lawrence Erlbaum Associates, 1997, 287.

Scott D. Weingart. "Critical Decision Making in Chaotic Environments." Chapter 30 in *Patient Safety in Emergency Medicine*. Pat Croskerry, Karen S. Cosby, Stephen M. Schenkel, Robert Wears (eds). Philadelphia, Pennsylvania: Lippincott Williams & Wilkins, 2009, 209-212.

Susan Bond, Simon Cooper. "Modelling emergency decisions: recognition-primed decision making. The literature in relation to an ophthalmic critical incident." *Journal of Clinical Nursing*, August 2006 Vol. 15, No. 8: 1023-32.

a method used by soldiers in combat and firefighters at the scene, based on the need to make critical decisions in dynamic situations under extreme time pressure with only limited information.[574] With respect to clinical practice, subsequent research has shown that RPD's application, particularly in emergencies, enhances clinical effectiveness."[575]

According to Klein and his colleague Caroline E. Zsambok, the RPD model bears the hallmarks of NDM. The model involves highly trained, experienced persons who (1) work in complex, uncertain conditions and (2) face serious consequences for their actions. RPD *describes*, rather than *prescribes*, how decisions are actually made in the naturalistic (real world) setting and recognizes that situational awareness and problem solving are integral parts of the decision-making process.

> The function of the RPD model is to describe how people can use their experience to arrive at good decisions without having to compare the strengths and weaknesses of alternative courses of action....People can use experience to size up a situation, providing them with the sense of typicality (i.e. recognition of goals, cues, expectancies and courses of action).[576]

This is the "pattern matching" concept Endsley refers to—a "pattern recognition sub-skill" that catalyzes a plan of action.[577]

Although the RPD model places significant emphasis on experience, it also has valuable utility as "guidance for training people to make better decisions and for designing [processes] that will support decision making."[578,579] Thus, the RPD model

574. Weingart 2009, 212.

575. Susan Bond August 2006, 1023.

576. Caroline E. Zsambok 1997, 287.

577. Peter J. Fadde. "Instructional design for advanced learners: Training expert recognition skills." *Educational Technology Research and Development*. DOI 10.1007/s11423-007-9046-5. 2007. [Fadde 2007]

is more than a description; it informs and promotes the development and deployment of CRM tools and techniques for improving situational awareness as a prerequisite to decision making.[580] Putting it another way, because the RPD model "emphasizes the growth of experience on sizing up situations rather than the use of strategies for making rational choices among courses of action,"[581] RPD skills are "practical skills" that can be taught as part of CRM training to accelerate expertise, even in novices.[582]

Although the current research generally rejects the old analytical model, many authorities are reluctant to emphasize the role intuition plays in the RPD model and, by extension, NDM. As previously noted, Endsley leans that way, preferring to attribute pattern matching to ingrained memory as opposed to a mere hunch. On the other hand, a substantial array of respected research supports the proposition that "intuitive

---

578. Caroline E. Zsambok 1997, 287.

579. In their article, Currey and Botti cite an example of how the NDM framework can guide the design of practical processes and tools. They describe study of the cues that experienced nurses in a neonatal ICU actually use to make complex decisions. That NDM-based study revealed assessment cues indicating early sepsis in neonates that either had not been previously reported in the literature or conflicted with cues that had been reported. Significantly, the elicited cues were used to create a guide for assessing sepsis in neonates. That guide enabled less experienced staff, in effect, to apply and benefit from expert knowledge in detecting sepsis. (Currey and Botti 2003, 209, referring to Crandall and Getchell-Reiter,"Critical decision method: a technique for eliciting concrete assessment indicators from the intuition of NICU nurses." *ANS Advances in Nursing Science*. September 1993 Vol. 16:42-51.)

580. On the other hand, Klein and Zsambock also recognize that the RPD model has limitations. It does not embrace all relevant factors that affect naturalistic decision making, such as the "influence of team and organization constraints." Also, the RPD model does not reflect "memory or attentional or metacognitive processes." (Caroline E. Zsambok 1997, 287)

581. Caroline E. Zsambok 1997, 287. For simlar themes in a combat context, see Karol G. Ross, Ph.D., Gary A. Klein, Ph.D., Peter Thunholm, Ph.D., John F. Schmitt, and Holly C. Baxter, Ph.D. "Recognition-Primed Decision Model." *Military Review*. July-August 2004, 6-10, 6. [Karol G. Ross July-August 2004]

582. Michael Leonard 2003, 2; Fadde 2007; Simpson January 2001 (Executive Summary).

decision processes result in higher performance than do analytical processes."[583]

The distinction, in the end—and for practical purposes—seems more semantic than substantive. No matter the label, given a combination of sufficient training and experience, the research on RPD holds that an expert decision maker faced with almost any situation will pick up cues that almost automatically and subconsciously trigger and tap a reservoir of internal information that he or she recognizes as a similar or analogous pattern that matches, thereby priming a decision—a course of action—aimed at achieving the desired outcome.[584]

The pattern is nothing other than a *mental model* developed through training and experience. A pattern-matching decision maker is not guessing, but is, in effect, running a mental simulation of the proposed course of action against what he or she knows has worked before. In simulating, the decision maker will generally—and logically—consider (1) the consecutive steps to be taken, (2) the potential outcome of these steps, (3) the problems that are likely to be encountered along the way, and (4) how those problems can be handled. After simulating, the decision maker rejects, modifies, or implements the action.[585] If the action is rejected, a second action script is chosen and simulated.[586] "Because NDM emphasizes satisfactory rather than optimal decision outcomes," these serial simulations occur very rapidly and are in essence a "go/no-go check".[587,588]

> If time is not adequate for a complete mental simulation, the decision maker will simply implement the decision action that experience has generated as the most likely to be successful and make subsequent changes as

---

583. Karol G. Ross July-August 2004,6.

584. Along these lines, see Michael Leonard 2003, 2.

585. Simpson January 2001, 10-11.

necessary to maintain a satisfactory outcome.[589]

If, as noted above, making decisions in the clinic depends first on situation assessment, then NDM/RPD strategies condense that phase, saving considerable time without sacrificing accuracy.[590] Situation assessment, of course, goes hand in hand with situational awareness. Both are crucial to "intuitive decision strategies."[591] In this regard:

> Situational awareness is a prerequisite for good decision making, correlating positively with decision accuracy.[592]

In light of the above analysis, even if one believes that a type of intuition drives NDM/RPD, a decidedly rational component is nevertheless involved. Again, the expert decision maker is not merely guessing, but running a series of rapid pattern matches and mental simulations:

---

586. Theoretically, this process can be rapidly repeated as necessary—although research has suggested that an expert decision maker's first choice is usually the best. For the "image theory" take on decision making, see the text box labeled "Classical Decision Theory vs. NDM-Inspired Image Theory."

    The RPD model thus exposes a critical difference between experts and novices. Novices will tend to cycle, rather slowly and in trial-and-error fashion, through more possible courses of action, which might exacerbate the risk of untimely decision. (See, for example, Michael Leonard 2003, 8.) From a pattern matching perspective,

    A novice or inexperienced [person], no matter how relatively skilled they are, simply will not have enough templates of situations, encounters or circumstances in memory to pattern match current situations....[T]he biggest difference between experts and novices, especially in terms of NDM, is their ability to assess and evaluate the situation, rather than their ability to generate and choose among options. (Simpson January 2001,15-16)

    These points underscore the importance of training in RPD to condense the expertise curve.

587. Id.

588. As Simpson tersely puts it, "The [NDM/RPD] decision making process is relatively rapid, as either the current situation is in some way recognizable to another, or it is not." (Simpson January 2001,15)

589. Id.

590. Id.

> NDM requires a continual series of decisions, rather than a single, one-off decision. The decisions are interdependent, with one decision affecting those that occur after.[593]

> RPD is one model of NDM involving decisions for which alternative courses of action are directly derived from the recognition of critical information and prior knowledge. These alternatives are serially evaluated, so there is no need for the decision maker to compare options.[594]

> Decision making becomes a matter of providing direction for the continuous flow of behaviour and monitoring one's progress toward some goal, rather than discrete episodes involving choice dilemmas.[595]

Since, as explained above, a mental model supports situational awareness and decision making, then in a team context, a shared mental model supports team situational awareness and team decision making.

> Shared mental models allow crews to function efficiently because they serve as an organizing framework, allowing the crew to anticipate events as well as each other's actions; [this is] vital for effective NDM and RPD.[596]

Thus, contrary to the concern stated at the outset of this chapter, the RPD model does not preclude, but actually aligns with, collaborative decision making. If the main decision maker cannot initially arrive at a course of action, perhaps because of

---

591. Id.

592. Id.

593. Simpson January 2001, 4.

594. Simpson January 2001, 5-6.

595. Simpson January 2001, 13.

596. Simpson January 2001, 10.

an unfamiliar or developing situation, he or she can quickly seek input from other team members[597] through the CRM tools and techniques described in this book. When a course of action is identified, other team members can use their own RPD skills to test it, critique it, or offer other options. Unlike the analytical decision making model, the RPD model is not degraded by but "capitalizes on time constraints."[598]

As already suggested, NDM and RPD explain and inform decision making in dire, "life threatening"[599] emergencies. However, "risky and irreversible decisions"[600] must also be made in less emergent situations where the consequences of poor decisions are equally dire:

> Consider however a paediatric cardiac surgeon weighing up the risks of operating on a young baby: anatomy of the heart, pulmonary artery pressure, findings from the echocardiogram and a host of other features may be considered to assess the likely short and long term outcomes for the child of operating now, operating in six months or not operating at all. This decision involves complex calculations, weighing of different factors and combining them to produce a judgment between two or more choices. Numerous studies have shown that people vastly overestimate their ability to make such judgments and that we also overestimate the number of factors that we take into account. Using statistical methods and models (whether paper or computerised) is

---

597. This point is adapted from Karol G. Ross July-August 2004,7-8.

598. Karol G. Ross July-August 2004,8.

599. Eric L. Grogan 2004, 845.

600. Imperial College London. "More Details on Clinical Judgement and Decision Making." *Imperial College London/Faculty of Medicine*. 2009. http://www1.imperial.ac.uk/medicine/about/divisions/sora/biosurg/csru/csruresearch/clinjudgement/moredetails/ (accessed June 11, 2009)

nearly always superior to using unaided clinical judgment. [601, 602]

Surgery aptly illustrates this point on non-emergencies. Surgeons, in concert with patient and colleagues, make critical decisions that directly impact patient safety before, during, and after a procedure, and "at all levels of patient care, including the hospital (organisational level), the surgical/operating theatre team (group level) and the individual surgeon (individual level)." Viewed through this lens, decision-making skill is as important as "the surgeon's technical skill, the operating theatre team performance and the quality of the pre- and post-operative ward care." For this reason, "surgery has been said to consist of 75% decision making and 25% surgical skill."[603]

Consequently, it seems that the NDM model would also prevail in "non-life threatening"[604] situations. And this is apparently the case: as a practical matter, experienced people do rely on NDM as a matter of course in *all* decision making. For example:

> Several studies on experienced engineers found that even under no time pressure, they still relied heavily on NDM type strategies, regardless of information characteristics, problem difficulty, familiarity and structure.[605]

---

601. Id.

602. The last two sentences of this block quote also, in effect, argue against reliance on intuition. This argument is broached in greater detail later in this chapter.

603. Id.

604. Eric L. Grogan 2004, 845.

605. Simpson January 2001, 1.

NDM and Metacognition

Metacognition is relevant to both CRM in general and SA and decision making in particular. The term has been defined countless times,[606] but for the purposes of this book, "metacognition" means, quintessentially, self-awareness: knowledge or consciousness of one's own cognitive processes and thoughts and the factors that influence them. Metacognition thus also entails an awareness of one's own biases and limitations. This is a "big picture," EI-resonant concept.

Attuned self-awareness enables people to:

- Plan and prioritize their activities.

- Continuously monitor them.

- Analyze them.

- Regulate and adjust them (correct mistakes).

- Ultimately, direct (or re-direct) their activities to a desired end.[607]

For these reasons, metacognition is considered critical to learning and improvement. Of particular importance in the CRM/patient safety domain, metacognition is also considered a

---

606. The definition used in this paragraph has been synthesized from several diverse (and many overlapping) sources. See, for example:

MSN. *Encarta Online Dictionary.* http://encarta.msn.com/dictionary_1861629491/metacognition.html (accessed June 15, 2009).

Annenberg Media. "Teaching Reading K-2 Workshop, Key Terms." *Learner.org.* http://www.learner.org/workshops/readingk2/front/keyterms2.html (accessed June 15, 2009). [Annenberg Media]

San Diego State University. http://coe.sdsu.edu/eet/Articles/metacognition/start.htm (accessed June 15, 2009). [SDSU]

Flavell, J. H. "Metacognitive aspects of problem solving." In *The Nature of Intelligence* by L. B. Resnick (Ed.), 231-236. Hillsdale, NJ: Lawrence Erlbaum Associates, 1976, 232.

607. Annenberg Media; SDSU.

teachable skill.[608, 609] According to Simpson, metacognitive training is useful not only for making decisions but also changing them, when appropriate, to "avoid cognitive lockup."[610]

Circling back to Naturalistic Decision Making, metacognition training would:

> ...allow [clinicians] to be more aware of their capabilities and limitations [and] have an overall better idea of their strengths and weaknesses, and potential problems, and hence can factor this into NDM to be more effective and flexible....[Training this skill] will aid decision making.[611]

By now, it is plain that metacognition training and CRM training are "closely related."[612] To paraphrase Simpson's analysis on NDM:

- Effective resource management can help hospital teams reduce the demands on their own cognitive resources, especially at times of high workload.

- Effective resource management allows for situational flexibility, which is an important part of NDM.

- Teaching CRM includes helping clinicians better understand what must be done in most decision situations, how to identify and use all available resources, how to effectively manage time and resources (including team members), and how to prioritize tasks.

---

608. SDSU.

609. Not surprisingly given the above discussion of NDM, expert learners generally have better metacognition than novices (SDSU).

610. Simpson January 2001, 19.

611. Id.

612. Simpson January 2001, 20.

Hence, "the teaching of this area of NDM [metacognition] can be modeled from the CRM courses."[613]

Following the tapestry image introduced above, decision making in both emergencies and non-emergencies weaves into the CRM fundamentals stressed throughout this book. For example, the various factors that contribute to poor surgical decision making and therefore threaten patient safety, including the unclear presentation of symptoms, clinician knowledge and expertise, individual traits (including subjectivity), and difficult working conditions, can be mitigated by seeking help or advice to gather the relevant information needed to make effective decisions— simply put, by collaborating. This, in turn, means having sufficient individual situational awareness to recognize when and how much collaboration is called for.

In sum, making good decisions is an acquired skill.[614] Regardless of the specific threat to patient safety, it depends on and combines (1) the level of urgency, (2) technical acumen, (3) experience, (4) situational awareness, and (5) above all, the right information.[615] As already noted, imparting the right information involves a skillful balance:

> Too little information results in poor risk assessment by the decision maker and results in errors, injury and death.[616]

On the other hand, since (as noted above) "the human memory and attention system are limited, and deteriorate when overloaded,"[617]

> Too much information overloads the decision maker and makes it difficult to make effective

---

613. Simpson January 2001, 20.

614. Simpson January 2001, 15.

615. International Association of Fire Chiefs 2003, 5; Simpson January 2001,8.

616. International Association of Fire Chiefs 2003, 5.

617. Simpson January 2001, 15-16

decisions. CRM training concentrates on giving and receiving information so appropriate decisions can be made.[618]

Heuristics

Heuristics are "quick," "intuitively sensible,"[619] "simple decision-making rules"[620] that are developed over time through experience and can help guide rapid decisions in the face of complexity or uncertainty. Variously characterized as predictive rules of thumb, educated guesses, intuitive judgments, or simple common sense, heuristics are used to "reduce the complex task of assessing probabilities and predicting values."[621]

Heuristics become especially germane in emergencies, when there is little time for conscious deliberation, and intuitive (semiconscious and subconscious) decision making (NDM/ RPD) becomes reflexively engaged.[622] According to some scholars, "in naturalistic environments, heuristics may be both less effortful and more accurate than classical decision models."[623] In aviation, virtually all cockpit decisions are heuristics.[624] In the clinic, they help "on most occasions."[625]

As the word "most" in the phrase just quoted implies, the use of heuristics can be problematic. In computer parlance, a heuristic is "an algorithm that usually, but not always, works or that gives nearly the right answer."[626] As this vague,

---

618. International Association of Fire Chiefs 2003, 5; along these same lines, also see Simpson January 2001, 15-16.

619. Simpson January 2001, 13.

620. Imperial College London 2009.

621. Simpson January 2001, 13.

622. See, for example, Currey and Botti 2003, 209.

623. Simpson January 2001, 15.

624. Simpson January 2001, 13.

625. Imperial College London 2009.

unsatisfying definition suggests, like most "simple" guides, heuristics can also *mis*guide:[627]

> Various decision-making biases influence what information is available, including that which is provided by the patient, what information is sought, and what investigations and tests are ordered to enable the clinician to make his or her judgment.[628]

> Heuristics and biases cause people to sample and process information in a selective, subjective manner...[and therefore] can sometimes lead to systematic and predictable errors. Such errors may include sampling only salient data, ignoring data that conflicts with initial situation assessment, and basing situation assessment and diagnosis on recently occurring events because they come to mind easily.[629]

The lesson here as related to CRM is this: although CRM promotes the use of mental models, aids, and tools to guide decisions, CRM does not teach blind adherence to them.[630] The dictates of the situation and the clinical judgment of those at the sharp end drive decisions, and proper deployment of CRM in any organization would not supplant those imperatives.

---

626. "Dictionary of Algorithms and Data Structures." National Institute of Standards and Technology.

627. Amos Tversky and Daniel Kahneman. "Judgment under Uncertainty: Heuristics and Biases." *Science*, September 1974 Vol. 185. No. 4157, 1124-1131, 1124.

628. Imperial College London 2009.

629. Simpson January 2001, 13.

630. For more on the ongoing debate about the use of evidence-based guidelines and how they might best be used as part of the clinical decision-making process, see the section titled "Decision Making and Evidence Based Medicine."

Planning is Essential

For any clinical team, planning is vital. Whether manifested as a briefing, a "stop the line" reassessment, or otherwise, planning promotes team performance by helping to:

- Create or reinforce mental models.

- Share relevant information.

- Set goals and expectations.

- Prioritize tasks.

- Clarify each individual member's roles and responsibilities.

- Address environmental characteristics and constraints.

- Prepare for the unexpected.

For example, the hospital is notified that a critical car crash patient is on his way to the emergency room. The attending resident assembles the team. She prepares the team for the patient's arrival by sharing what she knows so far, setting out and prioritizing tasks, establishing and clarifying each member's role and responsibilities, and advising them that she just heard that one of the x-ray machines is down. She also prepares them for the unexpected by letting the team know the patient is a female with a shaved head.

Decision Making Models

Despite the emergence and asserted primacy of NDM, analytical or "rational" decision making has played, and continues to play, a useful role in the pursuit of safety. Until this decade, most decision strategies in aviation (including CRM-trained strategies)[631] and also in healthcare have been represented by "structured" and "prescriptive" mnemonic tools such as those described below:

- **DECIDE**
  Define, Establish, Consider, Identify, Develop, Evaluate

- **IMSAFE**
  Illness, Medication, Stress, Alcohol, Fatigue, Eating

- **SADIE**
  Share, Analyze, Develop, Implement, Evaluate

- **GRADE**
  Gather, Review, Analyze, Decide, Evaluate

In aviation, the IMSAFE model is intended for a pilot's preflight use to answer the question: "Am I fit to fly?"[632] The "share" component of the SADIE model implies collaboration with others.[633] The DECIDE, SADIE, and GRADE tools have a learning component; each calls for evaluating a decision's outcome.

As suggested above, some proponents of NDM (notably Klein) worry about the reflexive and unthinking use of these analytic decision-making devices.[634] They may work adequately when stress is low, but in emergent, highly complex, or

---

631. "Mental is everything: New research on decision making poses some questions for single-pilot operations." *Flight Safety Australia*, March-April 2001, 22- 27, 22.

632. Federal Aviation Administration Flight Standards Service. *Instrument Flying Handbook*. Oklahoma City, OK: United States Department of Transportation, 2007, 1-13.

633. Mental is everything, 2001, 22.

634. Simpson, for example, cautions that analytical, prescriptive decision-making aids such as DECIDE, SADIE, and IMSAFE represent "a cognitive black box" of over-simple inputs and outputs: "The correct choice or outcome indicates good judgement, and the wrong choice or outcome indicates poor judgement." (Simpson January 2001,2)

unfamiliar situations, or under extreme workload, they create too many options, take too long, or simply unravel—it's simply not how people really decide things, particularly under duress. As stated in an aviation article comparing traditional and NDM decision models:

> It is difficult to see how a complex incident...could be "shoe-horned" into a generic rational choice model like GRADE, DECIDE, PILOT or SADIE....[I]f this pilot had rigorously applied any of these models to every decision, he may not have survived. He just would not have had the time to go through all the options.[635]

That same article quotes a paper by Klein, who wrote:

> ...under time pressure, pilots often look for the first workable option, and don't have the luxury of finding the absolute best...in a variety of natural settings, skilled decision makers rarely compared options. Even a watered-down version of the rational choice method may be used less than five to ten per cent of the time for critical decisions.... Unlike a controlled study environment, or the majority of simulations, reality poses its own unique set of difficulties that can impinge on the processes of any rational choice model, including time pressure, high stakes, ill-defined problems, shifting goals....[636]

Notwithstanding the lingering worry about classical theory and the advent of NDM, "NDM is not a panacea for real-world decision-making problems."[637] The model is still emerging.[638] Stating it in the reverse, analytic decision-making tools and aids

---

635. Mental is everything, 2001, 25.

636. Id.

637. Id.

638. Currey and Botti 2003, 206.

still have value and utility in the clinic. Even Klein's own NDM Process Model (reproduced above as Figure 15.3) reserves a place for "Analytic Decision Models."

Analytic tools, by extension, play a useful role in CRM training and practice, particularly as initial screening mechanisms. Mnemonic tools, for instance, are uniform and are easy to learn, incorporate into practice, and instill unit or organization-wide. They can be used as part of a team-wide lexicon to develop or reinforce a shared mental model or a decision-making protocol.

In addition to this "top down" use, mnemonic aids offer practical sharp-end help. For example, the IMSAFE self-assessment tool can be used:

- By a surgeon to assess whether he or she is able to operate without threatening a patient's safety.

- As part of a pre-shift or pre-operative briefing to confirm that all members are ready to perform at a high reliability level.

- By team members to monitor and cross-check their peers and spot red flags.

According to a 2008 study, the DECIDE model is a "closed loop," "step-by-step process for decision making," offering a "resource for health care managers" that enables them "to improve their decision-making skills, which leads to more effective decisions." The study follows the logic through, concluding that health care managers making "more quality decisions... ultimately determines the success of organizations."[639] DECIDE is also used as a "self-reinforcing" training tool for decision making.[640]

---

639. Guo April-June 2008.

Despite the reservations detailed above, analytic tools may also serve in emergencies. It makes sense that if clinicians can use NPD-type pattern matching to guide rapid decisions, the repeatable and eminently recognizable pattern of a mnemonic tool can serve a similar purpose—particularly for those less expert—to rapidly orient them and superimpose rational structure onto uncertainty.

Synthesizing Models

As this chapter on decision making suggests, the hand-wringing and wrestling continues between the advocates of analytical/classical decision theory (referred to by some as "CDT") and proponents of NDM. The former condemn NDM as intuitive, "fuzzy," or imprecise "seat-of-the- pants" practice that ignores the technological advances and the vast array of information and evidence (including specified "evidence-based best practices") that are now available to support sound decisions. Champions of NDM suspect clinical practice that relies on analytic tools, guidelines, and checklists, often dismissing it as "cookbook medicine" contrary to patient-centered practice. NDM champions would instill a framework rather than a prescription for making decisions and leave the final judgment calls to the clinicians at the scene.

---

640. Russell Lawton. "The DECIDE Approach to Training Pilots in Pilot Decision Making." *The Third International Pilot Decision Making Conference*. Ottawa, Canada: Aircraft Owners and Pilots Association [AOPA] Air Safety Foundation, December 2-3, 1986. 1-10, 5.

Evidence-Based Medicine

Recent analyses led by Falzer have examined the CDT/NDM divide and how it has hindered the evidence-based medicine (EBM) movement. These analyses have also suggested a way to balance the two poles and promote the adoption of evidence-based practices (EBPs) through NDM methods,[641] a recommendation which renders Falzer's ideas both instructive and directly relevant to CRM and this portion of the book.

More specifically, in a 2008 article about the problems in implementing EBM guidelines for psychiatry,[642, 643] Falzer starts by acknowledging the well-documented health care quality gap, the

> disparity between knowledge and its implementation [which] is adversely affecting quality of care.

Falzer also notes the advent of the EBM movement and the subsequent development of guidelines for EBPs, intended to close the gap. There is no controversy in this; most practitioners "acknowledge that clinical decisions and practices should be based on the best available evidence."

---

641. Paul R. Falzer. Cognitive schema and naturalistic decision making in evidence-based practices."*Journal of Biomedical Informatics*, April 2004, Vol. 37, No. 2: 86-98, 86.

642. Paul R. Falzer, Brent A. Moore, and D. Melissa Garman. "Incorporating clinical guidelines through clinician decision-making." *Implementation Science* 2008, Vol. 3, No. 13. The pages in this source are not separately numbered for citation. This section draws extensively from this source, and unless otherwise indicated, quoted language is taken from it.

643. Although Falzer's article specifically addresses EBPs in psychiatry and mental health, his comments are nevertheless expressed as applicable to most clinical disciplines.

The problem Falzer articulates has arisen because the use of EBM guidelines has strayed from the original intent and purpose to "inform and assist clinical practice":

> [G]uidelines serve a valuable function as decision tools, and substantiate the importance of decision-making as the means by which general principles are incorporated into clinical practice.

Using guidelines as decision tools fits the previously detailed concepts about shared mental models, decision training, and intelligent use of mnemonic aids and is therefore consistent with CRM principles.

However, in many instances—somewhat as Klein had worried—guidelines have been recast as standards of performance.[644] Failure to strictly conform to them has become equated with substandard practice. Thus, clinicians have bristled:

> EBPs have not been received with the enthusiasm that was anticipated...[and] the implementation of EBPs is a polarizing issue....Battle lines are drawn when clinicians are told, in one way or another, that the quality of their work can be gauged by how closely they conform to guidelines that were developed for the express purpose of aiding their decisions rather than directing them.

---

644. Endsley, for his part, wrote: "[I]t should be carefully noted that one should ensure that SA on one aspect of the situation is not gained at the cost of another, equally important aspect. If ideal SA is perfect knowledge on all relevant aspects of the situation, then this establishes a yardstick against which to measure. People rarely will reach this level; however, it allows us to determine the degree to which different system designs allow the operator to approach the ideal level of SA. This may vary for different elements of the situation, as SA has generally been found to be a multi-dimensional construct and not a unitary one." (Endsley 2000, 20)

Some researchers have therefore become concerned that EBPs might ultimately have a "deleterious effect" on the quality of care and that "the implementation of EBPs is on a collision course with the movement to individualize care and promote patient-centered health care."

Falzer balances the argument by referring to studies for the other side, which would justify using guidelines as metrics because

> ...almost universally,...clinicians lack the consistency and the perceptive and integrative power that are requisite to sound decision-making. In short, they tend be "suboptimal" decision-makers who, as such, perform less capably than statistical models.

This problem underscores the inherent tension between the CDT and NDM approaches to decision making. Falzer proposes to break the impasse and advance the unquestionably noble purpose of EBM by moving away from blind adherence to guidelines as performance standards and toward encouraging clinicians to incorporate EBPs and guidelines into their practice via their decision-making protocols—similar to the CRM-centered checklists and mnemonic aids described above. Falzer surmises that

> [t]he diffusion of EBPs will lead to greater utilization insofar as they fit the cognitive processes of decision-makers.

This last caveat squarely aligns Falzer with the NDM camp. He repeats the practical inadequacies of CDT, arguing that CDT models

> ...have limited application to the task of understanding how clinicians make treatment decisions, particularly under practical constraints such as having limited information, working with complex disorders that have

heterogeneous outcomes, and prescribing for patients who have treatment-resistant conditions. The principal problem with CDT is its all-consuming interest in making optimal decisions, which putatively result from the proper employment of a logical model.[645]

Ignoring those limitations, some scholars have argued for "an explicit link between EBM and CDT," asserting that a particular treatment decision is by definition evidence-based "when it has a higher probability of achieving a desirable outcome than a non-evidence-based alternative." The idea behind this argument is that the best clinical outcome will be achieved by choosing the treatment that conforms to a pre-arranged expectation of maximum value.

This argument, despite its veneer of logic, is nevertheless discordant with the guiding principles of patient safety and the tenets of CRM expressed in this book. Predictably, Falzer also rejects this position. At the sharp end, optimal or ideal decisions yield to real-time, and often decidedly un-formulaic, imperatives that mandate the best decision under the circumstances. Through the prescriptive CDT lens, a clinician's performance will, again by definition, fall short a good part of the time—even if his or her decisions work and the outcomes are positive. A measure of "how frequently decision-makers fall short of an ideal...does not suffice as an explanation of how, where, and why decision-making goes wrong" and does not serve when "the objective is to correct and improve decision-making." Retrospectively comparing actual practices against EBP guidelines elevates them to "standards of optimality and involves a test of conformance."

---

645. Falzer also echoes the above analysis, tracing the marked differences between the decision-making approaches and skill of experts and novices. He alludes to studies of pattern learning and clinical judgment which have concluded that "these differences affect their use of clinical guidelines."

Once again, the CDT construct and the use of EBP guidelines as bright-line performance benchmarks seem overly fixated on what clinicians *ought* to be doing, rather than what they are *actually* doing and how to improve on it.

Falzer also dismisses later iterations of CDT such as "cognitive heuristics,"[646] which posit that "decision-making is suboptimal because people simply do not follow normative strategies" and that "cognitive short-cuts inevitably lead to inaccurate judgments." As explained above, this notion is at odds with the research of numerous eminent authorities, Klein included. Falzer writes:

> Moreover, the notion that decision-makers function as transducers, and employ a cognitive apparatus that works like a choice-selecting mechanism, is not a desirable or reasonable way of depicting clinical practice. When decisions are made with limited information, uncertainties are incalculable, and there is no universally correct answer, cognition plays a role more akin to active problem solving than passive optimizing.

As already established, active problem solving is inherent in CRM's proven situation-awareness-driven approach to decision making. Also consistent is Falzer's suggestion that

> ...clinicians incorporate EBPs into their decisional processes through the mechanism of screening. Instead of, or at least prior to, their using a guideline to assist in making a choice, they assess the guideline's applicability to the case at hand by using pertinent clinical facts as screening criteria.

---

646. Falzer does so while recognizing that cognitive heuristics theory has gained support in medical research.

Falzer opines that if his suggestion is followed, then when clinicians—with good reason—depart from treatment guidelines (such as a patient's unwillingness to change medications or non-adherence; the stability of the patient's current condition; or the need for more time to evaluate treatment response), they are, in effect, stating their commitment to follow the EBP guidelines unless there is good reason not to. That way, the clinician retains the power to decide if the guidelines are not appropriate for a given case or in a given situation. The decision would not constitute a wholesale rejection of EBP guidelines, because even if ultimately rejected through the screening process, it would have played a direction-finding, "crucial role at the beginning."

Falzer's approach would allow clinicians to embrace EBPs without having to follow them blindly or surrender clinical judgment. This position is crucial to CRM principles of paying attention to maintain situational awareness and being adaptable to dynamic and ever-changing circumstances.

In harmony with this theme, Falzer concludes by turning the tables on those who would equate any departure from EBP guidelines as poor practice. He says that since a guideline is not a rule, then "expecting clinicians to follow it automatically"—especially when the available evidence is unclear—"is tantamount to poor practice. But if the guideline is incorporated into a decision strategy, it can become a valuable means of transcending the [EBP] dissemination gap and improving quality of care."

Pulling It All Together

The debate about decision making is relevant to, and informs, the development and evolution of CRM theory and practice. But for all its passion, the debate is—after all—essentially academic. To deliver genuine results in patient safety, CRM stays tethered to the real world waiting at the end of the scalpel. It is no accident that CRM theory and evolution have, in effect, taken into account and adapted to the strengths and weaknesses of both the CDT and the NDM decision-making approaches. CRM readily endorses the local adaptation and use of tools such as checklists and mnemonic aids to standardize safe practices and to reinforce or create shared mental models to avoid the threats posed by human fallibility. Following Falzer's reasoning, EBP guidelines fit this mold well.

At the same time, however, CRM recognizes the indispensable value of hands-on clinical judgment and even creativity as the situation dictates. CRM training fortifies judgment skills, both individually and through team collaboration and communication of all relevant information, which includes the available technology and medical monitoring devices.[647]

In a practical sense, therefore, CRM-based decision-making principles bridge the divide between CDT and NDM by overcoming what each demonstrably lacks standing alone. This construct resembles what Robbins and Judge call "bounded reality"—combining traditional methods with intuition and creativity for better decisions, and in doing so assessing and adjusting to situations as they unfold and remaining mindful of organizational goals.

---

647. In this regard, see Currey and Botti 2003, 210.

In the CRM context, this approach stands to reason. If CRM is about using all available resources, then picking a side in the decision-theory debate would by definition take potentially valuable resources off the table.[648]

Common Biases and Errors

Distilling and summarizing the previous analysis in this book,[649] here is a listing and description of the most common decision-making biases and errors:

- **Heuristics**
  Over-reliance on short cuts or "rules of thumb" to simplify decision making.

- **Overconfidence**
  Unwarranted and unrealistic belief in the ability to make good decisions, even outside one's own expertise. A problem with metacognition (poor self-awareness). Not asking for help or consultation.

- **Selective Perception**
  Selecting, organizing, and interpreting information based on one's own filters and roadblocks. Another metacognition problem.

- **Immediate Gratification**
  Choosing the option that offers the most immediate results or avoids immediate costs.

---

648. Moreover, recent research suggests that the human mind is quite capable of simultaneously processing and synthesizing both rational and so-called "intuitive" inputs. (See, for example, Hodgkinson, Langan-Fox, and Sadler-Smith February 2008, 1-27)

649. The concepts presented in this section have been distilled or extrapolated from earlier text and numerous other sources, and are considered a representative or consensus overview. Therefore specific citations do not appear unless specific credit is warranted; that said, most of the ideas listed here are brilliantly summarized by Robbins and Judge (2008).

- **Anchoring**
  Fixating on the information first received as the basis for all decisions, ignoring or refusing to consider subsequent information.

- **Confirmation**
  Selecting and using only those facts that support one's decision, and discounting contrary information.

- **Tunnel Vision**
  Related to confirmation: focusing on certain aspects of a situation and ignoring others. This is related to what some have referred as a "mission mindset.

- **Availability/Recency**
  Over-emphasizing the information most readily available, most recent, or most vivid (the most easily recalled).

- **Escalating Commitment**
  Staying stubbornly with a decision, and increasing the commitment to it, even in the face of evidence that it was wrong. This often happens to those who are responsible for the decision. And is also related to a mission mindset.

- **Emotional Link**
  Related to escalating commitment: becoming emotionally invested in the outcome.

- **Illusion**
  Pattern matching pitfalls: one sees what he or she expects to see, sees matches where none exist, creates unfounded meaning from random or unconnected facts or events.

- **Jumping the Gun**
  Acting too fast.

- **Stuck in the Blocks**
  Acting too slowly.

- **Hindsight**
  Believing that an outcome, after it is already known, could somehow have been predicted.

- **Stunted Growth**
  Failing to review, critique, or seek feedback on decisions.

Decision Making Algorithm

The previous analysis also permits a distilled, refined, and annotated CRM-centered algorithm for making decisions in the clinic as defined below:[650]

- **Pay Attention**
  Attuned situation awareness—*paying attention*—will help ensure the appropriate degree of vigilance to spot cues and red flags. Most of the time, problems that require difficult decisions "don't just sneak up.

- **Detect**
  A strong (and shared) mental vision and proper preparedness (through CRM training and briefing) can help avoid problems in the first place, but if a problem arises, team members will be "spring loaded" to act.

- **Assess**
  To understand the problem, use all resources, technological and human (including NDM pattern matching and intuition) to gather the relevant data, evidence, and information. Collaborate and consult as appropriate.

---

650. Table 15.7 also draws from and analogizes to the very straightforward and digestible article titled "Do the Right Thing: Decision Making for Pilots." *Safety Advisor, Operations & Proficiency No. 11.* Aircraft Owner and Pilots Association [AOPA] Air Safety Foundation, 2006: 1-8.

- **Weigh Options**
  If time and circumstances permit, develop and consider all options and their potential outcomes, using NDM or CDT approaches. Clinicians accustomed to concrete answers—for whom NDM may be "too fuzzy"—are likely to favor the latter. In emergencies, however, use serial NDM pattern matching, simulation, and screening approach. Collaborate and consult as appropriate to the situation.

- **Identify Best Option**
  The optimum solution may not be in the cards. In the clinic, decision making is about doing the right thing at the right time.

- **Decide**
  Make a decision before the situation further deteriorates or changes altogether. "In a rapidly deteriorating situation, every passing minute robs you of options—options that likely won't come back."

- **Plan**
  Plan what to do next.

- **Act**
  Implement the plan.

- **Monitor**
  Maintain SA: monitor the situation to see if the plan is working or if things change enough to require a change in the plan. Use peer cross-check. Clinical practice, particularly once a treatment protocol or surgical procedure has begun, represents an active and "continuous decision-making cycle.

- **Review**
  Via debriefing while events are still fresh (or relatively so), review and critique what just happened; seek team feedback. Discuss what might be done better the next time.

Chapter 16

Briefing and Debriefing Skills

Key Points in this Chapter

- Briefing and debriefing represent another essential CRM skill. Recent studies have confirmed that briefing (1) helps establish and maintain shared mental models and thereby situational awareness, (2) is a critical component of effective teamwork, and (3) has become a main technique for improving patient safety.

- Briefings promote intra-team communication and collaboration. Team members can compare notes, identify goals and obstacles, and obtain the information they need to perform. Team leaders can quickly ascertain the problems of the day.

- Briefings are used before surgery, at the beginning (or end) of a shift, and at patient handoffs. They can also be used to "huddle" *ad hoc*, to help a team refocus under duress.

- In 2004, The Joint Commission in effect mandated a team briefing by adopting the Universal Protocol for Preventing Wrong Site, Wrong Procedure, Wrong Person Surgery.™ Surgical teams must, before beginning any procedure, conduct a "time-out" during which team members verify the intended patient, the procedure, and the procedure site and confirm that the site has been correctly marked.

- Team briefings should cover seven basic topics which are discussed in detail below. This chapter also offers tips on how to conduct them.

- The SBAR method is particularly suited for briefing.

- Debriefings, which occur after completion of a shift or procedure (while the events are fresh), are no less valuable than briefings. They provide an institutionalized, standardized, and structured platform for performance feedback, and therefore promote constant learning and improvement—both attributes of an HRO.

Briefing is another essential CRM skill that has proved effective for establishing and maintaining situational awareness and, by extension, promoting and enhancing patient safety.

Briefing: Setting the Stage

In aviation, a shared mental model (driven by the goal to reduce preventable errors) inspired the development of team briefings[651] as a fundamental tool of CRM for sharing information, promoting planning, and increasing overall situational awareness.[652] Briefing has proved extremely effective and is now recognized as "a critical part of effective teamwork,"[653] offering a structured protocol for team interaction and ongoing dialogue. As previously noted, team briefings and meetings also help to build and consistently reinforce shared mental models,[654] and by extension SA.

Briefing has proved no less valuable in the clinic and has become recognized as a main technique for improving patient safety.[655] For example:

- A 2005 study showed that preoperative briefings (1) improved communication in the OR, (2) detected previously missed patient risk factors "as the last checkpoint before proceeding with the surgery," and (3) improved performance measures and patient outcomes by enabling and "ensuring" more timely and appropriate prophylactic use of antibiotics and DVT sequential compression devices, and (4) improved medical records documentation.[656]

---

651. The most widely recognized type of aviation briefing is the pre-flight checklist (Maureen Ann Wright Spring 2005, 35).

652. Stephen M. Powell 2005.

653. Stephen M. Powell 2005; Jon Allard March 2007, 190.

654. See, for example, Jon Allard March 2007, 192.

655. See, for example, Jon Allard March 2007, 204-205.

- A previously cited 2007 study of UK operating theaters reported that 78% of OT practitioners agreed that briefing improves teamwork and 82% agreed that briefing improves patient safety;[657] a 2008 University of Virginia study drew a similar conclusion.[658]

In operating room practice and along with clear procedures and checklists, briefings "are of direct relevance" because they help every team member know exactly what to do and how.[659] In L&D practice, "a team meeting gives providers the needed awareness of the situation, allows clinicians to articulate patients' care plans, and provides an opportunity to create a shared vision or a 'shared mental model.'"[660] That said, in the SA context the term "briefings" is preferred to "meetings": in the high-stress, dynamic environment of the clinic, team discussions must be short in duration and to the point.

The purpose of briefings is to assemble team members at prescribed points in time or in processes. Team members compare notes, identify what they want to accomplish, identify resources, and anticipate obstacles; team leaders can quickly learn the immediate problems to be addressed that day. Briefings thus promote a sense of collaboration, set the tone for open communication, and make sure that all team members

---

656. Awad S.S., Fagan S.P., Bellows C., Albo D., Green-Rashad B., De la Garza M., Berger D.H. "Bridging the communication gap in the operating room with medical team training." *American Journal of Surgery*, November 2005 Vol. 190, No. 5: 770-774.

657. Jon Allard March 2007, 196.

658. Stephanie Guerlain; Florence E. Turrentine; David T. Bauer; J. Forrest Calland; Reid Adams. "Crew resource management training for surgeons: feasibility and impact." *Cognition, Technology & Work*, September 2008, Vol. 10, No. 4:255–264, 255. In this regard, see also Eric L. Grogan, MD, MPH, Renée A. Stiles, PhD, Daniel J. France, PhD, MPH, Theodore Speroff, PhD, John A. Morris Jr., MD, FACS, Bill Nixon, MA, F. Andrew Gaffney, MD, Rhea Seddon, MD, C. Wright Pinson, MD, MBA, FACS. "The Impact of Aviation-Based Teamwork Training on the Attitudes of Health-Care Professionals." *Journal of the American College of Surgeons*, 2004, Vol. 199: 843–848, 844. (Eric L. Grogan 2004)

659. Alfred Cuschieri November 2006, 645.

660. Susan Mann January 1, 2006, 2-3.

have the information they need to perform. Briefings are effectively used, for example, before surgery, at the beginning of a shift, and at patient handoffs. They can also be used to "huddle" *ad hoc*, to help a team refocus during times of dynamic change, such as a sharp decline in patient status.

The team huddle was in effect mandated by The Joint Commission in 2004 under the Universal Protocol for Preventing Wrong Site, Wrong Procedure, Wrong Person Surgery.™ Immediately before beginning any procedure, the surgical team must conduct a "time-out" during which team members actively verify the intended patient, procedure, and procedure site and that the intended site has been correctly marked.[661]

Briefings: The Seven Basics

No universal prototype exists for team briefings, nor is one particularly desirable, since team briefings must be "customized to fit the organizational culture."[662] Many hospitals have, in fact, developed their own specific tools to get the most out of briefings and enable consistent transmission of information."

Some of those tools include:

- Briefing checklists.

- Briefing cards.

- White boards.

---

661. Implementation Expectations for the Universal Protocol for Preventing Wrong Site, Wrong Procedure and Wrong Person Surgery 2003.

662. Dunn, et al. June 2007, 324.

Despite the lack of a universal format, there are several fairly universal principles and elements that comprise an effective briefing approach.

First, and overall, all briefings necessarily involve both upcoming work and interpersonal concerns,[663] since both affect performance and patient safety. Second, as mentioned above, briefings must be structured, concise, and most certainly, brief.[664] In the latter regard, the Institute for Healthcare Improvement recommends that a safety briefing last no longer than five minutes and that the time limit be observed.[665]

To help the team establish or maintain SA and to head off latent threats, the following seven basics should be included in the team briefing:[666]

1. Team members: Who's on the team?

2. Clinical status of the team's patients. This includes:

   • Vital signs.

   • Diagnosis.

   • Emotional condition.

   • Care plan.

   • Actions taken under the plan.

   • Expected disposition.

3. Team goals and objectives

---

663. Jon Allard March 2007, 192.

664. See, for example, Michael Leonard 2003, 2.

665. "Safety Briefings." *Institute for Healthcare Improvement.* http://www.ihi.org/ NR/rdonlyres/971CB2E8-4E23-448D-92BD-D680B4F62EA3/639/ SafetyBriefings.pdf. (accessed May 27, 2009), 4. [Safety Briefings]

666. This list was culled from many sources, including: Dynamics Research Corporation 2004, 1-7; Susan Mann January 1, 2006, 2-3.

4. Team member roles, responsibilities, and individually assigned tasks

5. Issues affecting (or potentially threatening) the team operations, such as:

   - Available resources: personnel, equipment and physical plant (such as operating rooms).

   - Workload.

   - Fatigue.

   - Skill level.

   - Stress level.

6. Next steps

7. An explicit "safety statement" requesting input from team members.

How to Conduct a Briefing

The leader conducting the briefing should proceed generally in the following order:[667]

- Bring everyone together. Try to wait for everyone so no one misses.

- Get the person's or group's attention.

- Make eye contact.

- Introduce himself/herself.

- Remind everyone that the purpose is to increase awareness of safety issues.

---

667. Teamwork Takes Hold to Improve Patient Safety February 2005, 4; Safety Briefings, 9.

- Use other people's names.

- Ask only for knowable information.

- Provide information.

- Explicitly ask for input. Ask open-ended questions to spur participation.

- Talk about next steps.

- Encourage ongoing peer monitoring and cross-checking.

When to Brief

As previously mentioned, it essential to SA and patient safety that briefings occur at those times when clearly communicated information is essential to performance and at those times known to be the riskiest for loss of essential information.

Therefore briefings should occur at the following times:

- At shift changes.

- At scheduled staff breaks.

- When team personnel changes.[668]

- Before operating.

- At patient handoffs.

---

668. Dunn, et al. June 2007, 324.

SBAR as a Briefing Technique

As previously observed, the SBAR method is particularly suited for briefing. Leonard and colleagues are strong advocates, stating that "simple rules are best for managing complex environments" and that SBAR is a standardized method that encompasses "the tools and concepts that have proved the most valuable."[669] SBAR enables teams to quickly reassess the situation if people are getting overloaded. A clinician might, for example, initiate an *ad hoc* SBAR briefing by saying:

> "Let's talk a minute and go over all the patients on the deck. Who's got what patient, where are we with each patient, what are the issues that need to be addressed, and how do we prioritise?"[670]

Debriefing

Briefings occur beforehand. Debriefings are no less valuable,[671] and take place after completion of a shift or procedure. Debriefings are a "practical tool"[672] that provides an institutionalized, standardized, and structured platform for "performance feedback"[673]—and individual, team, and organizational learning—by allowing staff to discuss and

---

669. M. Leonard 2004, i85.

670. Id.

671. Leonard, for example, refers to a study of team learning in adopting MICS and observes that "debriefings were seen as one of the key success factors in the surgical team with the quickest learning curve and best clinical outcomes." (M. Leonard 2004, i87)

672. Michael Leonard 2003, 2.

673. Eric L. Grogan 2004, 845.

question what challenges were faced, what went well, what did not go well, and what might be done better the next time.[674]

Debriefings, like briefings, should be concise, consisting of, in Leonard's words, "spending a couple of minutes after a procedure, or at the end of a day…while the events are fresh."[675]

One of the most common briefing techniques in use in clinical and non-clinical settings is the three questions model:

1. What went well?

2. What did not go well and why?

3. How can we improve for next time?

In addition, hospitals have included process improvement actions and built-in accountability procedures to ensure that opportunities for improvement that are identified are acted upon and implemented.

The debriefing is the bookend to a briefing. It helps close the loop on the CRM skills that are put into practice during a case, procedure, operation, task or project. Like briefings and other CRM skills, it takes practice. However, it is easy to start. Like other CRM skills, debriefings can be implemented quickly and easily. But to affect change and contribute to an overall culture of patient safety, the skill and methodology should be standardized. With a standardized process, the debriefing process can be rolled-out organization-wide beginning with staff training and reinforced with direct observation and coaching.

---

674. This sentiment is consistent throughout the research, including in M. Leonard 2004, i85-i87; Eric L. Grogan 2004, 845; and Teamwork Takes Hold to Improve Patient Safety February 2005, 6.

675. M. Leonard 2004, i87; see also Teamwork Takes Hold to Improve Patient Safety February 2005, 6.

Part Five

CRM Training and
Program Tools

Checklists, Forms and
Instructional Aids

Critical Situation Report Checklist

Patient:	Time:	AM PM
Location:	Date:	/ /

Situation

- [ ] Introduce yourself
- [ ] The patient I am calling about is _____ *patient's name*
- [ ] The situation I am concerned about is _____
- [ ] The patient's code status is _____

Background

- [ ] Here is the supporting background information.
- [ ] The patient's vital signs are:
  - [ ] Blood pressure ____ / ____   [ ] Pulse: _____
  - [ ] Respiration: ____   [ ] Temperature: _____
  - [ ] Pain (Scale   1   2   3   4   5   6   7   8   9   10)
- [ ] The patient's mental status is...
  - [ ] alert and oriented to person, place and time
  - [ ] confused and...   [ ] cooperative   [ ] non-cooperative
  - [ ] agitated and / or combative
  - [ ] lethargic but conversant and able to swallow
  - [ ] stuporous / not talking clearly and possibly unable to swallow
  - [ ] comatose / eyes closed / not responding to stimulation
- [ ] The patient's skin is...
  - [ ] warm and dry   [ ] diaphoretic   [ ] mottled
  - [ ] pale   [ ] extremities are cold   [ ] extremities are warm
- [ ] The patient...   [ ] is not on oxygen   [ ] is on oxygen
  - [ ] The patient has been on _____ (L/min.) or (%) oxygen for _____ minutes (hours)
  - [ ] The oximeter reads _____ %
  - [ ] The oximeter does not detect a good pulse and is giving erratic readings
- [ ] The patient is allergic to: _____

Assessment

- [ ] In assessing the situation, I think the problem is _____ *state problem*
  - [ ] The problem seems to be   [ ] cardiac   [ ] infection   [ ] neurologic   [ ] respiratory
  - [ ] I am not sure what the problem is, but the patient is deteriorating
  - [ ] The patient seems to be unstable and may get worse. We need to do something.

Recommendation / Request

- [ ] I recommend or request that you _____
  - [ ] transfer the patient to critical care
  - [ ] come to see the patient right away
  - [ ] talk to the patient or family about the code status
  - [ ] add / change orders to _____
- [ ] Do you want to have any tests done?
  - [ ] CXR   [ ] ABG   [ ] EKG   [ ] CBC   [ ] BMP   [ ] Others
- [ ] If a change in treatment is ordered, ask...
  - [ ] how often do you want vital signs?
  - [ ] how long do you expect this problem will last?
  - [ ] if the patient does not get better, when would you want us to call again?

Notes

SaferHealthcare
Creating and Sustaining a Patient Safety Culture

To order additional copies of this checklist, visit us on the web:
www.SaferHealthcare.com or call toll-free: 1-866-398-8083

327

SBAR Communication Worksheet

This is not part of the medical record

Patient Name:

Patient Date of Birth: / /

Date: / / **Time:** AM PM **Location:**

Room Number:

Pre-call preparation: Gather the following information: Patient's name; age; chart. Rehearse in your mind what you plan to say. Run it by another nurse if unsure. If calling about pain, when and what was last pain medication? If calling about fever, what was the most recent temperature? If calling about an abnormal lab, what was the result of the last test? What is the goal of your call? Remember to start by introducing yourself by name and location. Use area below as a checklist to gather your thoughts and prepare.

Situation
Briefly describe the current situation.
Give a clear, succinct overview of pertinent issues.

Background
Briefly state the pertinent history.
What got us to this point?

Assessment
Summarize the facts and give your best assessment.
What is going on? Use your best judgement.

Recommendation
What actions are you asking for?
What do you want to happen next?

Follow-up Action (Next Steps): Document the call and "read back" orders to ensure accuracy.
Is there a change in the plan of care? Yes No

SaferHealthcare

SBAR Communication Worksheet

Patient Name:

Patient Date of Birth: / /

Date: / /   **Time:** AM PM   **Location:**   **Room Number:**

Pre-call preparation: Gather the following information: Patient's name; age; chart. Rehearse in your mind what you plan to say. Run it by another nurse if unsure. If calling about pain, when and what was last pain medication? If calling about fever, what was the most recent temperature? If calling about an abnormal lab, what was the result of the last test? What is the goal of your call? Remember to start by introducing yourself by name and location. Use area below as a checklist to gather your thoughts and prepare.

Situation
Briefly describe the current situation.
Give a clear, succinct overview of pertinent issues.

Background
Briefly state the pertinent history.
What got us to this point?

Assessment
Summarize the facts and give your best assessment.
What is going on? Use your best judgment.

Recommendation
What actions are you asking for?
What do you want to happen next?

Follow-up Action (Next Steps): Document the call and "read back" orders to ensure accuracy. Is there a change in the plan of care? Yes   No

SaferHealthcare
www.SaferHealthcare.com

SBAR Process / Quality Improvement Action Form

The purpose of this form is to document and outline an action plan to make an improvement to a process or work flow.

Your Name:	Date Submitted: / /

Proposed Improvement Project Title:

Situation (Use the back of this sheet if you need more room to provide explanation.)

Please provide a brief explanation of what the situation is: What is the process that you believe can be improved.

Where does this process and/or situation occur or what area is impacted? (Check all that apply)

- ☐ Preoperative Area (e.g., Holding Area, Inpatient Unit, Admit Area)
- ☐ Other Clinical Department (e.g., Pharmacy, Radiology) (Specify Below)
- ☐ Administrative Department (Specify Below)
- ☐ Other (Specify Below)
- ☐ Operating Room
- ☐ Procedure Room (e.g., Endoscopy Suite, Procedure Room)
- ☐ Labor and Delivery Suite
- ☐ PACU

Background (Use the back of this sheet if you need more room to provide explanation.)

What drew your attention to this? Is this an issue that happens frequently? Does it affect other people? Why make a change?

Assessment

This recommended change will positively impact the following: (Check all that apply)

- ☐ Improve Efficiency
- ☐ Reduce Paperwork
- ☐ Prevent Harm to Patients
- ☐ Increase Workplace Safety
- ☐ Cut Costs
- ☐ Eliminate Waste
- ☐ Increase the Quality of Patient Care
- ☐ Speed the Delivery of Care
- ☐ Improve Employee Morale
- ☐ Increase Patient Satisfaction
- ☐ Clarify a Policy or Procedure
- ☐ Standardize Care

This recommended change will make an impact and improvement(s) in the following: (Check all that apply)

- ☐ Communication between staff
- ☐ Staff Changes / Hand-offs
- ☐ Work Space Cleanliness
- ☐ Other (Please Specify):
- ☐ Reduce Rushing / Haste
- ☐ Teamwork
- ☐ Scheduling
- ☐ Equipment Storage
- ☐ Supplies and Stocking
- ☐ Room Changeover

Recommendation

Please use the back of this form or attach additional pages to answer the following:

- ☐ 1. What can be done to improve this situation / or process?
- ☐ 2. What changes need to happen to ensure that this is fixed or improved?
- ☐ 3. How can you help make this change a reality?
- ☐ 4. What is the simplest, fastest but most thorough way to make this happen?

Status

Stick status label here
- Red (Submitted)
- Yellow (Under Review)
- Green (Resolved)

SaferHealthcare

To order additional forms or status labels, call 303-298-9033 or visit us on line: www.SaferHealthcare.com

SBAR Nurse Shift Report Guide for Labor Patients

Use this checklist to gather your thoughts and structure your hand-off report. Use the note space below to make additional notes pertaining to the report as needed.

Note: The elements within this checklist are not intended to be comprehensive but rather a starting guide to assist in organizing a plan of communication.

Patient: _____

Location: _____

Date: _____   Time: _____

Notes:

Situation

- ☐ Patient name   ☐ Date / Time of Admission
- ☐ Age   ☐ Physician
- ☐ Room   ☐ Midwife
- ☐ Multiple birth ☐ yes ☐ no
- ☐ Previous C-section ☐ yes ☐ no
- ☐ Ruptured membranes ☐ yes ☐ no
- ☐ High risk for:
  - ☐ shoulder dystocia   ☐ pre-eclampsia   ☐ maternal post-partum hemorrhage
  - ☐ urine rupture   ☐ fetal distress
- ☐ Gestational age: _____
- ☐ Allergies: _____
- ☐ Comorbid conditions (i.e. diabetes, cancer, heart condition, etc.)

Background

- ☐ Gravida _____ para _____
- ☐ GBS status
- ☐ Allergies: _____
- ☐ rH
- ☐ Labor History
  - ☐ membranes / fluid
  - ☐ onset
  - ☐ contractions
  - ☐ dilated _____ effaced _____
  - ☐ station
- ☐ Medications
  - ☐ P-Gel   ☐ oxytocics   ☐ tocolytics (magnesium)   ☐ antibiotics
- ☐ Pain (scale / interventions)
- ☐ Epidural
- ☐ Lab work (when ordered / results back)
- ☐ IV
  - ☐ what   ☐ bag #   ☐ rate   ☐ site
- ☐ EFM

Assessment

- ☐ Patient is progressing within normal limits; no complications apparent
- ☐ I am concerned about: _____

Recommendation / Request

- ☐ I suggest or request that you _____
  - ☐ watch for _____
  - ☐ get test results
  - ☐ new orders
- ☐ On call / availability
  - ☐ physician ☐ midwife   ☐ pediatrician ☐ anesthesiologist

To order additional copies of this hand-off report guide, call 303-298-8083 or visit www.SaferHealthcare.com

SaferHealthcare
Creating and Sustaining a Patient Safety Culture

SBAR Shift Report Hand-off Guide

1. Situation

Use this checklist to gather your thoughts and structure your hand-off report. Use the note space below to make additional notes pertaining to the report as needed.

Note: The elements within this checklist are not intended to be comprehensive but rather a starting guide to assist in organizing a plan of communication.

☐ Patient   ☐ Room #
☐ Admitting Physician   ☐ Admitting Diagnosis / Secondary Diagnosis
☐ Most Current / Pertinent Issues

2. Background

Discuss only elements that have recently changed or are pertinent to this patient

Notes:

☐ Admit Date _____ Anticipated Date of Discharge _____
☐ Physician / Ancillary Consults
     ☐ Psych.   ☐ Surgical   ☐ PT/OT   ☐ Speech   ☐ Wound Care   ☐ Other
☐ Date / Time last seen by Physician _____
☐ Allergy _____
☐ Code Status / DNR _____
☐ Patient / Family Concerns
☐ Medications (pertinent issues / effectiveness)   ☐ Immunization status
☐ Recent Interventions / Effectiveness _____
☐ Abnormal Labs _____
☐ Vital Signs   ☐ Temp   ☐ Pulse   ☐ Respirations   ☐ O₂ Sat.
☐ Pain status   ☐ Location   ☐ Score   ☐ Modalities Used   ☐ Effectiveness
☐ IV   ☐ Type   ☐ Amount   ☐ Site   ☐ Issues
☐ Drains / Tubes
☐ Wounds / Dressings
     ☐ Type   ☐ Location   ☐ Color   ☐ Edema   ☐ Temp   ☐ Change in Size
☐ Decubiti   ☐ Stage   ☐ Location   ☐ Treatment

Systems: Discuss only systems pertinent to this patient

☐ Neurological / Mental Status
     ☐ Level of consciousness   ☐ Speech Pattern   ☐ Dementia   ☐ Confusion   ☐ Depression
☐ Lungs / Respiratory
     ☐ Lung sounds (rales, rhonchi, wheezes)
     ☐ Cough (productive (description), dry)
     ☐ Shortness of breath, difficulty breathing, orthopnea
     ☐ Respiratory rate
     ☐ Oximetry
     ☐ O₂ @ _____ liters / per _____
☐ Cardiovascular   ☐ Heart Rate   ☐ Regularity   ☐ SOB   ☐ Edema
☐ GI   ☐ Appetite changes   ☐ Diet type   ☐ Thickened Liquids   ☐ TPN   ☐ Weight
     ☐ Abdominal Tenderness   ☐ Distention   ☐ Vomiting   ☐ Nausea   ☐ I @ ___ ml / ___
     ☐ Last Bowel Movement   ☐ Constipation   ☐ Diarrhea   ☐ Colostomy
☐ GU   ☐ Catheter   ☐ Urine Color   ☐ Dysuria   ☐ Frequency   ☐ Last UTI   ☐ O @ ___ ml / ___
☐ Musculoskeletal   ☐ Pain   ☐ Mobility Issues   ☐ Positioning   ☐ Fall risk status
☐ Assistive Devices   ☐ Wheel Chair   ☐ Cane   ☐ Walker   ☐ Other
☐ Skin   ☐ Temperature   ☐ Condition   ☐ Edema   ☐ Hematoma
☐ Discharge Plan / Issues   ☐ Case Management   ☐ Patient / Family Education
☐ Other _____

3. Assessment

☐ What do you think is going on with the patient?
☐ Do you have concerns about this patient? If yes, are they mild, moderate or severe?
☐ Discharge planning issues or concerns that need to be addressed

4. Recommendation

☐ Care / Issues requiring follow-up
☐ Orders requiring completion / follow-up
☐ Pending treatment / tests
☐ Issues / Items left undone that require follow-up

To order additional copies of this hand-off report guide, call 303-298-8083 or visit www.SaferHealthcare.com

SaferHealthcare
Creating and Sustaining a Patient Safety Culture

SBAR **Near Miss Event / Situation Report Form**

The purpose of this form is to share information about a situation to promote shared learning and the exchange of critical information to make sure that a similar situation does not happen again. It is not meant to assign blame or be punitive; it is designed to encourage transparency and improve the quality and delivery of patient care.

What was the worst potential outcome of this event / situation? ☐ Rework/Inefficiency/Delays   ☐ Minor Harm   ☐ Major or Permanent Harm

Situation

Where did this event/situation occur?

☐ Preoperative Area (e.g., Holding Area, Inpatient Unit, A.M. Admit Area)
☐ Operating Room
☐ Procedure Room (e.g., Endoscopy Suite, Procedure Room)
☐ Labor and Delivery Suite
☐ PACU
☐ Other Clinical Department (e.g., Pharmacy, CPD, Radiology)
☐ Please Specify Other Clinical Department:

Provide some details about the event/situation (check all that apply):

☐ First Case
☐ Emergency Case
☐ Time of Day
☐ Laterality Involved
☐ Multiple Teams
☐ Multiple Procedures
☐ Other Factor(s)

Explain the story of this event or situation. Be as specific as possible without including names of persons. (Issues to consider: How did the event/situation arise; any contributing factors; actions/inactions; what drew your attention to the event/situation; perceptions, judgments, decisions; etc.)

Background

What specialty or specialties were involved (please check all that apply)?

☐ Anesthesia   ☐ Obstetrics   ☐ Thoracic
☐ Cardiac   ☐ Orthopedics   ☐ Vascular
☐ General Surgery   ☐ Ophthalmology   ☐ Urology
☐ GYN   ☐ Pediatrics   ☐ Dental
☐ Neurosurgery   ☐ Plastics   ☐ Other (specify):
☐ Obstetrics   ☐ ENT   _____

Tell us something about the team that was involved in the event/situation:

How many people were in the room? _____

What disciplines were involved (please check all that apply)?

☐ Surgeon   ☐ Physician Assistant   ☐ Resident/Fellows
☐ Surgical House Staff ☐ CRN   ☐ Med/Nursing Student
☐ Anesthesiologist   ☐ ARN   ☐ Surgical Technologist
☐ House Staff   ☐ Industry Rep.   ☐ Other

Do most members of the team work together on a regular basis?   ☐ yes   ☐ no

Assessment

In your opinion, did any of the following issues contribute to the situation?

☐ Communication / Miscommunication   ☐ Rushing / Haste
☐ Staff Changes / Hand-off   ☐ Fatigue
☐ Unfamiliar Work Space   ☐ Inadequate Assistance
☐ Unfamiliar Equipment   ☐ Inadequate Supplies
☐ Unfamiliar Procedure   ☐ Schedule Changes
☐ Distractions   ☐ Change in Rooms
☐ Inexperience with Event / Situation ☐ Other

Recommendation

What can be done to prevent this situation / or event from ever happening again? (What changes need to happen to ensure that this never happens to another patient or another team)

SaferHealthcare™

To order additional copies of this report guide, call 303-298-8083 or visit us on-line: www.SaferHealthcare.com

Shoulder Dystocia Checklist

☐ **Shoulder dystocia identified foot stool in room** ⬚ ⬚

☐ **Call for help** ⬚ ⬚
    ☐ OB Physician _____
    ☐ Extra Personnel _____
    ☐ Neonatologist / Pediatrician _____
    ☐ Anesthesia
    ☐ Nursery Nurse _____
    ☐ Surgical Tech (alert to possible C-section) _____
    ☐ Supervisor _____

☐ **Assign individual to call out time every 30 seconds** ⬚ ⬚

☐ **Assess Bladder** (Cath if necessary) ⬚ ⬚

☐ **Watch epidural** ⬚ ⬚

☐ **Position for McRoberts** (assign personnel to position legs) ⬚ ⬚

☐ **Apply suprapubic pressure** (use footstool to get leverage) ⬚ ⬚
    ☐ Pressure to side of suprapubic bone

☐ **Consider episiotomy** ⬚ ⬚

☐ **Woodscrew** ⬚ ⬚

☐ **Reverse Woodscrew** ⬚ ⬚

☐ **Rubins** ⬚ ⬚

☐ **Repeat as possible** ⬚ ⬚

☐ **Gaskit shift** (mother on all fours) ⬚ ⬚

☐ **Deliver the posterior arm** ⬚ ⬚

☐ **Zanvanelli with immediate C/S** ⬚ ⬚

☐ **Document completely and accurately ASAP** ⬚ ⬚

Notes

_____
_____
_____
_____
_____

CRM Poster Series

OR Team Briefings

1. Announce Briefing

2. Introduce All Personnel

3. Share Critical Information

4. Ask for Team Input

5. Conduct Time Out

6. Review Contingency Plans

7. Ask for Questions about Case

Every Case   Every Patient   Every Time

Practice these Simple Briefing Elements

- **Make eye contact**
  Person speaking should look directly into the eyes of the person whom he/she is speaking to.

- **Use team member names**
  Briefing leader should address team members by their name.

- **Explicitly ask for input from all team members**
  Briefing leader should solicit ideas, comments, or feedback from team members.

- **Express views at any time during briefing**
  Each team member should feel free to speak up and provide input regarding their concerns/issues when appropriate.

- **Use a participatory approach to the briefing**
  Team members should use open, receptive body language during the briefing.

- **Share critical background information including known risks about the patient**
  Team members should provide pertinent information related to patient's medical background, equipment or to the procedure.

- **Conduct a "Time Out"**
  Describe the current situation following "time out" protocols including: verifying the patient's name, the procedure about to be performed, and site and age if necessary.

- **Discuss contingency plans**
  (plans if a complication or unexpected event occurs)
  Team members address the potential for an alternate or additional plan of action for the patient to include setting a bottom line, assigning tasks or describing a back up plan.

- **Close the loop: Ask for questions and encourage continued cross-talk**
  Briefing leader should ask for any questions regarding the patient/procedure just discussed and encourage the team to continue to speak up if they have any questions or concerns throughout the procedure or to give report on progress.

SaferHealthcare

Speak Up for Patient Safety

See it

Say it

Fix it

Empower Your Voice: Speak up, Be Heard, Get Action.

Teaching people how to speak up and creating a dynamic environment where they will express their concerns is a key factor in establishing a culture of patient safety. Frequently the lack of a common mental model or perceived hierarchy gets in the way of people saying what they should. Team members need to state a problem or potential issue politely and persistently until they get an answer. The common practice of speaking indirectly (the "hint and hope" model) is fraught with risk. It is important to focus on the problem at hand and avoid the issue of who is right and who is wrong.

Safer Healthcare

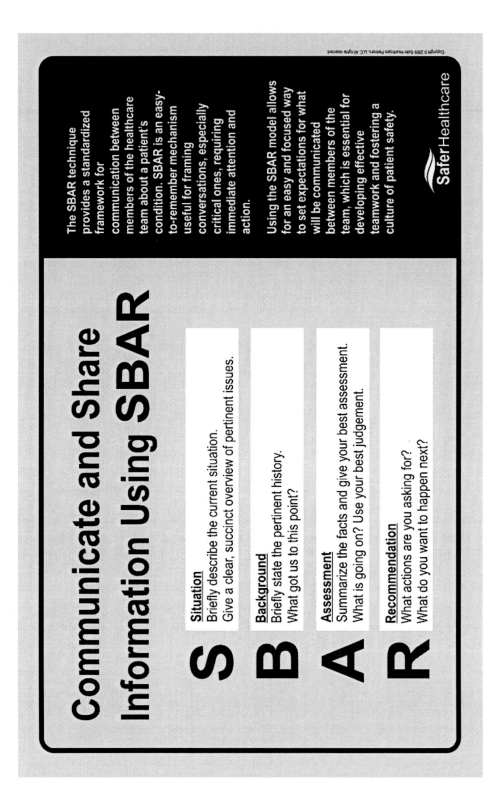

Communicate and Share
Information Using SBAR

S
Situation
Briefly describe the current situation.
Give a clear, succinct overview of pertinent issues.

B
Background
Briefly state the pertinent history.
What got us to this point?

A
Assessment
Summarize the facts and give your best assessment.
What is going on? Use your best judgement.

R
Recommendation
What actions are you asking for?
What do you want to happen next?

The SBAR technique provides a standardized framework for communication between members of the healthcare team about a patient's condition. SBAR is an easy-to-remember mechanism useful for framing conversations, especially critical ones, requiring immediate attention and action.

Using the SBAR model allows for an easy and focused way to set expectations for what will be communicated between members of the team, which is essential for developing effective teamwork and fostering a culture of patient safety.

Safer Healthcare

Be Alert for Red Flags

Deviating from the Normal Procedure

Unresolved Issues

Interruptions

Task Saturation

Preoccupation

Fatigue

Verbal Violence

"This doesn't feel right"

Ambiguity

Rushing

Poor Communication

Trying Something New Under Pressure

A gut feeling that things are not right is one of the initial signs that Situational Awareness is being lost. This "Red Flag" is one of the most reliable indicators because the body is able to detect stimulus long before we have consciously put it all together. In other words, trust your feelings. Call it intuition, but we have all experienced that feeling or sense that tells us subconsciously that something is not quite right.

Act on this feeling or instinct. Ask a fellow team member for clarification or voice your concern. Don't hesitate to speak up and be heard.

SaferHealthcare

Remain Alert

Situational awareness is the ability to identify, process, and comprehend the critical elements of information about what is happening to the team with regard to the mission.

More simply stated, situational awareness is knowing at all times what is going on around you.

SaferHealthcare

Maintain Your
Situational Awareness

- Know the Game Plan
- Anticipate Possible Events
- Follow Known Procedures
- Cross Check and Verify
- Verbalize "Red Flags"
- Provide On-going Updates

The loss of Situational Awareness usually occurs over a period of time and will leave a trail of clues. Be alert for clues or red flags that will warn of lost or diminished Situational Awareness. Remain alert at all times.

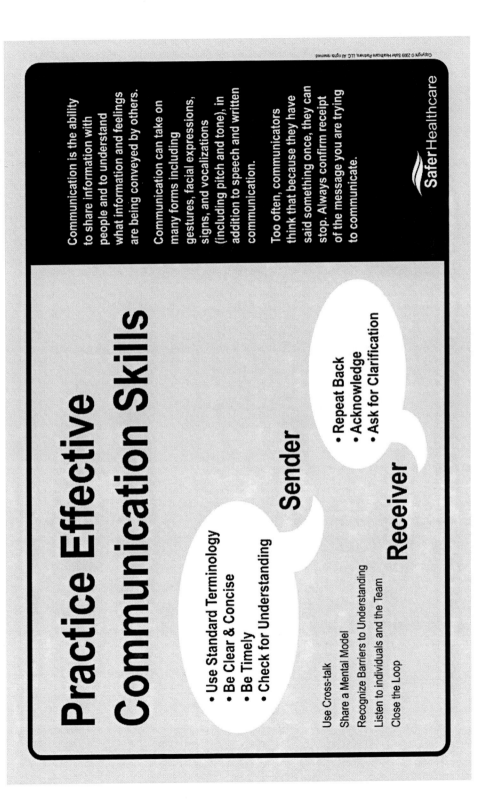

Working toward a Common Outcome

Teamwork is a joint action by two or more people in which each person contributes with different skills and is free to express and contribute his or her individual opinions or concerns to the unity and efficiency of the group in order to achieve common goals.

In a team environment, all members of the team contribute towards a common goal or outcome. The most effective teamwork is produced when all the individuals involved communicate and coordinate their contributions.

SaferHealthcare

Effective Teamwork
It is Everyone's Responsibility

10 Common Traits of Highly Effective Teams

1. There is a clear unity of purpose

2. The group is self-conscious about its own operations

3. The group sets clear and demanding performance goals

4. The atmosphere tends to be informal, comfortable and relaxed

5. There is task-oriented discussion in which everyone participates

6. Everyone is free to express his/her feelings and share ideas

7. There can be disagreement (and this is viewed as good)

8. Decisions are made at a point where there is general agreement

9. Each individual is respectful of each member of the team

10. Criticism is frequent, frank, but impersonal

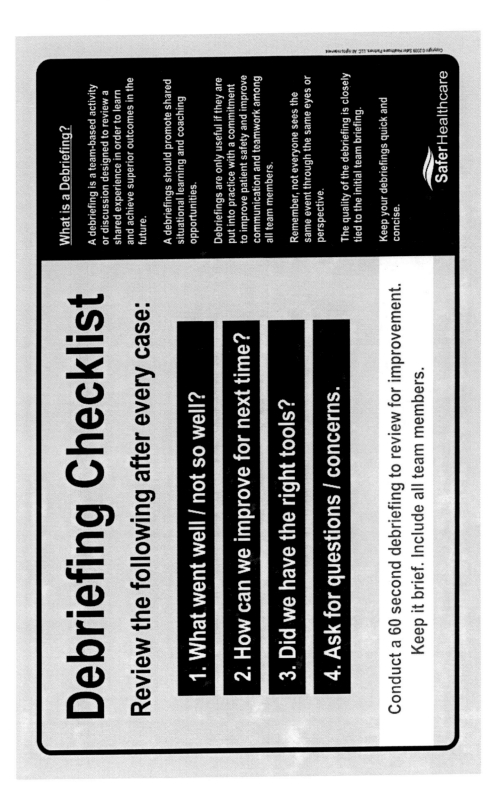

Debriefing Checklist

Review the following after every case:

1. What went well / not so well?

2. How can we improve for next time?

3. Did we have the right tools?

4. Ask for questions / concerns.

Conduct a 60 second debriefing to review for improvement.
Keep it brief. Include all team members.

What is a Debriefing?

A debriefing is a team-based activity or discussion designed to review a shared experience in order to learn and achieve superior outcomes in the future.

A debriefings should promote shared situational learning and coaching opportunities.

Debriefings are only useful if they are put into practice with a commitment to improve patient safety and improve communication and teamwork among all team members.

Remember, not everyone sees the same event through the same eyes or perspective.

The quality of the debriefing is closely tied to the initial team briefing.

Keep your debriefings quick and concise.

SaferHealthcare

Safe Practices Tool Card

Use this card as a resource and a guide. It is designed to encourage discussion and be used to help solve problems as they emerge. Remember to stay alert and help a fellow team member who is trying to follow these steps in order to maintain patient safety at all times.

Before every team activity
PRE **Stop and Hold a Team Briefing**
Be sure to follow the Briefing Checklist

After every team activity
POST **Stop and Hold a Team Debriefing**
Be sure to follow the Debriefing Checklist

Listen for "CUS" Words
Level 1: "I am **Concerned**!" Level 2: "I am **Uncomfortable**!" Level 3: "I do not feel **Safe**!"
Use these words to get the attention of other team members. Escalate levels as situation dictates.

Decision Making and Problem Solving
Use the following model to make a decision and review after to make improvements for next time.

1	2	3	4	5	6
Identify Problem	Suggest Solution(s)	Choose the Best	Execute and Take Action	Review for Improvement	Problem Resolved

Have You Learned Something? Share it with the Team
Have you learned something during or after a case? Share it with the rest of the team. Help them learn from the same experience. Be sure to include compliments as well as necessary suggestions for improvement next time. Don't be afraid to tell someone they did a good job.

Conflict Resolution: Be Proactive
Are you uncomfortable? Is there conflict? Is communication strained? If so, speak up and mention it right away. Don't be afraid and don't keep it inside. Address it now before it becomes worse or adversely affects patient or practitioner safety. Still feel there is conflict after addressing the issue? Speak to a manager or team member right away and get their help.

Speak Up for Patient Safety
Empower Your Voice. Speak up, Be Heard, Take Action. Use the "Assertion Model" on the back of this card for helpful hints to take action. Be respectful and professional at all times.

See it   Say it   Fix it

Be the Voice of the Patient

Safe Practices Tool Card

Team Briefing Checklist

1. Announce briefing
2. Introduce all team members
3. Share critical information
4. Ask for team Input
5. Review contingency plans
6. Ask for questions about case

Team Debriefing Checklist

1. Ask: What went well?
2. Ask: What did not go well?
3. Discuss: How can we improve for next time?
4. Ask for questions from team members.

Debriefing is a team-based discussion and review of a shared experience designed to give participants the opportunity to learn and achieve superior outcomes in the future. Debriefings promote situational learning and teaching.

Be Alert for Red Flags

Pre-occupation or fixation
Reduced / poor communication
Interruptions
Unresolved issues
Verbal violence
Rushing, feeling pressured
Boredom or fatigue
Task saturation
"Hairs stand up on back of neck"
Deviating from normal procedure
Trying something new under pressure

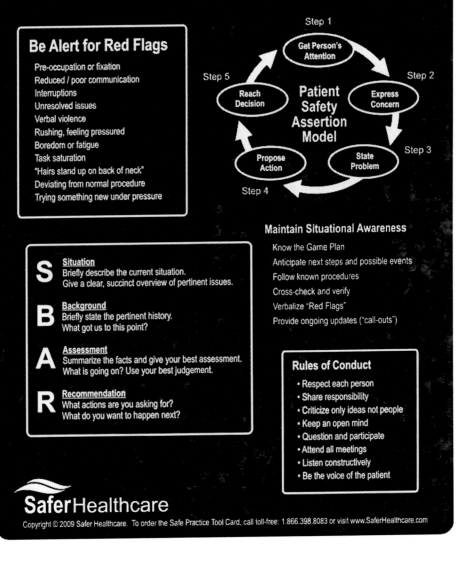

Patient Safety Assertion Model

- Step 1 — Get Person's Attention
- Step 2 — Express Concern
- Step 3 — State Problem
- Step 4 — Propose Action
- Step 5 — Reach Decision

Maintain Situational Awareness

Know the Game Plan
Anticipate next steps and possible events
Follow known procedures
Cross-check and verify
Verbalize "Red Flags"
Provide ongoing updates ("call-outs")

S — **Situation**
Briefly describe the current situation.
Give a clear, succinct overview of pertinent issues.

B — **Background**
Briefly state the pertinent history.
What got us to this point?

A — **Assessment**
Summarize the facts and give your best assessment.
What is going on? Use your best judgement.

R — **Recommendation**
What actions are you asking for?
What do you want to happen next?

Rules of Conduct

- Respect each person
- Share responsibility
- Criticize only ideas not people
- Keep an open mind
- Question and participate
- Attend all meetings
- Listen constructively
- Be the voice of the patient

SaferHealthcare

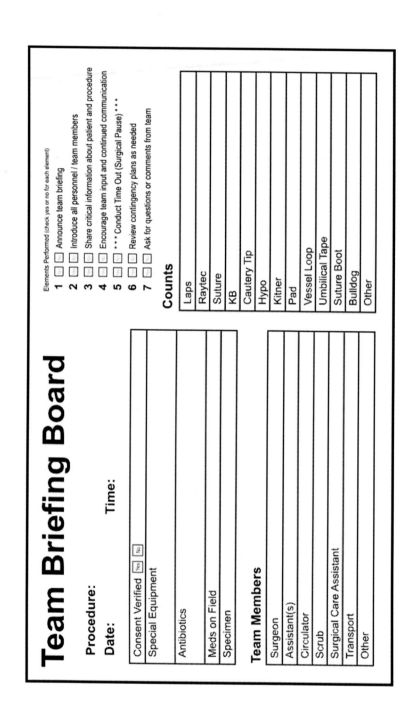

Team Briefing Board

Procedure:

Date: _____ **Time:** _____

Consent Verified [Yes] [No]

Special Equipment

Antibiotics	
Meds on Field	
Specimen	

Team Members

Surgeon	
Assistant(s)	
Circulator	
Scrub	
Surgical Care Assistant	
Transport	
Other	

Elements Performed (check yes or no for each element)

1 ☐ ☐ Announce team briefing
2 ☐ ☐ Introduce all personnel / team members
3 ☐ ☐ Share critical information about patient and procedure
4 ☐ ☐ Encourage team input and continued communication
5 ☐ ☐ *** Conduct Time Out (Surgical Pause) ***
6 ☐ ☐ Review contingency plans as needed
7 ☐ ☐ Ask for questions or comments from team

Counts

Laps	
Raytec	
Suture	
KB	
Cautery Tip	
Hypo	
Kitner	
Pad	
Vessel Loop	
Umbilical Tape	
Suture Boot	
Bulldog	
Other	

Patient:

Date: /   /   **Time:**   AM PM   **Location:**

Surgical Team Briefing Checklist

Elements Performed (check yes or no for each element)

- Yes / No Announce team briefing
- Yes / No Introduce all personnel / team members
- Yes / No Share critical information about patient and procedure
- Yes / No Encourage team input and continued cross-talk / communication
- Yes / No * * * Conduct Time Out (Surgical Pause) * * *
- Yes / No Review contingency plans as needed
- Yes / No Ask for questions or comments from team

Before Surgery

Surgical Team Debriefing Checklist

Elements Performed (check yes or no for each element)

- Yes / No Announce team debriefing
- Yes / No Discuss what went well and not-so-well during surgery
- Yes / No Ask how / what the team can improve for next time
- Yes / No Ask if the team had the right tools at the right time
- Yes / No Assign follow-up roles and responsibilities
- Yes / No Ask for any last questions or comments

After Surgery

Notes / Follow-up / Action Item #1:

Assigned to:

Notes / Follow-up / Action Item #2:

Assigned to:

SaferHealthcare
Creating and Sustaining a Patient Safety Culture

Safer Healthcare Training Resource Center
4200 East 8th Avenue, Suite 5, Denver, Colorado 80220
Phone: 303.298.8083 Toll-free: 1.866.398.8083

www.SaferHealthcare.com

Increasing Patient Safety through Effective Communication and Teamwork

Surgical Team Briefing Checklist

Elements Performed (check yes or no for each element)

- Yes No   Announce team briefing
- Yes No   Introduce all personnel
- Yes No   Share critical information and patient and procedure
- Yes No   Encourage team input and continued cross-talk
- Yes No   ***Conduct Time Out***
- Yes No   Review contingency plans
- Yes No   Ask for questions

Surgical Team Debriefing Checklist

Elements Performed (check yes or no for each element)

- Yes No   Announce team debriefing
- Yes No   Discuss what went well and not-so-well
- Yes No   Ask how team can improve for next time
- Yes No   Ask if the team had the right tools at the right time
- Yes No   Assign follow-up responsibilities
- Yes No   Ask for any last questions or comments

SaferHealthcare
Creating and Sustaining a Patient Safety Culture

These stickers are designed to be utilized as reminders of key human factors elements in the care of surgery patients and can each be used as checklists before and after the patient's procedure. These stickers are designed to increase levels of teamwork and communication in the OR and help ensure the delivery of safe and reliable care.

To order additional copies, call toll-free: 1-866-398-8083 or visit us on-line: www.SaferHealthcare.com

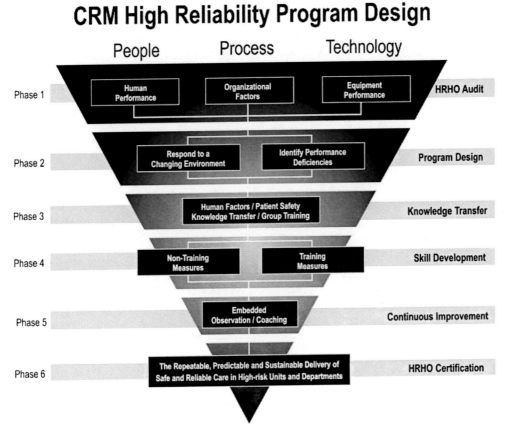

CRM High Reliability Program Design

Create highly reliable teams and standardize communication in your organization today.

Order bulk copies of
"Everyday CRM Skills Handbook"

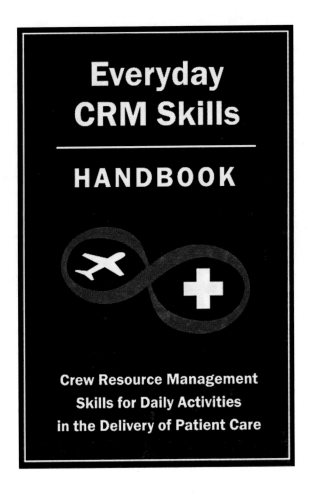

Call Toll-free: 1-866-398-8083

Order on-line:
www.SaferHealthcare.com